ENGLISH PLEASURE GARDENS

The Terrace, Annesley.

ENGLISH
Pleasure
GARDENS

ROSE STANDISH NICHOLS

With a New Introduction by
Judith B. Tankard

DAVID R. GODINE, PUBLISHER
BOSTON

To

AUGUSTUS SAINT-GAUDENS

Published in 2003 by
David R. Godine, Publisher
Post Office Box 450
Jaffrey, New Hampshire 03452
www.godine.com

Originally published in 1902 by The Macmillan Company, New York
Introduction copyright © 2003 by Judith B. Tankard

Library of Congress Cataloging-in-Publication Data
Nichols, Rose Standish
English pleasure gardens / Rose Standish Nichols ;
with a new introduction by Judith B. Tankard.
p. cm.
Originally published: New York : Macmillan Co., 1902.
With new introd.
Includes bibliographical references (p.).
ISBN 1-56792-232-5 (pbk. : alk. paper)
1. Gardens—England. I. Title
SB466.G7N55 2003
712'.0942—dc21   2003040817

Plans drawn by Allen H. Cox and reproductions of original
photographs and drawings by the author

First softcover printing 2003
Printed in the United States of America

Contents

List of Plans

Illustrations in the Text

LIST OF ILLUSTRATIONS

LIST OF ILLUSTRATIONS

Introduction

WHEN ENGLISH PLEASURE GARDENS was first published in 1902, one reviewer observed that the volume stood "like a solid and substantial dowager among the lighter and more frivolous garden-sisterhood."[1] That comment could also be applied to the young author of the book, Rose Standish Nichols (1872–1960), one of the country's earliest professional garden designers and author of three outstanding books about gardens that were the fruits of her extensive travels around the world. She was also a connoisseur of art and antiques, an outspoken social reformer, and a confirmed pacifist. While Rose Nichols' name has fallen into obscurity because so few of her gardens survive, her books remain remarkably fresh and articulate today. Long out of print, *English Pleasure Gardens* in this new edition will introduce new genera-

1. *Watercolor portrait of Rose Standish Nichols by Taylor Greer, 1912. Courtesy Nichols House Museum, Boston.*

2. *The Nichols House Museum, 55 Mount Vernon Street, Boston. Photograph by Higgins and Ross. Courtesy Nichols House Museum, Boston.*

tions to the redoubtable Miss Nichols and to the pageantry of Britain's garden heritage, which shaped her own ideas about garden design.

The eldest of three daughters of Dr. Arthur Nichols and Elizabeth Homer (who was related to the artist Winslow Homer), Rose Nichols lived for most of her life in Boston's dowager-filled society enclave on

3. *Oil portrait of Rose Standish Nichols by Cornish Colony artist Margarita Pumpelly Smyth, c. 1890. Courtesy Nichols House Museum, Boston.*

Beacon Hill. Her home at 55 Mount Vernon Street is now the Nichols House Museum, established in 1961 by a legacy in her will. Furnished with ancestral portraits, historic needlework, and antiques collected on trips abroad, the museum offers a rare glimpse of early twentieth-century life on Beacon Hill as well as a personal view of one of New England's most distinguished garden designers.[2]

As a young child, Rose was introduced to gardening through her grandfather Thomas Johnston Homer, who allowed her to cultivate a small corner of his garden in Roxbury, near Boston. In 1889 the Nichols family began spending summers in Cornish, New Hampshire, where they were exposed to some of the most beautiful gardens in New England, created by artists such as Thomas Wilmer Dewing, Stephen Parrish, and sculptor Augustus Saint-Gaudens, Rose's uncle and the founder of the Cornish Art Colony. It was Saint-Gaudens who encouraged his favorite niece to take up garden design after he admired the walled garden she created in 1896 at Mastlands, the Nichols family's home in Cornish.[3] Filled with luscious plantings of foxgloves,

4. Rose Standish Nichols in her garden at Mastlands, now the Cornish Colony Gallery and Museum. Century Magazine, May 1906.

5. The reflecting pool and fountain at Mastlands. Lowell, American Gardens, 1902.

irises, Oriental poppies, delphiniums, asters, phlox, and other traditional New England favorites, the garden also featured crisp rows of
dwarf crab apples and a small reflecting pool in the center. Nichols'
touch in combining the fragrant blossoms and the fruit of the trees
transformed a simple country garden into an old-time pleasure ground
that harked back to an earlier era of gardening.

Nichols was among an elite group of mostly East Coast women who
brought residential garden design to national acclaim in the early
1900s, when the profession of landscape architecture was in its forma-
tive stage and largely dominated by men. Nichols, like her female con-
temporaries, had to devise her own program of self study, as few
options were open to them at the time. She tutored privately with architect Charles A. Platt, a summer resident of Cornish and the country's foremost proponent of houses and gardens modeled on the Italian
villa principles. Platt also was a mentor to another distinguished landscape architect, Ellen Biddle Shipman.[4]

Nichols studied drafting and took lessons in horticulture from Ben-
jamin Watson at the Bussey Institution, then a department of Harvard
University adjacent to the Arnold Arboretum in Boston. In 1899 she
was admitted as a special student at the Massachusetts Institute of
Technology in Cambridge, Massachusetts, taking an upper-level design studio. She capped off her studies in England, where she met
some of the country's leaders in garden design, such as Reginald
Blomfield. His book, *The Formal Garden in England* (1892), extolled
"Old English" gardens of the Elizabethan and Stuart eras, known for
their strong geometric form. As Nichols later wrote, "All the artists in
Cornish . . . became champions and exponents of the so-called 'formal'
school and were among the first to revive old-fashioned gardens in this
country."[5] Her own garden at Mastlands, which bore a remarkable resemblance to the sunken garden at Hampton Court (illustrated on
page 93), was "formal" in all aspects, from its geometric configuration to
its restrained plantings. Nichols was less inspired by the naturalistic
school as advocated by Blomfield's adversary, William Robinson.[6]
Throughout her career, Nichols drew upon her vast knowledge of

6. The sunken garden at Hampton Court, England, which inspired the garden at Mastlands. Photograph by Judith B. Tankard.

English and European gardens, coupled with her excellent command of American horticulture.

After landing her first commission in 1904 for a Beacon Hill neighbor seeking her advice on her Newport, Rhode Island, garden, Nichols worked for approximately seventy clients. Most of her work was concentrated along the East Coast, especially the New England states where she had social connections, as well as Lake Forest, Illinois. Little is known about most of her commissions, since her professional papers were discarded sometime after her death in 1960. By that time most of her gardens had already disappeared; they were either altered beyond recognition or fell victim to housing subdivisions or other destructive measures. The recent restoration of her garden at Mastlands and a handful of private gardens has sparked an interest in Nichols' career and the formidable contribution women made to residential garden design in the first half of the twentieth century.[7]

Unlike her better-known colleagues, Beatrix Jones Farrand, designer of the gardens at Dumbarton Oaks in Washington, D.C.;

7. *Rose Standish Nichols (far left) with members of the Beacon Hill Reading Club, 1953. Courtesy Nichols House Museum, Boston.*

Marian Cruger Coffin, designer of Winterthur in Delaware; and Ellen Biddle Shipman, who designed nearly 600 gardens nationwide, Nichols pursued many activities. In 1896, when she was just beginning her studies, she was busy establishing the Beacon Hill Reading Club "to create a feeling of neighborliness on the Hill," inviting women to engage in lively discussions of new books or read drafts of their own works.[8] In later years she turned her attention to world peace, attending peace conferences in Europe with Jane Addams and starting a discussion group called The League of Small Nations.

Her firm belief that the universal love of gardens, especially among women, could be used as a tool for improving international relations fostered friendships with influential women. These included First Lady Edith Wilson, Queen Margherita of Italy, and Queen Sophie of Greece, the latter two of whom had remarkable gardens.[9] Nichols used such friendships to great advantage. After being initially turned away from Bernard Berenson's Florentine villa, for instance, she rejoined that she was traveling with "three queens." When Berenson looked out the window to find Queen Margherita, Queen Sophie, and Queen Alexandra of Jugoslavia in tow, he immediately welcomed the royal party.[10]

* * *

It was Nichols' books and articles that won her lasting fame and recognition. An inveterate traveler, she made nearly thirty trips abroad to visit gardens and research books and articles. The publication of *Italian Pleasure Gardens* in 1923, followed a year later by *Spanish and Portuguese Gardens*, as well as the reissue of *English Pleasure Gardens* in 1925, spread her name in elite gardening circles and brought her too much work. As she wrote to her sister Marian, "The trouble is that I have so many jobs in different states all of which ought to be tackled about the same time. It is very hard for me to know where to begin."[11] Some of those states were Arizona, California, Connecticut, Georgia, Illinois, Massachusetts, New Hampshire, New York, Pennsylvania, Rhode Island, and Wisconsin.

Rose Nichols specialized in the design and planting of flower gardens, loosely based on Elizabethan gardens. As she wrote in *English Pleasure Gardens*, "a love of flowers is the natural foundation on which to build all gardens." Like many women of her era, she rarely had the opportunity to lay out entire estates and more typically was part of a team with the architect and landscape architect who defined the broader landscape.

One of her most spectacular commissions was the water court at the House of the Four Winds in Lake Forest, loosely modeled after the Generalife gardens in Granada, which she later illustrated in *Spanish and Portuguese Gardens*. This garden is a good example of how she drew

8. The water court at House of the Four Winds, Lake Forest, Ill., designed by Howard Van Doren Shaw and Rose Standish Nichols. Courtesy Smithsonian Institution, Archives of American Gardens.

upon her extensive travels abroad and knowledge of historic gardens. Her striking, but understated plantings accentuated the geometry of the garden's layout.

At Haven Wood, the twenty-acre Edward L. Ryerson estate in Lake Forest, Nichols worked closely with the architect Howard Van Doren Shaw (a follower of Platt with whom she collaborated on several projects), who laid out the terraces, and Jens Jensen, the landscape architect who provided the landscape definitions. Nichols described her sunken walled garden there as "a very beautiful garden, laid out in four

9. Haven Wood, Lake Forest, Ill., designed by Jens Jensen and Rose Standish Nichols. Shelton, Beautiful Gardens in America, *1924.*

quarters. Accents were provided by pyramidal evergreens and with standard heliotropes and roses. Along with a definite color scheme, emphasis was placed on contrasts of sunlight and shadow."[12]

In Milwaukee, Nichols worked alongside architect David Adler on a lakeside garden for executive Lloyd R. Smith to complement the Italian Renaissance-style house. She designed a long water cascade, leading from the terrace to the lakefront, echoing the famous one at the Villa Cicogna in the Italian Lakes, about which she had written.[13] The building is now the Villa Terrace Museum of Decorative Arts and the garden has recently been resurrected, although none of the original planting plans have been found.[14]

At Grey Towers in Milford, Pennsylvania, Cornelia Bryce Pinchot, wife of Gifford Pinchot (noted forestry expert and two-term governor of Pennsylvania) and an important garden club member, asked Nichols to prepare planting plans for a swimming pool border: "What I want from you is . . . the benefit of your expert knowledge and wide experience."[15] The Pinchots, being restless clients, had called upon

10. *Forecourt at the Italian Renaissance-inspired Lloyd Smith estate, Milwaukee, Wisc.,*
designed by David Adler and Rose Standish Nichols (now the Villa Terrace Museum of
Decorative Arts). Courtesy Dennis R. Buettner FASLA.

11. *The water-staircase at the Villa Terrace Museum. Courtesy Dennis R. Buettner FASLA.*

several other designers over the years before contacting her. Unfortunately Nichols' recommendations were not acted upon due to lack of funds.

* * *

English Pleasure Gardens, Rose Nichols' first and most important book, is extraordinarily perceptive, embracing the thirty-year-old author's wide-ranging knowledge of art, architecture, decorative arts, history, and literature. "She is brilliant on the subject," Lady Nancy Astor wrote after her visit to Cliveden in 1930.[16] It was one of the first comprehensive treatments of the history of English gardens and earned the author a considerable reputation in her own lifetime. In recent years, scholars have delved more deeply into the subject, but few have done so with such graceful prose and insightful design analysis.[17] Alicia Amherst's *A History of Gardening in England* (1895), which predated *English Pleasure Gardens* by several years, was a drier, more scholarly tome without the critical eye that Nichols brought to her book. A. Forbes Sieveking's book, *In Praise of Gardens* (1899), was based primarily on quotations from garden literature rather than analytical, although the author did accuse Nichols of drawing up his research.[18]

As early as June 1895 Nichols confided to her sister Marian that she was "working on a book" and by 1900 it had progressed to the point that she was approaching publishers, both American and British.[19] "Lots of publishers are asking to see the manuscript, but nothing is quite ready to show them yet," she wrote to her sister.[20] Throughout 1900 and 1901 Nichols was spending most of her time in England, visiting gardens and spending long hours at the British Museum. She scoured museums, libraries, and archives for illuminated manuscripts and antique tapestries to illustrate her book. She used some of her research in two articles about English manor house gardens that were published in 1901, although her mother urged her not to publish them until after her book came out.[21] In July 1901, when her book was nearly finished, she sent a prospectus to Grant Richards, one of the foremost literary publishers of the early twentieth century, whose authors included Arnold

Bennett, A. E. Housman and George Bernard Shaw.[22] Acting as an agent, he asked that she deliver the manuscript by October that year, and the following year *English Pleasure Gardens* was published by Macmillan.

Dedicated to her uncle, Augustus Saint-Gaudens, *English Pleasure Gardens* is a treasure trove of garden lore, written in an intelligent, but not overly intellectual manner that is still as compelling reading today as it was one hundred years ago with much to offer gardeners, armchair travelers, and historians alike. The book's attractive presentation, with garden plans, photographs, and hundreds of the author's own line drawings, makes it all the more special. Her sketches of ornament and garden features—dovecotes, arbors, sundials, and the like—bear an unmistakable resemblance to those rendered by F. Inigo Thomas in Blomfield's book, *The Formal Garden in England*.[23] Nichols' original artwork for the book's evocative cover, depicting the topiary garden at Brockenhurst, is used in this reissue.

English Pleasure Gardens champions the formal garden, especially Elizabethan flower gardens and the Medieval pleasaunce—at one time Nichols was even considering "The English Pleasaunce" as the book's title.[24] In addition to her comments on England's monastic gardens and formal Tudor gardens, she offers a fresh discussion of the diverse influences of French, Dutch, and Italian traditions on English garden design. The book gives short shrift to William Kent, "Capability" Brown, and their successors who were responsible for destroying many of England's great formal pleasure grounds. From a modern-day perspective, it is interesting to note that most of the gardens Nichols extolled—Longleat, Penshurst, Montacute, Melbourne Hall—were late nineteenth-century restorations.

In her final chapter, devoted to "today," Nichols singles out the influential work of modern garden architects, such as John Sedding, Reginald Blomfield, Edwin Lutyens, F. Inigo Thomas, and landscape architect Thomas Mawson, all of whom adhered to the "formal" school of design. She was one of the first to praise Gertrude Jekyll's gardens, which were only just beginning to be known, for their successful grouping of both wild and cultivated plants. One wonders what Rose Nichols would have thought of the revival of interest in formalism one hundred years after the publication of her book? Her rare knowledge of English garden design, both historical and modern, played a decisive role in her own design career. Today's gardeners and historians are sure to find inspiration in Nichols' remarkable book and its delightful illustrations.

JUDITH B. TANKARD

12. Rose Standish Nichols in her early eighties at Rye Beach, N.H. Photograph by George Taloumis, 1952. Courtesy Nichols House Museum, Boston.

NOTES

1. H. W. Boynton, *Atlantic Monthly* 91/547 (May 1903), 705.

2. Rose Nichols had envisioned her home as a museum along the lines of Boston's Isabella Stewart Gardner Museum. On a much more intimate scale, the Nichols House Museum displays examples of Rose Nichols' own crewelwork and wood-carving as well.

3. Mastlands is now the Cornish Colony Gallery and Museum and Rose Nichols' garden was recently restored after lying in ruin for many years. See Judith B. Tankard, "Restoration Drama: A New Hampshire Pleasure Garden Blooms Again," *Horticulture*, June 2001, 54–58.

4. Charles A. Platt (1861–1933) was the author of *Italian Gardens* (1894), an important book that influenced the formal garden style that dominated America in the early 1900s. His dozen or so properties in Cornish embodied the harmonious relationship of house and garden.

5. "A Little Garden Hunt in England," *House Beautiful*, July 1923, 29.

6. William Robinson (1838–1935) was an important advocate for naturalism in garden design. His book, *The Wild Garden* (1870), served as inspiration for the prairie style of landscape gardening in the Midwest.

7. See Judith B. Tankard, "Defining Their Turf: Pioneer Women Landscape Designers," *Studies in the Decorative Arts*, 8/1 (Fall-Winter 2000–2001): 31–53.

8. George Taloumis, "Rose Standish Nichols: Sixty Years Ago She Organized the Beacon Hill Reading Club (1896)," *Boston Globe*, 16 September 1956.

9. Nichols wrote about Queen Sophie's garden in "A Glimpse of the Pro-American Queen and Her Gardens," *House Beautiful*, August 1922, 110–11, 150.

10. Southard Menzel, "Sketches of the Life and Character of Rose Standish Nichols . . .," *Rose Standish Nichols as We Knew Her* (Nichols House Museum, 1986), 17.

11. Letter, Rose Nichols to Marian Nichols, 1 September 1931, Box 5, Folder 87, Nichols Family Papers, Schlesinger Library, Radcliffe College, Harvard University. Thanks to Alan Emmet for sharing her notes on the Nichols Family correspondence.

12. Taloumis, *Boston Globe*.

13. "The Terraced Gardens at the Villa Cicogna," *House Beautiful*, May 1929, 688-90, 692.

14. A new Renaissance-style water garden, designed by Buettner and Associates, was launched in 2002. The Villa Terrace Decorative Arts Museum is located at 2220 North Terrace Avenue, Milwaukee, Wisc.

15. Letter, Cornelia Bryce Pinchot to Rose Nichols, 6 October 1938, Pinchot Papers, Library of Congress, courtesy of Grey Towers.

16. "I have just seen a charming Miss Nichols from Boston . . . She has not seen English gardens for some years . . . Could you tell me of any good gardens nearby that

she could see?" Letter, Nancy Astor to Norah Lindsay, 7 August 1930, Papers of Viscountess Nancy Astor, Reading University Library, courtesy of Allyson M. Hayward.

17. The most notable recent publication is Sir Roy Strong's *The Renaissance Garden in England* (London: Thames and Hudson, 1979).

18. Sieveking requested that a preface be added to later editions of *English Pleasure Gardens* acknowledging his work, but nothing seems to have come of it. Letter, A. F. Sieveking, 15 May 1903, Box 5, Folder 96, Nichols Family Papers.

19. Letter, Elizabeth Homer Nichols to Arthur Nichols, 13 June 1895, Box 3, Folder 54, Nichols Family Papers.

20. Letter, Rose Nichols to Marian Nichols, 28 March 1900, Box 5, Folder 85, Nichols Family Papers.

21. "Old Manor House Gardens," *Century Magazine* 61 (April 1901), 906–912, and "The Longleat Flower Garden," *Architectural Review* 8 (January 1901), 2–4.

22. "Book is progressing slowly, but steadily. It must be finished and handed in to Mr. Richards by October 1st." Letter, Rose Nichols to Marian Nichols, 20 July 1901, Box 5, Folder 86, Nichols Family Papers.

23. In 1899, Mrs. Nichols asked her daughter if she had given up her plan of going into Mr. Thomas' office, introducing the possibility that Rose Nichols may have studied privately with him. Letter, Elizabeth Nichols to Rose Nichols, 10 October 1899, Box 3, Folder 57, Nichols Family Papers.

24. Letter, Elizabeth Nichols to Rose Nichols, 25 April 1901, Box 3, Folder 58, Nichols Family Papers.

A SELECTION OF
ROSE STANDISH NICHOLS' GARDENS

Ballyshear, for Charles B. Macdonald, Southampton, New York

Bonnymede, for Mrs. Gardiner Hammond, Montecito, California

Ellslloyd, for Louis L. Laflin, Lake Forest, Illinois

Green Meadow Farm, for George A. Cluett, Williamstown, Massachusetts

Grey Towers, for Cornelia B. Pinchot, Milford, Pennsylvania (now
Grey Towers National Historic Landmark)

Haven Wood, for Edward L. Ryerson, Sr., Lake Forest, Illinois

Highfield, for Mrs. Francis Peabody, Milton, Massachusetts

House of the Four Winds, for Hugh J. McBirney, Lake Forest, Illinois
(occasionally open to the public)

Mason Garden, for Ellen Mason, Newport, Rhode Island

Mastlands, for Arthur S. Nichols, Cornish, New Hampshire
(now Cornish Colony Gallery and Museum)

Morningside, for Alfred S. Bourne, Augusta, Georgia

Pirie Garden, for John T. Pirie, Lake Forest, Illinois (occasionally open to the public)

Rosewood, for Mrs. Julius Rosenwald, Highland Park, Illinois

Schweppe Garden, for Charles H. Schweppe, Lake Forest, Illinois

Sopra Mare, for Lloyd R. Smith, Milwaukee, Wisconsin
(now Villa Terrace Museum of Decorative Arts)

Stone Ashley, for Miss Florence Pond, Tuscon, Arizona

Tivoli, for Mrs. Preston Davie, Tuxedo, New York

———

ENGLISH PLEASURE GARDENS

The Argument

NATURE SUPPLIES THE LIVING MATERIAL, and this is the best part of a garden; craft can vary its growth, art can accentuate and frame its charm, but its ever changing beauty is the gift of God.

In the world's history, horticulture as a craft has never before reached its present state of perfection and has never included such an amazing variety of trees, shrubs, and plants. The scientific spirit of the age has impelled botanists to seek new specimens at the ends of the earth and to naturalize the most far-fetched exotics on English soil. But if all this wealth of vegetation, indigenous and outlandish, is to answer other than practical and scientific purposes, it must be taken in hand by art as well as by craft and science. To give the utmost pleasure to people neither horticulturists nor botanists, a collection of plants, forming a garden, should be treated as an artistic composition.

Unfortunately, garden design has not advanced at the same rapid pace as horticulture and botany; in fact, until within the last few years it has gone backward rather than forward in England, ever since the period of the Italian Renaissance, although then as now it was the last of the arts to succeed, although then as now it was the last art to succeed. As Bacon wisely predicts, "Man shall ever see that when ages grow to Civility and Elegancy: Men come to Build Stately sooner than to Garden Finely: As if Gardening were the Greater Perfection."

Ornamental gardening for centuries in Japan has been reduced (rather monotonously from our point of view) to an almost exact science; in a different form it was practiced as a fine art in classic Greece and Rome, was revived throughout Europe at the time of the Renaissance, and still continues to be studied in France along the same lines under the head of architecture. But in England to-day it is not generally understood as more than a craft. Theories have been advanced to raise its standard, but in such a partisan spirit and from such a one-sided standpoint that they have accomplished little. Each Englishman who attempts to explain how a garden should be planned and planted seems to have agreed to differ from every other expert who has previously expounded his theory on the subject. If two garden-designers think alike, the fact has hardly been acknowledged, although it may be surmised that their differences are more apparent than real.

The result of this divergence of opinion is that scattered over England are a great variety of gardens almost impossible to classify. Some are planted as if upon untrodden Alpine peaks remote from every trace of civilization, although in reality a sumptuous mansion is not ten feet away. Others are the perfection of "mosaïculture," a term invented by a Frenchman to denote the most complicated plant patchwork, forming the last word of floricultural artificiality.

Between these two extremes are many delightful gardens, neither imitations of a wilderness nor rigidly conventional, where plants can grow freely and people are not out of place. Often they have been designed with less rhyme than reason, but are only more charming because they are useful as well as ornamental, to be "lived in" as well as "looked on." Unlike the great French gardens, they are not brilliant intellectual achievements laboriously constructed to form a vista from the windows of a palatial château and to afford a gay crowd of courtiers a parade-ground; nor have they the melancholy beauty of those early Italian villas whose romantic effect has become intensified by neglect and decay; at present in their perfection the English gardens are in appearance flourishing, of moderate dimensions and unassuming style. Their homelike atmosphere gives them individuality and a charm more endearing than that of other more pretentious performances. Of many of the simplest and most pleasing of these no examples will be given, either because their peculiar attraction is due to their skilful adaptation to a particular situation and their spirit only could be reproduced elsewhere, or because they belong to a class existing by every country roadside, of which the general scheme is too familiar to require explanation. Others have been excluded as being too consequential and elaborate to answer any but princely requirements.

Nothing can be prettier than a cottage garden, or in its way perhaps more magnificent than Chatsworth, but neither of these comes within the scope of this work. One is too practical, the other too ornate.

The origin and early growth of all gardens are purely conjectural, but in their first stages those in England were not probably dissimilar to those in other parts of uncivilized Europe. In the Middle Ages, after the Norman Conquest, they developed certain distinctive features. Later they passed more or less under the influence of the Italian Renaissance, French, Dutch, and Chinese styles, and to understand them it is necessary to understand the characteristics of these different schools.

As their connection with the manners and customs of the day is even more intimate than that of architecture proper, to realize their purpose one must be able to picture them peopled with the characters, many of them historic, who made them what they were in their prime.

The celebrated gardens are filled with historic associations. Without being able to imagine the life of the French court in the eighteenth century, who can appreciate Versailles? It only exists as a background for artifice and artificiality, for elegant ladies, their powdered hair erected à la Pompadour, their hoop-skirts sweeping the broad paths, coquettishly shielding their eyes with their painted fans, and gossiping with the gentlemen in attendance about, perhaps, the recent disappearance of the king and the de Montespan down a covered alley set aside for the royal flirtations.

Plans and photographs can only partially show the form of these gardens, words are still more inadequate to express their spirit, but perhaps some suggestion can be given of their arrangement and their charm.

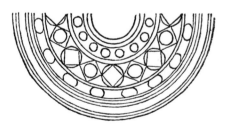

Acknowledgments are due to so many people, that the author cannot even begin to name her indebtedness. Garden-owners everywhere have thrown open their gates with a hospitality which has not been unappreciated, while facts have been obtained with and without permission from almost every writer about gardens, whether living or dead. For all these opportunities to add to her stock of information she can only say that she is truly grateful.

CHAPTER ONE

Classic Pleasure Grounds

 T is not such a far cry as might be imagined from the famous pleasure grounds of remote antiquity to the gardens, both "wild" and "formal," in England at the present day. Our environment more closely resembles the luxurious surroundings of our Roman conquerors than the comfortless domains of our own forefathers after they were freed from the Roman yoke and had lost sight of Roman culture. Without much effort we modern Anglo-Saxons in England or America can picture ourselves revelling in an elegant Pompeian villa or in an airy Athenian peristyle; but we should dread being doomed to suffocate in a smoky ancestral hut or to be cooped up in the thick, almost windowless walls of an Anglo-Norman fortalice. Precedents not ours by direct inheritance have become so by adoption.

Æsthetically, we are still held fast by classic traditions, taught the Britons by the Romans early in the Christian era, degraded, if not utterly destroyed, during the Dark Ages, but revived at the time of the Renaissance. To see our sense of beauty expressed in perfect form, we continue to look back to the masterpieces of the Greeks and Romans. It is to them that we turn now to find the derivation of many charm-

A MOSAIC PAVEMENT found in a Piece of Ground call'd the Black Friars in the Borough of LEICESTER, belonging to ROGERS RUDING, Esq.ʳ October 1754.

ing details in addition to the general plan of the formal garden. Hundreds, almost thousands, of years ago the classic garden makers realized our ideals, combining architecture with sculpture and horticulture to produce gardens unsurpassed in the perfection of their design. A lack of our variety and abundance of flowers was their only deficiency.

A knowledge of the arts and sciences spread with the growth of the Roman provinces throughout Europe. Civilization made great progress in Great Britain after the conquest of Claudius; architecture and horticulture were practiced from both an ornamental and a useful standpoint. Villas, or country seats, including extensive residences with spacious courtyards, vineyards, orchards, kitchen and pleasure gardens, were laid out all over the province. These constructions were similar to those relinquished by the Romans in Italy, and hardly less carefully finished, though on a somewhat smaller scale.

In Great Britain, the contemporary description of Tacitus relates that, even before the close of the first century, there were plantations of luxuriant vegetation. The olive and the vine seem to have been the only fruits for which he considered the climate unsuitable. Later, however, there were vineyards, and, when the Romans were at the height of their power, almost every kind of fruit now cultivated in Northern Europe, with the exception of pine-apples, gooseberries, currants, and raspberries, is said to have flourished. Thirty-eight Anglo-Saxon and English names of plants are distinctly of Roman origin, among them the rose, lily, poppy, mallow, laurel, mulberry, and feverfew.

Unfortunately, no equally interesting records of the architecture in Britanno-Roman gardens have been handed down to us. But we can form some idea of the extent of ground covered with lavishly ornamented plantations from the general outlines of the villas and from the elegance of the architectural remains excavated on their sites. Statues, vases, and fountains of marble and bronze, almost as fine as those in Italy, have not infrequently been discovered. Numbers of the most remarkable of these relics are on exhibition in the British Museum and elsewhere. Others remain *in situ*.

Mosaic pavements, formerly ornamenting the living rooms, the peristyle, and other courtyards, are found in excellent condition. These were composed of *tessellæ*, or small cubes of coloured marble, forming geometrical designs or depicting scenes from everyday life or mythology. Such mosaics were called *opera segmentata, opus musivum*, and *musaceum*. The illustration [opposite] shows a good specimen, which was unearthed near Leicester in 1754. It is Græco-Roman in style, like most of the Romano-British art. The labyrinth or fret border enclosing the design is of very ancient origin, and may be intended to suggest the celebrated labyrinth of Crete. On other mosaics the story of Theseus, Ariadne, and the Minotaur has been obviously reproduced. The axe of

Lycurgus also forms part of many designs. Modern reproductions of these mosaics are commonly placed in the hallways of houses and on the thresholds of shops; even more appropriately, they might be made to pave the paths or to inlay the basin of a fountain in a formal garden.

To obtain a more complete picture of the Romano-British gardens we must return to their prototypes in Italy, and thence inquire into the gardens of those countries which inspired Rome during the centuries before Christ. Horticulture in primitive Italy, as in other uncivilized countries, was at its beginning merely intended for practical purposes. But *autres temps, autres mœurs*. Gradually the Latin word *hortus*, applied in the days of republican simplicity to a field of vegetables, was stretched to signify in the plural, at the time of the luxurious emperors, pleasure gardens of the utmost magnificence. At this latter period the source of every new form of Roman art, including garden-architecture, was Greece, which in its turn had received inspiration from Egypt, Persia, and Assyria.

A religious significance was attached to almost every feature in these pre-Christian gardens. Beasts and birds might be the living incarnations of the gods for whom they stood as representatives, while trees and religious flowers were revered as godlike attributes. In Egypt the cat was as closely connected with Isis, as the peacock in Italy with Juno, or doves in Greece with Aphrodite. Tree worship was observed in all these countries. Count Goblet d'Alviella says in the *Migration des Symboles*, that the sacred tree as it migrated from country to country was changed into that which was most precious in the estimation of the people. Thus the date-palm in Chaldea, the vine or the fir tree in Assyria, the lotus in Egypt, and the fig in India were regarded with the utmost veneration.

Egyptian gardens are the earliest of which definite records remain. Pictures and inscriptions, dating far back in the centuries before Christ, show that every Egyptian dwelling was built around a series of courtyards containing vegetation both useful and ornamental. Originally, a row of trees along the inner wall of the building shaded it and the enclosed quadrangle. Later, the tree trunks gave place to solid columns, and the overhanging branches to projecting rafters, which resulted in a general effect foreshadowing the Greek peristyle and the monastic cloisters. In the centre of the quadrangle was a fountain or a basin for fish, where many-coloured lotuses rose above the level of the water. Grape-vines and ivy, entwining the columns and clustering over the rafters, formed a shady tunnel on the outer edge of the area, while blossoming plants, set out symmetrically, brightened the inner space. Roses, jessamine, myrtle, and cistus, growing directly in the soil or cultivated in flower-pots, presented a simple conception of a floral parterre.

Secluded in these courtyards the ladies of the harem loitered, with their pet monkeys for playmates, under the shady colonnade or beside the cool fountain, then as now jealously guarded from any contact with the outer world. At a very early period, therefore, the idea of seclusion came to be connected with Oriental pleasure grounds, as it was later with those of the Greeks and Romans, with the mediæval pleasaunce, the monastic cloister-garth, and the garden called old-fashioned nowadays.

When Egyptian horticulture flourished extensively—from the eighth to the third centuries before Christ—plantations overran the courtyards and spread into the grounds without. The scheme of these plantations has often been found incised upon ancient blocks of stone. It appears to have consisted of a collection of walled, rectangular parallelograms, covering many acres. Among these interesting representations is the plan of a garden belonging to one of the pharaohs engraved upon part of the tomb of Tel-el-Amarna, formerly exhibited at the British Museum. Riat, in *L'Art des Jardins*, says of this:"The plantation, as was usually the case, lay near the Nile to facilitate its irrigation, and was divided by walls into sections, each devoted to a special culture. In the centre lies a rectangular basin occupied by fish and ducks and tufted with lotuses. A fringe of trees–dates, sycamores, and palms–veils the boundary walls of the enclosure, containing within many other species, such as figs, pomegranates, willows, acacias, and tamarisks. A large door flanked by two smaller ones, as was common, formed the

main entrance. Several kiosks, near the basins or under the shade, were inviting for a peaceful siesta."

Dating from about 1500 B.C., various mural paintings in tempera show garden scenes where, beside the fish-ponds or under the palm trees and sycamores, guests are being entertained by musicians playing on the flute and by dancing girls. One especially interesting example, preserved at the British Museum, shows a gentleman with two companions in a boat like a gondola towed by slaves along an oblong-shaped pond, overhung by several rows of trees. Another, sketched in the illustration, depicts a similar pond on a smaller scale, where fish and ducks disport themselves among the sacred lotuses.

In ancient Egyptian literature, gardens are often poetically described as the meeting place of lotus-eating lovers, whose "flowery food caused sweet forgetfulness." The following extract is from a poem written about 1300 B.C.

"She led me, hand in hand, and we went into her garden to converse together.

There she made me taste of excellent honey.

The rushes of the garden were verdant, and all its bushes flourishing.

There were currant trees and cherries redder than rubies.

The ripe peaches[1] of the garden resembled bronze, and the groves had the lustre of the stone *nashem*.[2]

The *menni*[3] unshelled like cocoanuts they brought to us; its shade was fresh and airy, and soft for the repose of love.

---

1. The Persea fruit, a species of sacred almond. 2. Green Felspar. 3. An unknown fruit.

'Come to me,' she called unto me, 'and enjoy thyself a day in the room of a young girl who belongs to me, the garden is to-day in its glory; there is a terrace and a parlour.'"

—"The Tale of the Garden of Flowers," translated by
M. François Chabas (*Records of the Past*, Egyptian texts).

The Assyrians and Persians, whose intercourse with the Egyptians was intimate at least fourteen centuries before Christ, were celebrated for their marvellous gardens at a very early period, and passed on a share of their knowledge to the Greeks and Romans. Pliny says in his *Natural History*, as it was translated by P. Holland at the time of the Renaissance, "The Syrians are great Gardiners, they take exceeding pains and bee most anxious in gardening; whereupon arose the proverb in Greek to this effect, 'Many Woorts and Pot-herbs in Syria.'"

These Eastern pleasure grounds were known to the Greeks as *paradeisoi* (παράδεισοι) Sir William Temple in the *Garden of Epicurus* writes:

"A Paradise seems to have been a large Space of Ground adorned and beautified with all Sorts of Trees both of Fruits and of Forest, either found there before it was enclosed or planted after; either cultivated like gardens for Shade and for walks with Fountains or Streams and all sorts of Plants usual in the Climate and pleasant to the Eye, the Smell or the Taste; or else employed like our Parks for Inclosure and Harbour of all sorts of Wild Beasts, as well as for the Pleasure of Riding and Walking: And so they were of more or less extent and of differing Entertainment according to the several Humours of the Princes that ordered and inclosed them."

There are several representations of such *paradeisoi* incised on marble slabs brought from Kouyunjik to the British Museum. The most interesting of these is placed on the east wall of the Assyrian basement, and depicts a grove of trees where both King Asshur-bani-pal reclining upon a couch and his queen sitting beside him erect in an armchair are banqueting. Above, a bower of grape-vine shades their heads, and behind each stand attendants waving fans to cool the air. Others bring plates of food and play upon musical instruments. Birds are perched on the trees, a part of whose foliage is being devoured by a huge grasshopper, while from one of the branches swings the captured head of an enemy.[1]

At Babylon, the Hanging Gardens built or restored under the Persian dynasty in the sixth century B.C., famous as one of the Seven Wonders of the world, were located in the heart of a crowded city and raised above the traffic of the streets upon massive arcades. The gardens were formed of four terraces covered with trees, shrubs, and flowers. Each terrace diminished in extent as its height above the ground increased; thus the shape of the whole had somewhat the appearance of a pyramid. Strabo mentions the lowest of these platforms or terraces as being four hundred feet square with a height from the base to the apex of about one hundred feet. These dimensions, however, vary greatly according to different authorities. Indeed, our idea of both their age and appearance is very vague. There were other hanging gardens on a smaller scale at Thebes, Syracuse, and various places of less importance.

In the fifth century B.C. the Greeks were familiar with the gardens of the Persian satrap, Cyrus the Younger, at Sardis. Xenophon described how Cyrus showed this "Paradise of Sardis" to the Grecian ambassador Lysander, who was in ecstasies at the "beauty of the trees, the regularity of the planting, the evenness of their rows, and their making regular angles one to another, in a word, the beauty of the quincunx order in which they were planted and the delightful odours issuing from them." But his admiration was redoubled when, seeing his astonishment at the skill with which all this had been accomplished, Cyrus remarked: "All the trees which you here behold are of my own appointment. I it was who contrived, measured, and laid out the ground for planting these trees, and I can even show you some of them that I planted with my own hand."

The earliest Grecian gardens, existing before Greece had come into close contact with foreign countries, were characterized by an extreme simplicity, much like that of a modern orchard or kitchen garden. We

---

1. This is shown in the illustration at the beginning of this chapter.

may draw the conclusion that even the royal gardens were far less elaborate than those described as existing at the same time in the East, from a description in *The Odyssey* of the garden of Alcinous, similar to that of Laertes in Ithaca, and typical of the Homeric Age.

"And without the courtyard, hard by the door, is a great garden, of four ploughgates, and a hedge runs round on either side. And there grow tall trees blossoming, pear trees and pomegranates, and apple trees with bright fruit, and sweet figs, and olives in their bloom. The fruit of these trees never perisheth, neither faileth, winter or summer, enduring through all the year. Evermore the west wind blowing brings some fruits to birth and ripens others. Pear upon pear waxes old, and apple on apple, yea and cluster ripens upon cluster of the grape, and fig upon fig. There too hath he a fruitful vineyard planted, whereof the one part is being dried by the heat, a sunny plot on level ground, while other grapes men are gathering, and yet others they are treading in the winepress. In the foremost row are unripe grapes that cast the blossom, and others there be that are growing black to vintaging. There too, skirting the furthest line, are all manner of garden beds, planted trimly, that are perpetually fresh, and therein are two fountains of water, whereof one scatters his stream all about the garden, and the other runs over against it beneath the threshold of the courtyard, and issues by the lofty house, and thence did the townsfolk draw water. These were the splendid gifts of the gods in the palace of Alcinous."[1]

After the fifth century, however, there began to develop in Greece pleasure gardens of a more studied appearance, bearing greater resemblance to those of Persia, Babylon, and Egypt. This change, no doubt, was partly caused by the progress of civilization and partly by the closer relations established between the East and the West. Greek colonists returned from these foreign countries, bringing with them new plants and increased information as to their culture and the architectural features appropriately placed in their vicinity. The peristyle, or principal house court, was ornamented with pavilions, fountains, and colonnades, interspersed with low beds of rare exotic plants. There were groves of oaks, cypresses, poplars, willows, and elms, sometimes

---

1. *The Odyssey*, VII. Done into English prose by S. H. Butcher and A. Lang.

THE GARLAND-WEAVERS

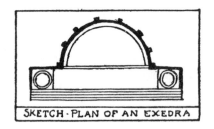

SKETCH · PLAN OF AN EXEDRA

set out in public parks, and sometimes in the consecrated grounds ad-joining the temples of the gods. The prophetic oak grove of Dodona was one of the most ancient Grecian sanctuaries, while many other trees and plants were considered as habitations of living spirits. Fauns and dryads seemed to animate the forest trees, and a transmigrated soul might find a resting-place in clumps of laurel or mulberry, or even dwell in such delicate flowers as the hyacinth or crocus. Floral decora-tions ornamented every ceremony, religious or secular. In mourning or rejoicing, the heads of the participants were crowned with roses, laurel, or bay leaves. Flowers were so much used in their religious ceremonies that the early Christians despised them as characteristic pagan at-tributes.

In Athens, gardens both public and private were numerous. Many of these, intended as meeting-places for philosophers and their pupils, belonged sometimes to individuals, sometimes to the state. Pliny says, "Epicurus, that connoisseur in the enjoyment of a life of ease, was the first to lay out a garden at Athens; up to his time it had never been thought of to dwell in the country in the middle of the town." Plato and Theophrastus also owned famous gardens where their pupils assem-bled for instruction. In his will Theophrastus made the following be-quest, "As to my garden, the walk and the houses adjacent to the garden, I give them to those of my friends mentioned below, who de-sire to devote themselves in common to study and philosophy therein." His pupils were especially renowned for pacing up and down the gar-den walks during philosophic discussions, and accordingly were enti-tled members of the peripatetic school. In the Lykeion and the Akademion, beautiful parks contained canals, fountains, groves of elm and plane trees, and many buildings large and small. Beside the main thoroughfares were narrow winding paths, known as philosophers' walks, furnished with *exedra* or seats large enough for several wanderers to rest upon while engaged in conversation.

The most idyllic description of a Grecian garden was written in the third century by Theocritus, a Sicilian Greek, who lived partly in Sicily, partly in Egypt. "So, I and Eucritus and the fair Amyntichus turned aside into the house of Phrasidamus, and lay down with delight in beds of sweet tamarisk and fresh cuttings from the vines, strewn on the ground. Many poplars and elm trees were waving over our heads, and not far off the running of the sacred water from the cave of the nymphs warbled to us: in the shimmering branches the sun-burnt grasshoppers were busy with their talk, and from afar the little owl cried softly out of the tangled thorns of the blackberry; the larks were singing and the hedgebirds, and the turtle-dove moaned; the bees flew round and round the fountains, murmuring softly; the scent of late summer and of the fall of the year was everywhere; the pears fell from the trees at our feet, and apples in number rolled down at our sides, and the young plum trees were bent to the earth with the weight of their fruit."[1]

The classic Roman pleasure gardens began to come into existence during the latter half of the second century before Christ. Traditions of the earlier gardens, which have been described, had been handed down to the Romans, and added to the honour in which gardens were held. "For we find in remote antiquity even," Pliny says, "there was nothing looked upon with a greater degree of admiration than the gardens of the Hesperides, those of the kings Adonis and Alcinous, and Hanging Gardens, including those of Cyrus, king of Assyria." Cato and Varro treated gardening from a cultural standpoint, and their example was followed in verse by Virgil and Columella.

Between Greece and Rome the connection was at this time most intimate. Many parts of the Roman houses were fashioned after Grecian models and known by Grecian names. Often, however, the names appropriated were not used for the same objects in both countries, and this ambiguity led to confusion. Thus, while a gallery or colonnade

---

1. *Idyl* VII, "Thalysia," trans. W. Pater.

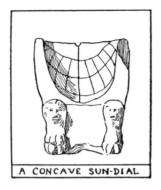

A CONCAVE SUN-DIAL

covered with vines like a pergola was called by the Greeks a *xystus*, this name, as Vitruvius has pointed out, was given by the Romans to a parterre composed of paths and flower-beds. *Peristylium, exedra,* and *hippodrome,* among other words frequently applied, rightly or wrongly, to different features in Roman gardens, denote their derivation from the Greek. Sometimes the transposition led to mistakes as curious as that which allowed the Romans to consult for a century a Grecian sundial, brought from Catana in Sicily to Rome, without realizing that the difference in latitude made it a useless timepiece in the more northern city.

This Græco-Roman style of garden was brought to its perfection in the first century before Christ—the period of the conquest of England—and hence is most interesting to us as showing the style likely to have been introduced by the Romans into Great Britain. In Italy, at this time, pleasure gardens were multiplying so rapidly that scant attention was being given to agriculture and market-gardening. Many querulous critics extolled the good old days when farming used to be held in high esteem, and bewailed a neglect entailing among other evils a food supply insufficient for the population. The cities, towns, and summer resorts were honey-combed with gardens, which gradually overran the suburbs and spread thickly throughout the country, until villas, including vast pleasure gardens, were notable from the Apennines to Mount Vesuvius.

In Rome, and in the smaller cities and towns, trees, shrubs, and flowers were planted everywhere. "That a man could not heretofore come by a commoner's house within the citie, but he should see the windowes beautified with greene quishins wrought and tapissed with floures of all colours; resembling daily to their view the gardens indeed which were in out-villages, as being in the very heart of the citie, they might think themselves in the country." [1] There were sacred groves and public parks like those at Athens, hanging gardens similar to those at Babylon, and garden courts with a far-away resemblance to those of Egypt, and in direct imitation of the Grecian peristyle. "A city garden, especially of one who has no other," says Cato, "ought to be planted and ornamented with all possible care."

When there was no ground to spare in crowded streets, the roofs of the houses were laid out with pergolas, ornamental plants, and fountains, while larger gardens were supported on masonry in mid-air. These pensile gardens were novelties as adversely criticised as the twenty-story buildings of modern American cities. "Live not they against nature," asks Seneca, "that plant orchards on their highest towers, that have whole forests shaking upon the tops and turrets of their houses, spreading their roots in such places where it would suffice them that the tops of their branches should touch?" [2]

If the dwelling was built purely after the Roman fashion, vegetation was cultivated in a court behind the house; but if the Grecian peristyle had replaced the ancient atrium, it contained the *viridarinm*, or herbage. Sometimes ornamental plants were grown in both the inner and outer enclosures, which, opening into each other, were similar in arrangement. Smaller courtyards, particularly one reserved for the women, contained flowers especially intended to be picked. Often when the space was too limited to contain a real garden, the illusion of seeing one was contrived by painting the enclosing walls with flowers and shrubs in perspective.

The Grecian peristyle differed from the Roman atrium as an elegant drawing-room differs from a homely living-room in a modern house. Most of the larger dwellings at the time of the Empire contained one and sometimes two peristyles. These courtyards were unroofed quad-

1. Pliny, *Natural History*, Book XIX, trans. P. Holland. 2. Seneca, *Epistles*. 122.

rangles enclosed by a portico adjoining the principal apartments occupied by the family, and in pleasant weather were more frequented by it than any of the indoor rooms. Ladies, who could not go freely abroad, made the courtyards the scene of most of their pleasures. It furnished them with both a sitting room and playground. Here we see the housewife pictured as seated under a sunshade working on some tapestry or feeding a pet dog or bird. Here a girl is balanced aloft in a swinging chair, and others are tilting or amusing themselves with other childlike sports and games. Playing on musical instruments was another favourite diversion practiced in the peristyle.

As Rome grew crowded and the space within the walls became costly, less room for urban gardens was available, and people began to build villas where the area was cheaper and more unrestricted, first in the suburbs of the city, along the banks of the Tiber, and over the Campagna, then gradually spreading throughout the peninsula. This led to the development of the *villa pseudo-urbana*, which almost superseded the *villa rustica* in many rural districts. The former was intended for townspeople who sought relaxation in a more or less quiet and secluded spot, where they could lead a peaceful and healthy life in all the luxury of their city houses; while the latter was a simple farm-house such as the Villa Rustica at Boscoreale. Seclusion was a desideratum. The charming arrangement of these pseudo-urban villas is most delightfully described in several of the younger Pliny's letters. He points out as the great advantage of his Tuscan property above all his other villa grounds that here "there is no need to put on your toga, no one wants you in the neighbourhood, everything is calm and quiet, and this in itself adds to the healthfulness and cheerfulness of the place, no less than the brightness of the sky and the clearness of the atmosphere."

Of Pliny's Tusculan villa, about one hundred and fifty miles from Rome, he wrote to his friend Apollinaris in the latter part of the first century:

"My villa is so advantageously situated, that it commands a full view of all the country round; yet you approach it by so insensible a rise that you find yourself upon an eminence without perceiving you have ascended. Behind, but at a great distance, stand the Apennine Mountains. In the calmest days we are refreshed by the winds that blow thence, but so spent, as it were, by the long tract of land they travel over, that they are entirely divested of all their strength and violence before they reach us. The exposure of the principal house front is full south, and seems to invite the afternoon sun in summer (but somewhat earlier in winter) into a spacious and well-proportioned portico, consisting of several members, particularly a porch built in the ancient manner. In front of the portico is a sort of terrace, embellished with various figures and bounded with a box hedge, from whence you descend by an easy slope, adorned with the representations of divers animals in box answering alternately to each other, into a lawn overspread with the soft—I had almost said the liquid—Acanthus[1]: this is surrounded by a walk enclosed with tonsile evergreens, shaped into a variety of forms. Beyond it is the Gestatio laid out in the form of a circus, ornamented in the middle with box cut in numberless different figures, together with a plantation of shrubs, prevented by the shears from shooting up too high: the whole is fenced in by a walk covered with box, rising by different ranges to the top. On the outside of the wall lies a meadow, that owes as many beauties to nature, as all I have been describing *within* does to art; at the end of which are several other meadows and fields interspersed with thickets. At the extremity of this portico stands a grand dining room, which opens upon one end of the terrace; from the windows there is a very extensive prospect over the meadows up into the country, from whence you also have a view of the

---

1. Probably a kind of moss.

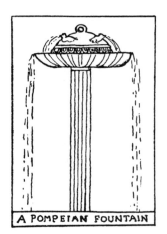

A POMPEIAN FOUNTAIN

A POMPEIAN BUST

terrace and such parts of the house which project forward, together with the woods enclosing the adjacent hippodrome. Opposite, almost in the centre of the portico, stands a square edifice, which encompasses a small area, shaded by four plane trees, in the midst of which a fountain rises, from whence the water, running over the edges of a marble basin, gently refreshes the surrounding plane trees and the verdure underneath them." Then follows a description of the hippodrome, the marble seats, summer-houses, and fountains, which added much to the beauty of the gardens. Other suggestions as to the appearance of the villa gardens may be gathered from the remaining ruins of Hadrian's superb villa at Tivoli, from the dwellings excavated at and near Pompeii, and from the writings of the classic writer Vitruvius.

Of the smaller pseudo-urban villas we are fortunate in being able to study those in and near Pompeii. At this watering-place, everything was so planned that the residents might enjoy a change from city life, by dwelling almost continually in the open air. As it was mostly frequented in summer, protection was provided from the heat rather than from cold. Courtyards occupied far more space within the walls of the house than the wholly enclosed apartments under its roof. The residence mainly consisted of a large central peristyle, surrounded by the various living rooms. All over the town, gardens filling the courtyards

Peristyle, House of the Vettii.

have been excavated, some of these enriched with a great variety of beautiful objects both useful and ornamental. Fountains (*fontes surgentes*), statuary of bronze and marble, besides stone sun-dials, tables, and couches, are to be seen in their original positions. Fish-ponds (*piscinæ*) lined with blue stucco, niches covered with shell-work or gayly-coloured mosaics, and little pavilions formed of marble columns are among the interesting features. The walls are covered with frescoes, often representing landscapes with gardens.

The Casa Nuova, or house of the Vettii, contains the best examples of a *xystus* and peristyle. Recently excavated, it has been left as far as possible in its former shape, and judiciously restored to complete the original effect. Even the pattern of the flower-beds was traced from the patches of richer earth, outlined by brick copings, showing the original design. At one corner of the quadrangle a little bronze boy squeezes under his arm a goose from whose bill water spouts into a circular basin. Similar infants, each holding a different bird or beast, stand be-

side corresponding basins at the three remaining corners, while in the middle of each side two statues of children direct water into an oblong trough. The lead pipe through which the water was conducted is still occasionally used; the marble tables upon which food was served still stand on the veranda, while classic flowers, planted in beds laid out on their original lines, still brighten the parterre. The photograph gives a good idea of the arrangement, but only a vague impression of the charm of the running water, the brilliant sunlight, and the wonderful blue sky of Italy, in contrast to the cool shade of the portico.

The medium-sized country-seat near Pompeii, known as the villa of Diomedes, is interesting as containing gardens both within and without the house. Its front door, as the celebrated classic architect Vitruvius advises, opens almost directly into a peristyle, the centre of which is divided into paths and flower-beds. At the left of the peristyle is a passage leading into a second garden not yet excavated. A third and much larger enclosure behind the house is encompassed by a portico, and was planted with trees and flowers. In the centre are the remains of a fish-pond ornamented by a fountain, and behind these there was a platform, over which vines were trained on a wooden framework supported by six stucco columns. Doubtless meals were often served under this delightful little pavilion when the air was refreshed by its

A RUSTIC ENCLOSURE

vicinity to the cool fountain. The illustration [opposite] is taken from an edition of the *Hypnerotomachia Poliphili*, published early in the sixteenth century, two centuries before excavations were begun at Pompeii. Curiously enough, it gives a very good impression of the Pompeian combination of a fountain and pavilion.

In the more palatial villas, added to the garden in the peristyle and to that behind the house, were various other enclosed pleasure grounds laid out on a much larger scale. The geometric patterns of the formal enclosures were arranged in sharp contrast to the studied wilderness of the park. Nothing could have been more harmonious than the general proportions of these gardens, or more elaborate than their details. Straight lines predominated and were designed to offer a series of long perspectives to the eye. If looked down upon from a considerable height, they would hardly have been distinguishable from the extensive pleasure grounds laid out by the great architects of the Italian Renaissance.

Even the kitchen gardens were planned with an eye to their ornamental effect. "But is the garden that is for use to avail of no ornament?" asks Quintilian; "by all means let these trees be planted in a regular order, and at certain distances. Observe that quincunx, how beautiful it is; view it on every side; what can you observe more straight or more graceful? Regularity and arrangement even improve the soil, because the juices rise more regularly to nourish what it bears. Should I observe the branches of yonder olive tree shooting into luxuriancy, I instantly should lop it; the effect is, it would form itself into a horizontal circle, which at once adds to its beauty and improves its bearing."

Wall-painting of a Garden, Villa Livia.

The architectural features were so varied and fanciful that it would be hopeless to try to describe them all, though few would be without interest. Pavilions, temples, grottoes, arbours, and greenhouses were common, and there was every kind of portico and colonnade, as well as water-works, including baths and fountains. The plan of the classic gardens was invariably the work of an architect; architecture predominated in the general scheme and in all its details. The vegetation near the house was always placed under a certain restraint, although in the park beyond it might seemingly run wild. The contrast between the formality of the garden and the exemption from restraint in the park is shown in the accompanying illustration. This is a reproduction of a wall decoration at the Villa Livia outside of Rome, giving a good idea of the general appearance of a Roman garden.

A casino, a form of pavilion consisting of two or three rooms, was considered almost a necessity. It was especially intended for games, banqueting, or repose. As the villa was removed from the bustle of town, so the casino was detached from the noise unavoidable in a country house, containing, besides the host, his family, dozens of guests, and hundreds of slaves. Pliny enthusiastically describes a casino at the

end of one of his violet-scented terrace walks, "which I am in love with
—yes, literally in love with, for I built it with my own hands." This contained two sitting rooms and a sleeping apartment. The last was heated
by a hot-air apparatus and was doublewalled, so that it was "impervious
to the voices of the slave boys, the murmur of the sea, the raging of
storms, the light of day, and even the flash of lightning unless the windows are opened." Continuing, he adds, "Here it seems to me that I
have got away even from my own villa, and I derive especial enjoyment
from it at the time of the Saturnalia, while the other parts of my establishment are ringing with the license and mirthful shouts of that
season, for there I am no hindrance to the gambols of my slaves, nor are
they to my studies."

Other smaller isolated pavilions were called *cubicula*, because they
were primarily intended for repose and contained a sleeping-place, usually a couch placed in a niche or alcove. Our word cubby-hole is of similar origin and significance. Pliny describes such a little edifice at his
Tusculan villa as "a summer-house of exquisite marble, the doors
whereof project and open into a green enclosure; so that from its upper
and lower windows the eye is presented with a variety of different verdures. Next to this is a little private recess (which, though it seems distinct, may be laid into the same room) furnished with a couch; and
notwithstanding it has windows on every side, yet it enjoys a very agreeable gloominess by means of a spreading vine which climbs to the top
and entirely overshades it. Here you may recline and fancy yourself in a
wood: with this difference only, that you are not exposed to the weather.
In this place a fountain also rises and instantly disappears; in different
quarters are disposed marble seats, which serve no less than the summer-house, as so many reliefs after one is wearied with walking."

There were various forms of unwalled constructions, consisting of
columns erected on platforms and supporting vine-covered rafters,
shading couches or seats, and a table where meals could be served. Several examples of these little banqueting pavilions remain at Pompeii,
and must have appeared when in perfect condition much like the [op-
posite] illustration, which shows a Renaissance reproduction of the

A POMPEIAN EXEDRA

same idea. Another similar pavilion, but in the shape of an alcove, is de-scribed by Pliny as terminating an acanthus walk. "At the upper end is an alcove of white marble shaded by vines, supported by four small Carystian pillars. From this bench the water, gushing through several little pipes, as if it were pressed out by the weight of the people who re-pose themselves upon it, falls into a stone cistern underneath, from whence it is received into a fine-polished, marble basin, so artfully con-trived that it is always full without ever overflowing. When I sup here this basin serves for a table, the large sort of dishes being placed round the margin, while the smaller ones swim about in the form of little ves-sels and water-fowl. Corresponding to this is a fountain which is in-cessantly emptying and filling; for the water, which it throws up to a great height, falls back into it by means of two openings, and is re-turned as fast as it is received."

Simplest of all was a seat, or exedra, sometimes covered and some-times uncovered, usually semicircular in form and placed on a slightly raised platform. This was especially intended for conversation. On the street of the Tombs in Pompeii are three or four of these seats, favourite places for a rendezvous. Similar exedræ were placed in the house courts, gardens, and parks.

Grottoes or artificial caves cooled by streams of fresh water served

as *musæa*, or thinking-places for philosophers, where they could medi-
tate in solitude, hidden from observation, protected from interruption,
and sheltered from the heat of the midday sun in summer. Such a
grotto surmounted by a pergola is shown in the accompanying illustration. Other caverns, warmed by hot air, were provided for winter occupation. The following account, by M.T. Varro, gives a good idea of
one of these out-of-door studies and its surroundings: "My study (*museum*) is situated at the spot where the stream springs, and from this
point, as far as an island formed by its junction with another water-
course, is a distance of eight hundred and fifty feet. Along its banks a
walk is laid out ten feet broad; between this walk and the country my
aviary is placed, closed in right and left by high walls. The external lines
of the building gave it some resemblance to writing tablets surmounted
by a capitol. On the rectangular side its breadth is forty-eight feet and
its length seventy-two, not including the semicircular capitol, which is
twenty-seven feet in diameter. Between the aviary and the walk, which
marks the lower margin of the tablets, opens a vaulted passage leading
to an esplanade (*ambulatio*). On each side is a regular portico upheld by
stone columns, the intervals between which are occupied by dwarf
shrubs. A network of hemp stretches from the outside walk to the architrave, and a similar trellis joins the architrave to the pedestal. The
interior is filled with birds of every species, which receive their food
through the net. A little stream supplies them with water."[1]

Greenhouses with panes of glass or of translucent stone were built
for the protection of the more tender plants in winter, and to force others to mature out of season. Here exotics from the East were grown.

Multitudes of birds, beasts, and insects, as well as human beings,
were made welcome to portions of the plantation and supplied with
suitable dwelling-places. In the early cult of sacred trees and pillars,
birds played an important part, and then, as Mr. Arthur Evans has remarked, as occurs to-day among primitive races, the spiritual being in
bird form was commonly supposed to descend on trees and stones.
Peacocks strutted along the alleys, swans sailed over the water, and
doves flew about the fountains, each the possible incarnation of a god

---

1. *Of Agriculture*, M. T. Varro.

or goddess. Song-birds are said to have been less esteemed than those which, like the turtle-dove, had "qualities recalling the great law of Nature, the law of love, a fundamental principle in the religion of antiquity." Sometimes they were confined in cages of hempen netting or wickerwork, but often they were permitted to roam at liberty. Beehives were also constructed of wickerwork and sometimes of earthenware.

In the scheme of the gardens, much importance was attached to various open-air constructions especially intended to promote muscular exercise. The largest of these was the *hippodromus*, a name given in the time of the Antonines, not to a building, but to an elongated rectangle terminated at one end by a semicircle, and defined by a broad path running around it like a race track. Here one could drive along a broad avenue shaded by planes and laurels, be carried in a litter on an alley firmly constructed for that purpose, or walk on a gravel foot-path. The central area was covered by turf intersected by narrow paths and sometimes planted with rose-bushes or geometrical flower-beds. Pliny the Younger gives a detailed description of a hippodrome of this kind at his Tusculan villa. It was enclosed by "plane trees covered with ivy, so that while their heads flourish with their own foliage, their bodies enjoy a borrowed verdure; and thus the ivy, twining round the trunks and branches, spreads from tree to tree and connects them together. Between each plane tree are planted box trees, and behind these bay trees, which blend their shade with that of the planes. This plantation, forming a straight boundary on both sides of the hippodrome, bends at the farther end into a semicircle, which, being set round and sheltered with cypress trees, varies the prospect and casts a deeper gloom; while the inward circular walks (for there are several), enjoying an open exposure, are perfumed with roses, and correct by a very pleasing contrast the coolness of the shade with the warmth of the sun. Having passed through these several winding alleys, you enter a straight walk, which breaks out into a variety of others divided by box hedges. In one place you have a little meadow, in another the box is cut into a thousand different forms; sometimes into letters expressing the name of the master; sometimes that of the artificer, whilst here and there little obelisks rise, intermixed alternately with fruit trees; when on a sudden, in the midst of this elegant regularity, you are surprised with an imitation of the negligent beauties of rural nature, in the centre of which lies a spot surrounded with a knot of dwarf plane trees. . . . Throughout the whole hippodrome several small rills run murmuring along, wheresoever the hand of art thought proper to conduct them; watering here and there different spots of verdure, and in their progress refreshing the whole."

Broad paths wide enough for a sedan-chair or a litter to be carried along them were called *gestationes*. Sometimes they surrounded the parterre or hippodrome, and sometimes they were placed on a terrace. Often they were planted with soft moss or with sweet-smelling herbs, which sent forth their fragrance when crushed under foot.

Narrow paths, called *ambulationes* separated the beds in the parterre. These were not wide enough for more than one or two people to walk abreast.

Other kinds of esplanades, open, or covered by a portico, were intended especially for the taking of exercise. In summer they were shielded from the bright rays of light and exposed to every cool breath of wind; in winter protected from unwelcome breezes and warmed by the sunshine. The length of each promenade was carefully measured,

A FORM OF TREE-WORSHIP

and posted up where the walker could easily calculate the extent of his stroll.

Sculpture added much to the decorative effect of the garden. Carved balustrades, benches, tables, bas-reliefs, and statuary were considered the most important part of many gardens, and were beautifully designed. To supply this ornamentation, ship-loads of the finest works of art were exported from Greece to adorn Italian pleasure grounds. At Lucan's villa, near Rome, marble sculpture was so predominant that his gardens were called by Juvenal *horti marmorei.*

As in Greece, statues were usually set up in honour of some appropriate divinity. Accordingly, images of the Graces, the Seasons, Pan, Sylvanus, Flora, Pomona, and Vertumnus were frequently erected. Oftenest of all Priapus was thus worshipped. Even the humblest peasants took pains to employ his image rudely carved from a tree trunk or a block of stone to act as a protective deity or sanctified scarecrow to frighten harmful birds away from their crops. Terminal statues with knobs below the shoulders, from which a votive garland of flowers might be hung, seem especially fit for the open air.

Refreshment being one of the most desirable luxuries for human beings and a necessity for the vegetation, an abundance of water was indispensably connected with out-of-door dwelling-places. In the baths, fish-ponds, and fountains great ingenuity was displayed to please the eye while the body was being reinvigorated. An *aquarius* was one of the most highly skilled slaves employed at the villa; under his direction many useful and ornamental water-works, designed by the ar-

chitects and engineers, were kept in order. From an elaborate *château d'eau* to a slender font of drinking-water, almost every form of ornamental hydraulics with which we are familiar, and many others now unknown, seem to have been employed by the ancients.

At Pompeii there are a variety of fountains in a good state of preservation. Hardly a peristyle is without a rectangular basin of water a foot or two deep, either lined with marble or mosaic. Usually they are placed entirely below the level of the pavement, but occasionally the edge of the basin is surmounted by a marble coping rising a few inches above the surface. A marble table or statue was often placed in connection with this fountain. Many garden courts were also ornamented with brightly coloured niches covered with mosaic and shellwork sheltering a spout of water or a miniature *château d'eau* and decorated with statues. Masks serving as lamps were placed on each side of one of these niches. At night flames bursting through the eyes and mouth must have produced a weird effect.

Fantastically clipped evergreen trees and shrubs were the principal "vegetate ornament" of the garden. This kind of sculpture is said to have been invented by Matius, a friend of the Emperor Augustus. The chief gardener was known as the *topiarius*, and it was his none too easy task to see that the evergreens were artistically shorn. Under his supervision pyramids, cones, wild animals, hunting scenes, and even a whole fleet of ships might be shaped by skilful shears. Of shrubs there were fewer species then, but the variety in form given by the topiary's art made up for any deficiency in their natural diversity. An illustration

from the *Hypnerotomachia Poliphili* shows the image of a man upholding a curious structure, all of which was supposed to have been clipped from a box tree. Other no less fanciful designs were reconstructed on supposedly classic lines by the archæologists of the Renaissance, and were probably not far from the mark.

The *xystus*, or parterre, was elaborately laid out in figures edged with box. Sometimes these outlines were left empty, and sometimes they were filled with flowers. The accompanying illustrations give an idea of the style of the design. According to our ideas, flowers, even in the *xystus*, would have seemed lacking in abundance and variety. From *coronamenta*, a word used to signify cultivated flowers, we can assume that they were intended to be picked to decorate with wreaths the heads of those reclining at a banquet, or to festoon the walls with garlands, rather than to give pleasure when growing. Thus the appearance of the parterre depended mostly upon the geometrical design of the beds, the topiary work, statuary, and fountains. The scarcity of vegetation brought the architectural features into great prominence.

The rose, the lily, and the violet were the three most distinguished flowers of antiquity; but the narcissus, anemone, gladiolus, iris, poppy, amaranth, immortelle, verbena, periwinkle, and crocus were also cultivated and much admired. Many flowerless plants like basil, sweet marjoram, and thyme were grown for their fragrance, while the acanthus was welcome on account of its beautiful foliage. Numerous flowers are mentioned by Pliny in his *Natural History* on account of their curative properties, among them the asphodel, nasturtium, and mallow. Others he praises as especially appropriate for chaplets and garlands, such as

roses, violets, and the never fading amaranth. Ivy covered the walls or was trained to form garlands between trees and columns.

Trees and shrubs were cultivated in the garden and park and were often sacred to the gods, especially if happening to have been struck by lightning. In front of these tables or altars were idols placed as shown in the preceding illustration. The first temples, according to Pliny, were trees. Among the favourites were the pine, the emblem of Cybele, the oak of Jupiter, the laurel of Apollo, the myrtle of Venus, the poplar of Hercules, and the olive of Minerva. Groves of sacred trees were often planted, especially in connection with temples. The cypress although an exotic was also grown in many places. Yew, although sufficiently common, was not much esteemed, and instead juniper and rosemary were often employed for topiary work. Box, too, was frequently clipped, and then, as always, considered the best shrub for edgings.

Labyrinths are said to have been originally constructed to conceal the royal Egyptian tombs. The word is of Egyptian origin. The idea of Greek and Roman labyrinths may have come from Egypt; but in the great prehistoric palace at Knossos most archæologists recognize the original of the traditional labyrinth; it was the house of the double axe, symbolizing Zeus and reverenced as the sanctuary of the god, as well as the palace of the king. In the centre of the building were two sacred columns engraved with double axes. The plan of this labyrinth is commemorated on the ancient money of Knossos. During the Roman Empire, labyrinths were often constructed to ornament gardens. One is sketched on a wall at Pompeii with the inscription *Labyrinthus hic habitat Minotaurus*. Others were used as designs to embellish the mosaic pavement of the peristyle.

Finally, in Italy during the third century, as in England at the close of the eighteenth, formality and artificiality were carried to meaningless extremes of magnificence, and provoked much abuse and ridicule. One writer complains that the cities have been invaded to such an extent by the country that they are turned into vast gardens. Another derides a fanatical amateur whose garden was made complete by sacrificing to it his bedchamber and dining-rooms. The poets Horace and Martial, like Pope and Addison in more recent days, wearying of the restraint imposed upon nature and the overluxurious, pompous life established in the *villa pseudo urbana*, advocated return to the simplicities of the *villa rustica*.

Hadrian's famous villa at Tivoli showed evidence of the degraded but magnificent taste of his time. It was the last word of artificiality and pomposity, and cast the golden house of Nero quite into the shade. Even now the ruins cover an area of about ten square miles. Gardens, groves, colonnades, shady corridors, high-roofed domes, grottoes, baths, lakes, basilicas, libraries, theatres, circuses built of varicoloured marble and filled with works of art, were crowded together near the imperial palace.

Here Gregorovius tells us the emperor beguiled his time in recollections of his Odysseus-like travels.

"For this villa, built according to his own designs, was the copy and reflection of the most beautiful things which he had admired in the world. The names of buildings in Athens were given to different parts of his villa. The Lyceum, the Academy, the Prytaneum, the Poecile, even the vale of Tempe with the Peneus flowing through it, and indeed Elysium and Tartarus, were all there.

"One part was consecrated to the wonders of the Nile, and was

called Canopus after the enchanting pleasure grounds of the Alexandrians. Here stood a copy of the famous temple of Serapis, which stood on a canal and was approached by a boat....

"At a sign from the emperor these groves, valleys, and halls would become alive with the mythology of Olympus; processions of priests would make pilgrimages to Canopus, Tartarus and Elysium would become peopled with the shades from Homer, swarms of bacchantes might wander through the vale of Tempe, choruses of Euripides might be heard in the Greek theatre, and in sham fight the fleets would repeat the battle of Xerxes."

CHAPTER TWO

Monastic Gardens

URING the tumultuous Anglo-Saxon period immediately succeeding the withdrawal of the Romans from Britain, their civilization died into a vague tradition of the past. "The villas, the mosaics, the coins which we dig up in our fields, are no relics of our English fathers, but of a Roman world which our fathers' swords swept utterly away." The peaceful arts were lost in oblivion. Horticulture, least of all, could flourish while the country was being devastated by internal anarchy and barbarian invasions.

The coming of St. Augustine to Canterbury in 597 A.D. was the beginning of a new era. "The civilization, arts, and letters which had fled before the sword of the English conquest returned with the Christian faith." Toil, which had sunk into the greatest dishonour, was raised from the dust by the monks. "It was the special glory of St. Benedict [the founder of the order to which St. Augustine belonged] to teach the men of his day that work sanctified by prayer is the best thing a man can do, and this lesson has never been lost sight of since his time." Thus within the walls of the Benedictine monasteries were large gardens cultivated by the monks in common, and often smaller ones as-

signed to the abbot and to the chief
almoner of the community. Here
flowers, despised by the earliest
Christians as symbols of paganism,
were now grown to decorate the
church. The rose was held in the
highest esteem. At Subiaco is still
preserved the *roseto*, a little rose garden set apart for St. Benedict. The
rose-bushes it contains are said to
be the same as those whose beauty
delighted his senses, and with whose thorns he was accustomed to
mortify his flesh when endeavouring to chase away thoughts of the
beautiful temptress.

With the cross the monks carried the plough. The Benedictines
were accordingly called by Monsieur Guizot the *Défricheurs* of Europe.
In England, to the Benedictine St. Augustine and to his disciples were
due the revival of horticulture and the introduction of several new vegetables and fruits. On the continent the monks are said to have incor-
porated fragments of the Roman villas into their monasteries, and to
have restored the former gardens. But in England there seems to have
been very slight connection if any between the classic and conventual
grounds. Although during the two centuries succeeding the advent of
the saint, gardening certainly flourished within the newly founded
monasteries, little is known except the mere fact of its existence.

In the convents for women, too, planned like the conventual establishments for men, there were gardens. Of these, one of the earliest was
constructed by St. Radegonde, wife of Clothair I, at Poitiers, whither,
in the middle of the sixth century, she escaped to take the veil. "Here
the delicate hands of the queen, of the Abbess Agnes, and of the nuns
cultivated roses and other flowers, that, woven into garlands or scattered on the table to form a perfumed covering, ornamented the refectory." Perhaps some of these blossoms had clustered over an arbour
there, where the poet Venantius Fortunatus (a rather Epicurean

Cloisters, St. John Lateran, Rome.

bishop with many pagan proclivities), surrounded by a group of ad-
miring "sisters," used to compose his sonnets and enjoy en *âme précieuse*
the sweetness of open-air life.

The nuns were required to be good gardeners. Many years later,
Héloïse, abbess of Paraclet, addressed a long complaint to Abélard,
stating that it was unreasonable to expect nuns to conform to the same
rules as monks in regard to agriculture and horticulture. Physically, she
contended, women were unfit for much rough manual labour.

In the tenth century, the darkest of the Dark Ages, another period
of great industrial depression reached its lowest ebb. Again civilization
suffered from foreign invasions. Monasticism, for the previous two
centuries on the decline, almost ceased the struggle to subsist; and horticulture, as before early in the Christian era, practically became a lost
art.

In the eleventh century, however, a revival of religious zeal, in England as elsewhere, brought about an improvement in the condition of

affairs. This development preceding the Norman Conquest is well described by Viollet le Duc:

"All Europe was under either religious or military rule, and as in this world moral force always finishes by overcoming material force, when there is a conflict between the two, the monasteries acquired more influence and more riches than the castles. They had on their side the voice of the common people, who, in the shadow of the convents, devoted themselves to industry and cultivated their fields in greater security than under the walls of the feudal castles; who found solace for their moral and physical sufferings within the great establishments, where all was well ordered, where prayers and charity were never wanting. Religious houses were the place of refuge for sick souls, for great repentances, for hopes deceived, for work and meditation, for feebleness and poverty, at the time when the first condition of earthly existence was a strong arm and a shoulder capable of carrying a coat of mail."

After the Norman Conquest, William and his followers brought with them, from across the Channel, new styles in architecture for the castles and monasteries which they established to promote the subjugation of England. The rage for founding monasteries, then at its height in Normandy, spread all over the conquered country. William himself began this movement by erecting and richly endowing several superb abbeys, and many of his subjects followed his example.

Again the Benedictine order was the first to flourish, and this time far more extensively than ever before. In order to avoid any unnecessary contact with the outside world, its rule prescribed that each community should contain all the essentials of life within its precincts. Since the flesh of no four-footed animal could be eaten, the raising of fish and fowl was customary, while that of vegetables was indispensable. Fish and duck ponds, poultry yards, orchards, vineyards, kitchen and physic gardens, were, if possible, connected with every religious foundation, and were often its greatest pride and glory. Manual labour was obligatory, and the monks adopted agriculture and horticulture as their favourite pursuits.

"Beside the spacious monastic buildings," Monsieur Joret says, "one always found a garden. Although it was destined above all to supply the needs of the convent with vegetables, which served for the nourishment of the cenobites, and with aromatic or medicinal herbs, cultivated for the remedies which they furnished, yet some flowers also were cherished for the pleasure they gave the eye and for their fragrance, as well as to deck the altar on a feast day."

Of these monastic gardens few actual traces or exact records have been preserved in England. But William of Malmesbury's delightful description of the cultivated grounds close to Thorney Abbey, near Peterborough, early in the twelfth century, will give an impression of their general appearance. "It represents a very Paradise, for that in pleasure and delight it resembles heaven itself. The marshes abound in trees, whose length without a knot cloth emulate the stars. The plain there is as level as the sea, which with green grass allures the eye, and is so smooth that there is nought to hinder him who runs through it. Neither is there any waste space, for in some parts are apple trees, in others, vines, which are either spread on the ground or raised on poles. A mutual strife is there between nature and art; so that what one produces not, the other supplies."

A twelfth-century plan of Canterbury, showing the cloisters containing a herbarium and a conduit, with the fish-pond, orchard, and vineyard outside the walls, gives only a rough idea of the planting and arrangement; but there is no other even as complete belonging to this early period. Since, however, the various parts of all monasteries, appertaining to the same order, were disposed with as much uniformity as the exigencies of the situation permitted, the general scheme of the English monastic gardens can be gathered from the plans and descriptions of those on the continent. The building was usually placed in a valley near a river, in order that the grounds might be easily irrigated. Among the important divisions the cloister-garth contained perhaps the most characteristic features, and is especially interesting on account of its resemblance to the classic Grecian *peristyle* and to the Roman *atrium,* or *impluvium* According to Viollet le Duc:

"It is probable that the first cloisters were porticoes of the same kind as those of antiquity, that is to say;—a sloping roof of carpentry borne upon columns, of which the base rests on the ground. We have sought vainly to discover at what period the well-known disposition of the Roman *impluvium* was modified to that which we see admitted in the most ancient cloisters. There must have been a transition which escapes us for lack of monuments described, or buildings still existing. For there is a well-defined demarcation between the Roman *impluvium* and the Christian cloisters of Europe. In the first, the columns rest directly upon the soil, and one can pass from the colonnade to the plot of ground in the area intervening between the columns; while in the second, the pillars or columns are always placed on a pedestal, or a parapet, separating the gallery from the open ground, and only interrupted by rare breaks serving as exits. This latter disposition and the lowness of the columns are characteristic of cloisters in the West, and form a particular style of architecture, which has less connection with the courts enclosed by porticoes of the Romans."

The cloisters were enclosed by the church and the other principal buildings of the monastery—the refectory, the dormitory, and the chapter-house—just as the classic peristyle was surrounded by the living rooms occupied in common by the family. These cloisters were ordinarily placed south of the church in order that, unshadowed by its lofty walls, the monks might have the full benefit of the sun as they paced up and down the corridor reciting their prayers, or sat on the benches either studying religious books or wrapped in contemplation. Ostensibly they were absorbed in their devotions, but in reality "carnal" thoughts often crept into their minds and were whispered about; hence forbidden gossiping in the corners of the cloisters often gave occasion for doing penance.

Spanish Garden Courts, Granada.

COURT OF THE LIONS : THE ALHAMBRA

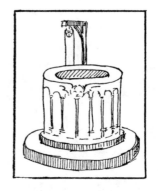

"The diversity of the dwellings and offices around the cloisters," says Guillaume Durand, "signifies the diversity of the dwellings and recompenses in the heavenly kingdom. 'For in my Father's house are many mansions,' said the Saviour. And in the moral sense the cloister represents the contemplation into which the soul withdraws itself and hides, after being separated from the crowd of carnal thoughts, and where it reflects upon the only real blessings — those of heaven. Around these cloisters are four walls symbolizing contempt for oneself, contempt for the world, love of one's neighbour, and love of God."

The walls of the cloister were usually painted with frescoes representing scenes from the Old and New Testaments, as those of the peristyle had been decorated with mythological subjects, landscapes, and garlands of flowers. On the walls of the Campo Santo at Pisa are some charming fourteenth-century frescoes, showing groups of people sitting and standing in an earthly paradise. Their surroundings are especially interesting, including a graceful hexagonal fountain with conventional flowers in the foreground, and orange and oak trees forming a charming background to the picturesque figures.

The grass plot in the midst of the cloisters was sometimes called "paradise," signifying to the monks, according to Wiclif, the greenness of their virtues. This verdant square was often thickly studded with flowers as represented in early manuscript illuminations. The flowers were under the charge of the sacristan, and were intended to be used by him to decorate the church at festivals and incidentally to give pleasure to

Gothic Fountain, from an Early Tapestry.

A·WELL·IN·THE·CERTOSA : FLORENCE·ᵗ·S·

the eye when growing. Two paths crossing each other at right angles divided the grass plot into quarters, and sometimes at their intersection was a tree, symbolizing to the brethren the ladder by which, in gradations of virtue, they aspired to celestial things.

More often, however, perhaps because cleanliness comes next to godliness, there was, in the centre, a *savina*, or tub of water, for washing purposes, or the simplest form of well, like the one reproduced from an early manuscript; at a later period this was replaced by a more elaborate, carved stone wellhead, or a fountain of drinking water, which became the most important architectural feature and ornament of the courtyard, whether designed in the Gothic or Renaissance style. The water was drawn up in a bucket suspended by a rope rolling on a pulley; this involved an iron support to the pulley, which was often ornamentally forged, as appears in the illustration of a well in the cloisters at the Certosa near Florence.

The plan of the ancient monastery of St. Gall in Switzerland, familiar to Charlemagne, still exists, and supplies much information as to the arrangement of a large religious establishment belonging to the Benedictines in the ninth century. Probably few alterations were made, except in details, during the later Middle Ages. Its name commemorates the Irish missionary before whom, at a still earlier time, "the spirits of flood and fell fled wailing over the waters of Lake Constance." The monastery was placed in a valley, and the cultivated grounds within the walls consisted of four divisions: the cloister-garth, the physic garden, the vegetable garden, and a combination of orchard and burial ground.

The cloister-garth was a square, planted with grass and possibly shrubs, divided by two intersecting paths into four equal quarters. In the centre was a *savina*, supplying water for drinking and washing purposes. These cloisters were south of the church, and surrounded by the other more important communal buildings.

For obviously logical reasons, the physic garden was placed close beside the house of the medical attendant. It was laid out in sixteen oblong beds, severally containing peppermint, rosemary, white lilies, sage, rue, corn-flag, pennyroyal, fenngreek, roses, watercress, cummin, lovage, tansy, kidney bean, fennel, or savory. All of these were regarded as herbs useful for medicinal purposes.

The kitchen garden was necessarily on a larger scale and contained eighteen oblong beds of identical shape, each planted with a different kind of vegetable or pot-herb: onion, garlic, parsley, coriander, chervil, dill lettuce, poppy, savory, radish, parsnip, carrot, cabbage, beet, leek, shallot, celery, or corn-cockle. Near by was the house of the head gardener or *hortulanus*.

In the burial ground, trees and shrubs were planted in the spaces between the graves, and must have produced the ornamental effect which in this connection we are apt to consider as modern. Mentioned as growing there were apple, pear, plum, service medlar, fig, quince, peach, hazelnut, almond, chestnut, walnut, laurel, and pine trees. Amidst such a luxuriance of foliage the graves must have been almost hidden from view.

Alexander Neckam, an Augustinian monk living in the twelfth century, is the earliest English writer on gardens. In his *De Naturis Rerum* he describes the herbs, trees, and flowers growing in a noble garden; but his list can hardly be taken to apply literally to plants then flourishing in England, for neither the pomegranates, almonds, dates, oranges, nor lemons mentioned by him could have survived there out of doors. On the other hand, "the drowsy poppy," the daffodil, and brank ursin (acanthus), peony, violet, rose, marigold, and lily, among other flowers he cites, we may well believe were grown in many gardens, as they are also described in the oldest English herbaries.

Battle Abbey, the first great monastery in England founded after the Norman Conquest, belonged to the Benedictine order, and was originally called "La Bataille." William the Conqueror ordered it to be built on the site of the decisive conflict between the Norman and Anglo-Saxon armies, in fulfilment of his vow, made as the battle raged, that if God should grant him the victory, a splendid chantry should be erected for the souls of the slain. The high altar is said to mark the spot where, in the thick of the fiercest fighting, Harold, the king, was killed and his body found by his betrothed, after nightfall.

A step away from this historic spot, stretching between it and the restored ruins of the monastery, are some beautiful modern gardens laid out by the late Duchess of Cleveland. The stiff, geometrical patterns of the parterre, bedded out with geraniums and edged with box, produce an effect harmonious with the building, although they are utterly unlike the homely plantations formerly cultivated by the monks. Another attractive arrangement is the terrace walk of grass intersected by gravel paths beside the Abbey, with embrasures in the thick wall for seats, where, walking or sitting, one overlooks a wonderful stretch of woodlands and downs once traversed by William and his army.

The Cistercians also, following in the footsteps of the Benedictines, as theirs was an offshoot of the older order, did much to further the progress of horticulture on the continent and in England. Their monasteries, as conspicuously bare of decoration as the Benedictines', were built in the hollows of valleys, where culture could fertilize the soil, and where there was an abundance of water to irrigate the land. St. Bernard founded the most famous of all their communities in the wild and gloomy valley of Clairvaux, beside a clear stream running through the midst of a thick forest. An ardent lover of nature, "Trust one who has tried it," he wrote; "you will find more in woods than in books, trees and stones will teach you what you can never learn from school-masters." One of the most sacred spots in the monastery, now sadly deprived of all its ancient glory, was a little plot of ground whose cultivation was his especial care. Large gardens belonging to the community lay within the cloisters, and outside others stretched over clearings in the forest, covering many acres. The several divisions of ground were separated by intersecting canals supplied by the river Alba. A glowing description of the orchard by a twelfth-century writer is worth quoting:

"If thou desire to know the situation of Clairvaux, let those writings be to thee as a mirror. . . . Then the back part of the Abbey terminates in a broad plain, no small portion of which a wall occupies, which surrounds the Abbey with its extended circuit. Within the enclosure of this wall many and various trees, prolific in various fruits, constitute an orchard resembling a wood. Which, being near the cell of the sick, lightens the infirmities of the brethren with no moderate solace, while it affords a spacious walking place to those who walk, and a sweet place for reclining to those who are overheated. The sick man sits upon the green sod, and while the inclemency of Sirius burns up the earth with his pitiless star, and dries up the rivers, he (the sick man) tempers the glowing stars, under leaves of the trees, into security and concealment and shade from the heat of the day; and for the comfort of his pain the various kinds of grass are fragrant to his nostrils, the pleasant verdure of the herbs and trees gratifies his eyes, and their immense delights are present hanging and growing before him, so that he may say not without reason,'I sat under the shade of that tree, which I had longed for, and its fruit was sweet to my throat.'The concert of the coloured birds soothes his ears with their soft melody; and for the cure of our illness, the Divine tenderness provides many consolations, while the air smiles with bright serenity, the earth breathes with fruitfulness, and he himself drinks in with his eyes, ears, and nostrils the delights of colours, songs, and odours."

The Carthusians, belonging to an order founded by St. Bruno in 1084, dwelt in monasteries planned to isolate, as completely as possible, each member of the community. This was to fulfil the rules peculiar to their order, obliging them to live in absolute silence and solitude. Each of the brethren, like the Egyptian monks, occupied a detached cottage, to which was added in the twelfth century a small garden cultivated by

Gothic Fountain in the Cloister-garth, Newstead Abbey.
Photograph by R. Keene.

its tenant. Numbers of these cottages and gardens surrounded the cloisters and obviated the necessity of having large pieces of ground under cultivation.

THE DOG'S GRAVE : NEWSTEAD

Among the orders of friars were the Dominicans, founded by the Spanish Dominic, and the Franciscans, by St. Francis of Assisi, in the thirteenth century. Both lived according to different lights from the monks, despised all luxury, and took less pride in owning beautiful buildings and fine plantations. Wanderers over the country, preaching and begging for food wherever they happened to stop, unlike the members of other orders, the friars required but small establishments, and few cultivated acres for their food supply.

An interesting abbey of exceptional beauty, once belonging to the Dominicans, or Black Friars, as they were called from the colour of their habits, is still standing at Newstead on the former estate of Lord Byron. Although altered in many of its details, the lay of the land is unchanged, and the general effect is probably much the same as in the time of the friars. A large, square sheet of water, called the Eagle Pond, remains untouched, and near it is the old "stew," where fish were bred for the friars' consumption; while the cloisters, restored by their present owners, and containing a good reproduction of a Gothic fountain in a square plot of grass, retain their conventual character.

Once battlemented walls are supposed to have enclosed the ground northeast of the Abbey now occupied by two parterres of flowers, edged with box and a square of grass planted with yew trees, shading a monument to the poet's favourite dog. Byron himself would also have been buried here, if his wish had not been disregarded on the supposi-

Eagle Pond, Newstead Abbey. Photograph by R. Keene.

tion that this was not holy ground; though, in fact, as the monks' ceme-tery, it had been consecrated long before.

Formerly, kitchen and physic gardens would naturally have been placed within the ancient enclosure where now are two box-bordered squares of flowers. Both are freely planted with all sorts of common annuals and perennials—larkspur, bachelor's buttons, foxglove, and the like—giving them the same delightful appearance as the quaint, old-fashioned gardens in New England.

Outside the walls, but as was frequently the case, within bow-shot for the sake of their protection, lies the large oblong sheet of water known as the Eagle Pond. Its name is derived from a brass, eagle-shaped lectern, probably hidden by the friars at the time of the disso-lution of their order by King Henry VIII, and discovered centuries afterward lying at the bottom of this pond. The broad, green margin of grass is a characteristic feature, while the summit of the bank, laid out in rectangular beds of flowers alternating with rectangular grass plots

LEADEN STATUE AT NEWSTEAD

STATUE : NEWSTEAD

each surrounding a walnut tree, is an unusually charming formal arrangement. In a plan of the Abbey made at the time it was sold, about fifty years ago, this scheme of planting is shown to have been the same as now, and it probably dates back to a much earlier period. A twelfth-century description of a similar piece of water helps us to picture its part in the lives of the monks:

"Here, also, a beautiful spectacle is exhibited to the infirm brethren; while they sit upon the green margin of the huge basin, they see the little fishes playing under the water, and representing a military encounter by swimming to meet each other. This water serves the double duty of supporting the fish and watering the vegetables."

A break in the wall beside the walk, above the pond, is well contrived to give a glimpse of the fine trees in the beautiful park outside the enclosure. Here, perhaps, the abbot was wont to chase the hart, for the ecclesiastics of old were very fond of hunting. The Bishop of Worcester writes in 1030 to his brother bishop of St. David's, who had promised him six couples of good sporting dogs, saying that "his heart languished for their arrival," and continuing with the following entreaty: "Let them come, O reverend father, without delay. Let my woods reecho with the music of their cry and the cheerful notes of the horn, and let the walls of my castle be decorated with the trophies of the chase."

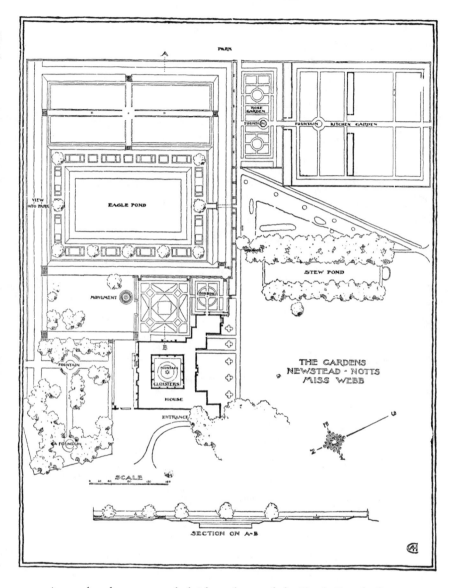

An orchard was recently laid out beyond the Eagle Pond after some overgrown bushes and half-dead trees had been cleared away from its site. One of the main grass paths separating the plantation into four sections is ornamented by two old leaden statues. These images of a faun and his mate were supposed by the ignorant country folk to have been worshipped by the uncle of the poet, popularly known as the wicked Lord Byron.

Other walled enclosures contain a rosary and a delightful flower-bordered kitchen garden. Their general arrangement is as simple as possible, but the position and design of the seats and fountains, and the planting of the beds, are contrived with so much taste and skill that the effect produced is exceptionally charming.

Beautiful plantations of exotics, row upon row of rare Japanese iris, Alpine gardens and thickets of bamboo, are also well worth a visit. Taken as a whole, the gardens at Newstead are extraordinarily interesting as showing great variety of treatment and as containing a collection of distinct types, each brought near perfection. To their beauty a weird charm is added by recollections of the sacrilegious Byrons and their pious predecessors. Shades of the friars seem to flit in and out among the more substantial figures of the lame poet and his friends, whose favourite diversion was to masquerade in monkish raiment.

Newstead, with many another monastery, lost much of the glory of its original gardens at the time of its dissolution by command of Henry VIII. Few others like it, however, have been restored and laid out again along their former lines. The curse, said to have been invoked by the monks upon their despoilers, is commonly believed to prevent monastic lands from being handed down in direct succession. This seems idle superstition, but it is strange how often such property changes hands, and how seldom are left any traces of the monastic gardens. At Shrublands there are some fine old Spanish chestnut trees, said to have been imported by the monks and supposed to be the oldest in the country. Here and there, in different places, are the outlines of an ancient stew-pond as at Harley-on-Thames and at Hatton Grange, or a portion of the cloisters once enclosing the garth as at Ashridge; but elsewhere in England it is difficult to discover more than a few scattered remains.

GARLAND MAKERS IN A PLEASAUNCE

CHAPTER THREE

The Mediæval Pleasaunce

NGLO-SAXON ways of living were greatly altered by the advent of the Normans in the latter half
of the eleventh century. Gallo-Roman, unlike Britanno-Roman, civilization had never wholly died out
even during the Dark Ages; hence in arts and crafts
the invaders came prepared to teach the inhabitants of England many
new and important lessons. After the withdrawal of the Romans, the
Frankish kings had continued to build villas in imitation of the classic
style, to which gardens were often attached. But of these gardens no detailed description written before the time of Charlemagne is extant.
Then, in 812 A.D., that emperor's capitularies were published, giving
particular directions concerning the maintenance of his numerous orchards and gardens. In the long list of vegetation he wished to have cultivated he mentions, among other flowers: lilies, roses, and poppies,
besides naming many fruit trees equally familiar to us. "We desire," he
dictated, "that in the garden there should be all kinds of plants."

The Carolingian orchard and garden were practically one and the

---

same. It was often the scene of the May-field and of other important assemblies, as well as of the more homely events of daily life. Here Charlemagne is described as receiving the ambassadors from the last pagan king of Spain. It must have been an impressive sight. "Fifteen thousand Frenchmen wearing satin tunics are stretched upon the white carpet. The king is seated on a massive golden throne, from which he overlooks all the barons with an almost priestly gravity; then suddenly the ten infidels enter the garden and make their way slowly through the crowd; they are mounted on white mules with bridles of gold and saddles of silver. They carry olive branches in their hands, Eastern fashion, as a token of peace. It is a scene worthy of Virgil."

> "Le roi Charles est en un grand verger,
> Avec lui sont Roland et Olivier . . .
> Ils sont assis sur des tapis blancs . . .
> Sous un pin, près d'un églantier
> Est un fauteuil d'or massif,
> C'est là qu'est assis le roi qui tient douce France."
> — *Chanson de Roland.*

In architecture, as well as horticulture, the Normans excelled the Anglo-Saxons at the time of the Conquest. The fortalices and monasteries first built by the conquerors were a decided improvement on any previous erections in England. These, however, were not the castles of which ruins now remain, but merely wooden towers or keeps, sometimes strengthened by palisades and ditches, used for defending important strategic positions formerly surmounted with earthworks by the Danes and Saxons. But, until the Normans had subdued the entire country, home life was an impossibility, and there was no occasion for domestic architecture. Thus, while the early monasteries were substantial stone buildings, commonly situated in the broadest and most fertile valleys, castles were ruder structures, generally erected on windy hilltops, where their inmates devoted both time and space to projects for offence and defence. To harbour in these bare strongholds such a peaceful pursuit as gardening would have been impracticable. After a

Castle with Terrace Walks, from Le Roman de la Rose.

few years, the danger of insurrection having lessened, the Normans replaced their first wooden structures by permanent castles built of
stone. Still until the twelfth century the times were far from peaceful,
and although agriculture and horticulture were among the favourite
occupations of the Normans, these cannot have flourished extensively
outside of monastic precincts. At Deeping, however, ancient records
show that a garden was laid out on the site of a ruined Roman villa by
one of William the Conqueror's followers. A few other gardens proba-

bly existed under exceptionally favouring circumstances, although frequently threatened with devastation. But as an abundance and variety of fish and game took the place of vegetables in the diet of the upper classes, except in monasteries, horticulture was of no vital importance.

A miniature on one of the pages of a beautiful fifteenth-century manuscript of the *Roman de la Rose*, belonging to the British Museum, represents a Norman castle of the earliest substantial design. Here the massive stone keep, strongly protected by double crenellated walls, and by both an inner and outer moat, is intended as a representation of the Louvre in the time of Philip Augustus. Then a marvellous treasure was guarded there, symbolized in the romance as the Rose. Hedges of roses, in extraordinarily full bloom, line the walks beneath the ramparts. Underneath, the moats are deep enough to have contained a large supply of carp to feed the garrison, and sufficiently broad to have permitted swans, also often eaten, to sail freely about on the surface of their smooth waters.

During a truce of hostilities, life in such a feudal castle must have been as dull and isolated as on board a sailing vessel becalmed at sea. The bored passengers crowding on deck to watch a flock of sea-gulls devouring scraps of food suggest the listless lord in a mediæval poem, seeking distraction by tossing bread and grain to the swans from his castle window into the moat below. Then, especially to the châtelaine and her women, a few plants must often have afforded as much diversion as the little flower whose care saved the reason of an imprisoned patriot and gave its name to the Italian story "Picciola."

Of the early Anglo-Norman style of architecture, Berkeley Castle is perhaps the most complete example now existing. The keep is said to date from the time of William the Conqueror. The whole castle is still inhabited and preserved in almost its original condition. Around the massive building runs a terrace intended both for a walk and to prevent the walls from being mined by besiegers. One of these terraces, covered with grass and flanked by an ancient yew hedge clipped in the shape of rude battlements, forms a quaint bowling-green. How long it has been laid out as such is unknown, but probably for several centuries.

Terraces, like the one adjoining these battlements, were, in those tumultuous times, the only safe place for the ladies to enjoy an airing. A portion was often reserved for their especial use, and, as at Castle Carlisle, called the "Ladies' Walk." There, at a much later period, Mary, Queen of Scots, when captive was allowed to take her exercise. At Bridgnorth, a pleasant terrace walk, much admired by Charles I, encircles the ancient castle walls and is more than half a mile in compass. On the borders of such a terrace, beside the hedge, a few herbs were usually cultivated by the châtelaine to be used in sickness, or to make a piquant sauce for whetting the satiated appetite.

At last the comparative cessation of internal warfare permitted the precincts of the castle to become still less restricted without loss of security. Then the pleasaunce (developing from the terrace walk containing the little collection of herbs already described) began to enjoy a less precarious existence. In France, earlier than in England, its form became more clearly defined, and, by covering more area, answered more varied requirements. From contemporary documents its appearance has been reconstructed and described in detail by M. Georges Riat in L'Art des Jardins:

"In the twelfth century the garden was habitually situated outside the ramparts, and was entered from the castle by a secret door in the fortifications. Later gardens, answering to the following description, were laid out in the courtyards of most seigneurial habitations. A fence, when the garden was in the courtyard, or palisades, when it was outside, surrounded it. A low wall, built in three parts so as to furnish a back for a grass-covered seat, formed a frame for intimate conversations. In a corner, a fountain in the Gothic style often served to water the parterre and the greensward. Sometimes a round flower-bed might be found in the middle of the *préaux* (*pratelli*), or flowered parterre. On the sides were cradle-shaped tunnels and trelliswork fastened to the walls. Sometimes a labyrinth, or *house of Dædalus*, twisted its tangled paths in conflicting directions.

"Flowers grown in the parterre, or in pots on the wall, brightened the enclosures. Several trees, clipped into balls, gave shade and freshness to the air. The ingenuity of the gardener, like that of the *topiarius* of ancient Rome, was exercised in clipping the shrubs to give them geometric forms. Finally, if the space permitted, there was a small basin of water for fish and swans. Great luxuries were to have an aviary for game-birds close by, and a number of peacocks strutting about under the eyes of the guests."

Intercourse with Palestine had marked effect in developing the gardens of the twelfth and thirteenth centuries. Many innovations were due to the Crusaders, who, in the peaceful intervals of their stay in the Holy Land, were often kindly received by their heathen adversaries and given many opportunities to study Oriental luxuries and add them to their bare homes in England. Not only the so-called Gothic arch, but many minor architectural features may have been due to Oriental influence. A great change was thus brought about in the details as well as in the general style of European architecture, and its result was shown, not only in the way the gardens of the knights hospitallers were laid out, but in adding to the ornamental appearance of the pleasaunce.

> "Sos sarmasane avoit un vergié ondoiant
> De ciprès, de loriers; moult sont soef flairant,
> Li oisel i font joie et demainent lor chant.
> Sous ciel n'avoit cière ente qui n'y fust voirement."

An Oriental garden of marvellous beauty was described by the celebrated Venetian traveller, Marco Polo. He visited Palestine in the thirteenth century; but the garden he speaks of with such admiration had already been in existence for probably nearly two hundred years. It was laid out for the famous Prince Hassan, from whose name and deeds were derived the words *assassin* and *hasheesh*. He was also called the Old Man of the Mountain because he dwelt on a mountain-side, where he had constructed the wonderful garden which his followers, bewildered by hasheesh, confounded with a heavenly paradise. After once having been entranced in this elysium, they were willing to become assassins and to risk their lives in attempting to murder Hassan's enemies for the sake of being rewarded by a return to his garden. The identity of the original "Old Man" became confused with that of his successors, and it is to the pleasure grounds belonging to one of these later princes that Marco Polo refers: "A very beautiful garden filled with all sorts of trees and fruits, and around these plantations stood different palaces and pavilions decorated with works of gold, paintings, and furniture all in silk. There, in the little canals, one saw running streams of wine, milk, honey, and very clear water. There were lodged young girls, perfectly beautiful and charming, who were instructed to play on all sorts of musical instruments; one saw them perpetually walking in these gardens and palaces."

Another description of a similar garden appears in the so-called *Travels* of Sir John Mandeville, a book first written in French and then translated into English at the close of the fifteenth century. The location of the garden he mentions was said to be the island of Milstrak.

"That isle is very rich. There was dwelling not long since a rich man, named Gatholonabes, who was full of tricks and subtle deceits. He had a fair and strong castle in a mountain, so strong and noble that no man could devise a fairer or a stronger. And he had caused the mountain to be walled about with a strong and fair wall, within which walls he had the fairest garden that might be imagined; and therein were trees bearing all manner of fruits, all kinds of herbs of virtue and of good smell, and all other herbs also that bear fair flowers. And he had also in that garden many fair wells, and by them he had many fair halls and fair chambers, painted all with gold and azure, representing many divers things and many divers stories. There were also beasts and birds which sang delectably and moved by craft that it seemed they were alive."

There are a few architectural features now to be seen in English gardens, which can be directly attributed to Oriental influence. Bathhouses, for instance, were an Oriental luxury. Edward I is said to have imported the idea of their use from Palestine, and to have built the one existing near Leeds Castle in the thirteenth century. It is now used as a boat-house. Tents were another accessory to a garden adopted by the Crusaders. They were made of rich tapestries, for which the English

Tent and Flowery Mede, from an Early Tapestry.

were among the first of European nations to obtain a reputation. Their usual form is shown in the illustration, reproduced from one of a series of tapestries in the Cluny Museum.

The planting of the Oriental gardens was also much admired by the Crusaders, and had its influence on European horticulture.

"La trovent un vergier qui fu tous ais d'olive,
Et de mout riches arbres qui sont de mainte guisse,
Et li vergiers fu jouenes et li ante florie."

Oriental flora were now cultivated throughout the west and north of Europe, as at an earlier period they had penetrated throughout Italy and other southern countries. The rose and the lily, both flowers of Oriental origin, had reappeared as early as the time of Aldhelm, the eighth century. The yellow Persian rose was especially celebrated by the ancient Mussulman writers, and its European naturalization is said to date from this period. Another variety known as the rose of Provence was brought back by Thibaut IV, Count of Champagne, to Provins, where it grew until recently in the suburbs of the town. The name of the rose of Damascus, or damask rose, also betokens its Eastern origin. Not long ago Syrian daffodils still grew upon the ancient site of Horseley Castle, and Armenian violets survived in several places. Many other exotics, now considered almost as native plants since they are so familiarly known in Europe, were the fruit of Crusaders' pilgrimages in the East.

At the close of the thirteenth and the beginning of the fourteenth century the connection between France and England was very intimate. The French language was spoken by the upper classes in both countries; and as to manners and customs in general, and their gardens in particular, the same fashions prevailed, although the French were somewhat in advance of the English. The description of a French garden in the twelfth century would answer for an English one during the two following centuries. Under the rule of the Plantagenets the Anglo-Saxons and the Normans had become fused into the English nation. The great lords of both races generally dwelt in peace with each other, if not always with their kinsfolk across the Channel, and as has been said, the Crusaders added much to their knowledge of how to live luxuriously. Frequently at home there was leisure to give attention to domestic comfort and to engage in the peaceful contests of chivalry. Then the castle, becoming more than a bare fortress, was treated as a commodious residence for the lord and the little court of retainers living under his protection. Sometimes, as at Tattershall, in one household, there were more than a hundred people.

To meet the new requirements, the enceinte of the castle was increased sufficiently to include within its walls and moat, besides more spacious living rooms, stables, outhouses, tiltyards, gardens, and orchards. At Framlingham the outer ballium, reached by a timber bridge from the postern, is shown in the thirteenth-century plan to have been laid out as a pleasaunce.

> "The grete tour, that was so thikke and strong,
> Which of the castel was the chief dongeoun,
> Was evene joynant to the gardyn wall."

As within the castle the wealthy lord sought to embellish the great hall, which often took the place of the ancient keep, with fine tapestry, richly carved furniture, and elaborately chased armour, so outside it he strove to decorate the gardens with fountains, arbours, and perhaps a maze. Often such a lord

> "Hadde, bihinden his paleys,
> A fair gardin of nobleys,
> Ful of appel-tres, and als of pirie
>
> Foules songe therinne murie.
> Amideward that gardyn fre,
> So wax a pinnote-tre
> That had fair bowes and frut;
> Ther under was al his dedut
> He made ther-under a grene bench,
> And drank ther under many a sschench [cupful]."
> —Weber, III, 23, "The Seven Sages."

Under Edward I the mediæval prosperity of the English may be said to have culminated. It declined under the weak or warlike reigns of his successors, until during the Wars of the Roses much that civilization had gained seemed to have been lost.

"The improvement in husbandry and horticulture was as satisfactory as the advance made in the fine arts. Here the influence of the king was specially felt. Though engaged in war or busy with legislative cares, Edward found time to attend to the cultivation of his desmesnes and the stocking of his gardens and orchards. Strangely mingled with the demands of the campaign against the Scots or with the requirements of the politician or the pleasures of the sportsman are directions to procure new cuttings of fruit trees and seeds of vegetables for the table. Fruit and forest trees, shrubs, and flowers introduced from the continent were naturalized in the king's gardens or in those of the nobility and the larger religious houses. In 'stately gardens' both the lemon and orange were common, which could not be grown without artificial heat. Many of these were neglected and forgotten after his death, until even the memory of them so completely passed into oblivion that their reintroduction after the Wars of the Roses is spoken of as though they had never been known before.

"Nor were the triumphs of horticulture limited to the improvement in our indigenous fruits. New varieties were introduced at this time. Figs, oranges, lemons, citrons, almonds, and even olives are noted among the fruits growing in the gardens of some of the large landowners of this country. These natives of a southern clime could not have ripened their fruits unless in exceptionally warm seasons or by means of hothouses; the evidence, however, that they existed is overwhelming."[1]

All classes of people now seem to have had gardens. Those belonging to the king were principally in the neighbourhood of London, at Charing, Westminster, Clarendon, the Tower, and at Windsor Castle. In them were grown peaches, first mentioned in 1276; pears and apples, of which several new varieties were introduced; quinces and strawberries, well known to the Anglo-Saxons, and gooseberries, which seem to have been a novelty. There were also royal vineyards at Windsor and Westminster. One of the great nobles, De Lacey, Earl of Lincoln,

---

1. *England in the Fifteenth Century.* Rev. W. Denton, M.A.

Bourgeois Garden, from the Profits de Rustican.

cultivated extensive market gardens on the top of Holborn Hill and received from them a considerable revenue. Fitzstephen, in his life of
Thomas à Becket, speaking of the suburban residences of the citizens
of London, says, "On all sides outside the houses of the citizens who
dwell in the suburbs there are adjoining gardens planted with trees,
both spacious and pleasing to the eye." As the various colleges were
founded, vineyards and *herbaria* (the beginnings of botanical gardens)
were laid out in their neighbourhood, so that by the early part of the
fourteenth century many fine orchards and gardens had become established, not only by the religious communities, but by the secular owners of the land.

An Englishman, John de Garlande, who lived in Paris during the
first half of the thirteenth century, gave a description in his *Dictionar-
ius* of the contents of a town garden in either France or England. "In
Master John's garden are these plants: sage, parsley, dittany, hyssop,

celandine, fennel, pellitory, the rose, the lily, and the violet; and at the side [*i.e.*, in the hedge] the nettle thistles and foxgloves. His garden also contains medicinal herbs; namely, mercury and the mallow agrimony, with nightshade and the marigold." There was besides a garden for pot-herbs, where grew borage, leeks, garlic, mustard, onions, cibols, and scallions; and in his shrubbery grew pimpernel, mouse-ear, self-heal, buglos, adder's-tongue, and "other herbs good for men's bodies." In the fruit garden were cherry, pear, apple, plum, quince, medlar, peach, chestnut, walnut, and fig trees, besides grapes.

The following fifteenth-century description by Lydgate of a rich churl's garden gives an idea of the arrangement in many smaller gardens a century before:

> "Whilom ther was in a smal village,
> As myn autor makethe rehersayle,
> A chorle, whiche hadde lust and a grete corage
> Within hymself, be diligent travayle
> To array his gardeyn with notable apparayle,
> Of lengthe and brede yelicke square and longe,
> Hegged and dyked to make it sure and stronge.
>
> Alle the aleis were made playne with sond,
> The benches turned with newe turves grene,
> Sote herbers, with cordite at the honde,
> That welled up agayne the sonne schene,
> Lyke silver stremes as any cristalle clene
> The burbly wawes in up boyling,
> Round as byralle ther beamys out shynyge."
> —"The Chorle and the Birde,"
> JOHN LYDGATE.

Dining in the garden was also common in warm weather.

> "Les napes metent pardeanz un jardin."
> —"Mort de Garin," p. 28.

Castle Garden, from a Picture by Dierick Boutts.

Afterward people were in the habit of playing chess there, as we see them in a garden scene reproduced from the *Romance of Alexander* [opposite]. Notwithstanding the rudeness of many of their habits, and their fondness for the brutal excitement of war and the chase, lives of

adventure had highly developed the imaginations of the upper classes and given them a taste for living amidst beautiful surroundings. Then, both by art and nature, people seemed made for gardens and gardens for people to an extent which we can hardly appreciate nowadays.

Above all, the pleasaunce was intended for the diversion of the châtelaine. As early as 1250 we learn from a contemporary record that Henry III, to gratify Eleanor of Provence, ordered his bailiff at Woodstock "to make round about the garden of our Queen two walls good and high so that no one can enter, with a well-ordered herbary befitting her position, near our fish-pond, where the said Queen may roam about freely." Here she might have meditated in solitude under a leafy bower, have enjoyed a tête-à-tête with a bosom friend enthroned on a turfed seat, or in pleasant company have paced up and down the sanded alleys.

As an agreeable alternative from the smoky castle hall, the pleasaunce was evidently the favourite place for recreation. It was often chosen for giving audience and receiving friends. In the *Romance of Garin le Loherain* the messenger found the great baron seated in a garden surrounded by his friends.

> "Trouva Fromont scant en un jardin
> Environ lui avoit de ses amins."
>
> — *Roman de Garin*, I, 282.

71

There entertainment was furnished by the troubadours, who sang their *Chansons de Geste*, interspersed with romances of the Crusades, of prowess, and of love; by the jugglers and tumblers, who performed wonderful tricks and gymnastic feats; and by the dancing-girls, whose graceful motions were of an Oriental character. The guests themselves also frequently carolled, or danced in a circle, sang songs, and played upon musical instruments for their own diversion.

> "Tho myghtist thou karoles sene,
> And folk daunce and mery bene,
> And made many a faire tournyng
> Upon the grene gras springyng.
> There myghtist thou se these flowtours,
> Mynstrales and eke jogelours,
> That wel to synge dide her peyne,
> Somme songe songes of Loreyne;
> For in Loreyn her notes bee
> Full swetter than in this contré."

Garland weaving was a favourite occupation for ladies. Both men and women wore chaplets of flowers on festive occasions, and they were also given as rewards for success in various sports. Chaucer speaks of the month of May as especially the season for weaving garlands. In "The Pastime of Pleasure," La Bel Pucel is described by the portress at the garden-gate as seated within thus employed:

> " 'Truly,' quod she, 'in the garden grene
> Of many a swete and sundry flowre
> She maketh a garlonde that is veray shene,
> Wythe trueloves wrought in many a coloure,
> Replete with sweteness and dulcet odoure
> And all alone, wythout company,
> Amyddes an herber she sitteth pleasauntly."

And again she is described weaving a chaplet or wreath to be worn on the head.

"Besyde which fountayne the moost fayre lady
La Bel Pucel was gayly sittyng
Of many floures fayre and ryally
A goodly chaplet she was in makynge."

In the "Lai d'Aristote" (Barbazon, III, 105, 107) King Alexander's beautiful mistress is described as descending early in the morning, walking in the garden alone, and making herself a chaplet of flowers. In another fabliau, cited by Wright and published by Keller, a Saracenic maiden descends from her chamber into the garden, performs her toilet at the fountain there, and then makes herself a chaplet of flowers and leaves, which she puts on her head. Then we read in *The Knight's Tale*, how the fair Emelie was wandering about in her garden at sunrise while:

"She gadereth floures, party white and rede,
To make a subtil gerland for hire hede
And as an aungel hevenysshly she soong"

The beauty of a jewel was never more enhanced by an appropriate setting than the loveliness of gentlewomen by the fanciful environment of this mediæval pleasaunce. Fresh as the "new flowers of sondry hewe," in her trailing robes fashioned "summerwise," her head wreathed with a chaplet of fragrant roses, her bright eyes sparkling in the sunshine, the "fayre ladye" was indeed the crowning joy of a very paradise. And as she was its most beautiful ornament, so was it her chief delight.

Le Roman de la Rose gives the best possible idea of both the French and English gardens of the Middle Ages. It was chiefly written by Guillaume de Loris, in the first half of the thirteenth century, and was probably well known in England before it was translated by Chaucer into English. There are several manuscript copies of it containing descriptions in the text, accompanied by illustrations giving vivid pictures of the pleasaunce. Its form, the walls enclosing it, with their surrounding moat; the subdivisions of latticework; the "flowery mede," shaded by fruit trees, with a fountain in its centre; and the stone-coped beds, containing clipped shrubs and other smaller plants, are clearly

Pleasaunce, from Le Roman de la Rose.

shown from various points of view. The arrangement is full of charm. In the most important of these illustrations (which is above , and was taken from a fourteenth-century Flemish manuscript preserved at the British Museum), the garden is shown as a whole, ornamented with many quaint details. It is enclosed by a crenellated wall, surrounded by a moat. The subdivisions are formed by a fence of wooden trelliswork, on the topmost railing of which is balanced a peacock. In the left-hand division is a copper fountain head, where the water, spouting from lions' mouths, drips into a circular basin, and runs off through a marble channel embedded in the turf. Velvety grass, thickly sprinkled with daisies, surrounds the fountain and forms a soft seat for the little company of merrymakers who are singing and playing upon musical instruments. The rich texture of such a carpet of turf was often dwelt upon in poetry:

> "About the brinkes of these welles
> And by the stremes over al elles
> Sprange up the grasse as thick y-set
> And soft as any veluet,
> On whiche men myght his lemman ley
> As on a fetherbed to prey."

Every kind of a plantation was contained in some form of an enclosure, as is evident from the different words applied to it; all, like the French *courtil*, suggesting its original location in a courtyard. A "garden," according to the derivation of the word from *zerd*, *garth*, or *yard* (three nouns from the same Aryan root as the French word *jardin*), originally signified a walled but unroofed enclosure containing cultivated vegetation. Usually this vegetation principally consisted of herbs, grass, or fruit trees. Thus there were *wyrt-zerds*, *grass-zerds*, *ortzers*, *cherry-zerds*, and *apple-zerds*, or "yards," the prefix specifying more or less exactly the contents of the circumscribed space.

This enclosure protected the vegetation from marauders, and secluded its occupants. Privacy was a very important characteristic of the garden. Inside the castle there was scant opportunity for confidential conversation. So when people wished to talk without being overseen or overheard, they were apt to retire to the pleasaunce. For lovers especially it was a favourite meeting-place.

> "Into the gardyn go we, and ye shal here
> Al pryvely of this a longe sermon:
> With that thei wenten arm and arm yfere,
> Into the gardyn from the chambre doun.
> And when that he so fer was, that the soun

> Of that he spake no man heren mighte
> He seyd hire thus, and out the letre plyghte."
> — Chaucer, *Troylus and Cryseyde.*

For the sake of seclusion as well as safety the garden was, therefore, surrounded by high and thick walls, fences, or a hedge, and usually still further defended by a moat.

> "And all was walled that none throu it wid were
> With posterns in pryvtie to pasen when him list
> Orche-ardes and erberes well clene."
> — Langland, *Piers Plowman.*

The walls were built of stone until brick came into use, and varied, of course, in height and thickness.

> "Amongst other of his honest thinges
> He had a gardyn walled al with stoon,
> So fair a gardyn wot I no wher noon."
> — Chaucer, *The Marchaundes Tale.*

Their summit was generally finished with battlements or crenellations.

> "I saw a garden right anoon,
> Full long and broad and everidele,
> Enclosed was and walled well
> With highe walls embattailed."

The earliest fences were commonly wattled, that is, woven of osiers. Others, more ornamental, were formed of rails or of pickets, and painted green.

Hedges often enclosed the later gardens, instead of walls. The bushes used for this purpose were privet (thus called perhaps because it served to insure privacy), thorn, sweetbrier, and yew.

"The hegge as thick as a castle wall,
That who that list without to stand or go,
Though he would all day prien to and fro
He shoulde not see if there were any wighte
Within or no!"

Moats were also common. In the *Chorle and the Birde*, Lydgate describes the garden of the rich churl as "hegged and dyked to make it sure and strong." The water served for fish and swans.

In form the enclosure containing the pleasaunce, garden, or orchard was preferably square or oblong.

"The gardyn was by mesurying
Right evene and square: in compassing
It was as long as it was large."

The entrance was through a postern or gateway in the wall sometimes surmounted by battlements, and always barred by a stout wooden door fastened with a massive iron lock. Idleness is shown, in the accompanying illustration [page 74] from *Le Roman de la Rose*, admitting the knight-errant through such a postern into the enchanted enclosure. A side door in the castle furnished another means of ingress. Through this side door, across the pleasaunce, and out the postern was a way of leaving the castle unobserved. It was thus that the beautiful pagan, Rosamond, descended to succour the wounded and insensible Elias of St. Giles, as described in one of the *Chansons de Geste*, and by the same means she and other *suaves pucelles* were in the habit of passing out in springtime to gather flowers.

"Quand vient el mois de mai por colir la florete."
—"Elie de St. Giles."

The flowery mede, or a grass plot thickly dotted with flowers, was perhaps the simplest form of a garden, and the one first known to our mediæval ancestors.

MAUGIS AND "LA BELLE ORIANDE"

"Ful gay was all the ground and queynt,
And poudred as men had it peynt
With many a fresshe and sondrie floure,
That casten up ful good savour."

There is a good representation of this kind of planting with but slight indications of beds in the wonderful series of fourteenth-century tapestries preserved at the Cluny Museum. The lady with her handmaiden, and her pet falcon, dogs, monkeys, and rabbits, is standing on a plot of flowery greensward, enclosed by a railed wooden fence overgrown with roses. This plot, as may be discerned, consisted of a circular bed carpeted with thick grass intermingled with low-growing flowers such as daisies, violets, hyacinths, and pinks. It is brought out more or less clearly in different sections of the tapestry. Such a *préau*, or bit of meadow conventionalized, was a common and very delightful portion of the pleasaunce. Of late years it has been reproduced in modern gardens.

Gradually, as the cultivated ground extended, it came to be divided into compartments. These subdivisions were usually formed of latticework with square or diamond-shaped apertures, more or less ornamental as during the classic era.

Then there were beds for plants, raised several inches above the level of the path, retained by a stone coping and fenced in with wattles, latticework, or open wooden railings. Fruit trees and herbs predominated, for as yet flowers were given no especial prominence in the garden.

"This yerde was large and rayled all th aleys,
And shadowed wel with blosmy bowes grene,
And benched newe and sanded all the wayes
In which she walketh arm in arm between."
— Chaucer, *Troylus and Cryseyde*, Liber Secundus, 820.

The main paths or alleys, as described in the last quotation, were covered with sand, and usually broad enough for two or three people to pace abreast. Narrower paths were intended to facilitate the weeding of the beds.

Resting-places in plenty were provided for those who found walking or standing tiresome. Simple benches cushioned with turf were built into embrasures or against the wall. Earth banked up around the trunk of a tree, grassed over and held in place by wattled osiers, formed a circular seat. In the centre of the garden a three-sided exedra constructed of stone or brick, covered with grass and flowers, often formed the most important feature. In the picture here given [page 81] the two seated figures are the lovers described in the following words:

"Oriande et Maugis se trouvèrent en ung jardin pour eulx esbattre et deviser en passe temps, après ce qu'ils avoient diné et que l'eure estoit de prendre un petit repos. C'est au mods de mai, le temps où tous les oysillons se dégoisent, et si sont tous vrais amans à penser à leur amour."

Arbours or bowers were wooden structures covered by shrubs and vines, and usually shading a comfortable seat. Originally in Anglo-Saxon times the bower, or *bur*, had been a small building containing a bedchamber, or a room especially intended for women. Thus we often read of the ladies' bower, and of a *bird in bure*, a lady in her bower. But gradually the word came to signify a summer-house in a garden.

...."A pleasant herber well ywrought
That benched was, and eke with turfes newe
Freshly turved, whereof the grene gras,
So small, so thicke, so short, so fresh of hew,
That most ylike green wool, I wot, it was;

A SEAT AN ARBOUR & A GALLERY

The hegge also that yede in this compas,
And closed in all the grene herbere
With sicamour was set and eglatere,
Wrethen in fere so well and cunningly
That every branch and leafe grew by mesure
Plain as a bord, of oon height by and by.

*   *   *   *   *

And shapen was this herber roofe and all
As is a prety parlour."

— Chaucer, *The Flower and the Leaf.*

Water in various forms was always, if possible, introduced into the garden. Fish-ponds, bathing pools, and fountains were common. Usually the central and most ornamental architectural feature of the pleasaunce was a fountain. The earliest of an ornamental appearance were apparently of Oriental design, similar to the well-known one in the cloisters of Monreale above Palermo and to that reproduced from a photograph taken of an early piece of tapestry in the South Kensington Museum. But, of course, architectural treatment of fountains, as of other details, underwent the same evolution from Romanesque to Gothic, and from Gothic to Renaissance, as did architecture in general.

A maze or labyrinth was frequently laid out in or near the garden.

Garden Scenes, from Le Roman de la Rose.

An early form seems to have consisted of a network of underground passages, making the approach to a hidden bower almost impossible to the uninitiated. Several of these mysterious subterranean labyrinths existed in England, the most celebrated one being that constructed by Henry II to conceal fair Rosamond's bower at Woodstock. The bower, in her case, was a small stone building enclosing a well, a large enough dwelling-place for one or two people.

Sometimes the fountain was covered with an arbour and placed in the centre of the garden.

"Amiddes the garden so moch delectable
There was an herber fayre and quadrante,
To paradyse right well comparable,
Set all about with floures fragraunt,
And in the myddle there was resplendys haunte,
A dulcet spring and marvaylous fountaine
Of golde and asure made all certayne."

Topiary work was not unknown, as is evident from the descriptions in various poems and the illustrations in many manuscripts. A clipped tree often formed the central feature of the garden.

"Amyddis the gardyn stode a fressh laurer
Theron a bird syngyng bothe day and nyghte."

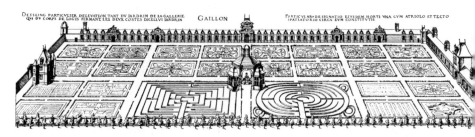

The Flower-garden, Château Gaillon, from Les Plus Beaux Bastiments de France, *by Androucet du Cerceau.*

Pious architects engraved labyrinths on the floors of cathedrals, as on the one at Chartres, so that the faithful, as has been ingeniously suggested, in following its tortuous ways might accomplish the semblance of a pilgrimage while their compatriots were on their way to the rescue of the Holy Sepulchre. Possibly the garden labyrinth may have originated in the same sentiment, though as time went on it came to be considered as merely affording diversion or purely as an ornament. Hedges edged the paths and an arbour marked the hidden centre.

Certain games were considered appropriate for the garden, among them tennis, bowling, and archery. But tennis-courts, archery and bowling-greens will be described in the account of Tudor gardens, where they were brought to greater perfection.

Other features of the garden, also con-structed at a later date, were menageries, aviaries, apiaries, and dove-cotes. Birds and bees everywhere added much to the charm of the garden. Swans swam in the basins and moat, peacocks strutted along the alleys and perched on top of the walls, and doves flew to and from their spacious homes. All these were served up as delicacies at meals. Of wild birds there were a great variety; some are mentioned in the *Romance of the Rose.*

> "For certys, as at my devys,
> Ther is no place in Paradys
> So good inne forto dwelle or be,
> As in that gardyne, thoughte me.
> For there was many a bridde syngyug
> Through-out the yerde al thringyng.
> In many places were nyghtyngales,
> Alpes, fynches, and wodewales."

If a large number of herbs were cultivated, they were sometimes set apart in an herbary. But many flowers which are now considered purely ornamental were then supposed to have healing properties, or to be fit ingredients for sauces and savouries; so the herbary was not strictly de-voted to the plants we should consider as herbs. Besides the plants grown for medicinal and culinary purposes, were others intended to be distilled into love philters and perhaps poisons.

The orchard in the Middle Ages was practically indistinguishable from the garden or pleasance. A precious description of it, which might equally well be applied to the garden of the period, was written by Albert the Great in a chapter of his *De Naturis Rerum*, called "De

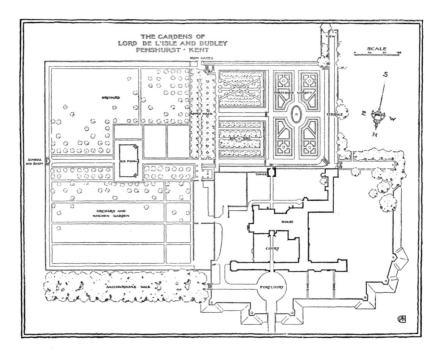

Plantatione Viridariorum." "In the first place," he says, "the whole site must be planted with the finest grass seed trodden into the ground by foot, forming an actual carpet of verdure, than which nothing could be smoother than the level surface.

"At one of the extremities facing the south, trees were grown, pears, apples, plums, laurel, cypress, and the like, interlaced with vines whose foliage protected the turf and furnished a fresh and agreeable shade.

"Behind the turf was planted a quantity of aromatic and medicinal herbs, for example, rue, sage, and basil, whose perfume would rejoice the sense of smell; then certain flowers, such as the violet, ancolie, lily, rose, iris, and others similar, which by their diversity charmed the eye and excited the admiration." Finally, at the extremity of the turf in the space reserved for flowers there was raised a seat formed of earth and covered with grass and flowers, where one could "rest one's body and re-fresh one's spirit."

The orchard in those days contained, besides a variety of fruit trees,

herbs for medicinal and culinary purposes and a few flowers, also fountains, seats, and the other architectural features of the pleasaunce.
Many fruit trees are said to have been imported from France, especially
in the thirteenth century, and hence were known by French names.
Among the varieties of pears were the *rule* or *regul*, the *passe-pucelle*, and
the *caloel* or *caillou*. Pearmain and costard apples were probably also of
French origin. Cherries had been reintroduced at the time of the Norman Conquest. Peaches, medlars, quinces, and chestnuts were commonly cultivated and imported from abroad.

Grafting was a craft well understood. Scions of ten or twelve distinct varieties of trees were grown upon an oak stock. Vines were
grafted on cherries and plums on vines.

The last of the castle gardens retaining a mediæval character were
those surrounding the great French chateaux. The difference between
them and the new order of arrangement arising from the Renaissance
was that each section was more or less isolated and treated as sufficient
unto itself, instead of being connected with a series of enclosures all
symmetrically disposed about the castle. But the approaching transition is apparent in the increasing symmetry of the plan as a whole.

In *Les Plus Beaux Bastiments de France*, written and illustrated with
many views and plans, Androuet du Cerceau gives an excellent idea of
these gardens as they appeared when upon the point of being superseded by the forerunners of Le Nôtre. According to his testimony
there were, especially at Blois, "quantities of large and fine gardens, differing from each other. Some having large alleys surrounding them,
others covered with carpentry, others with nut trees, others with vines
trained over them."

Gaillon, constructed under Louis XII for the Cardinal d'Amboise,
is perhaps the most interesting of these gardens, as can be seen from
the illustration [page 85]. Near the dwelling were two fine gardens separated by a terrace, adjoining "a gallery of sufficiently good arrangement
in the antique style, which looks out over the valley." One of these gardens was finished with "another fine and pleasing gallery worthy of being so called on account of its length and of the manner it is erected,

Parterre, Penshurst Place.

having a view on one side of the garden, and on the other of the said valley toward the river." In the middle of the garden was a pavilion, covering apparently a fountain of white marble. The other garden was placed in the valley. Near it the Cardinal had erected an "isolated or Carthusian dwelling-place, abounding in every pleasure."

But what of the mediæval pleasaunce remains in England to-day? Unfortunately, very little. More than half of the six or seven hundred castles built between the Norman Conquest and the reign of Henry VIII have entirely disappeared, many others have fallen into disuse, and of those still inhabited few retain their original surroundings.

Perhaps the most satisfactory survival is at Penshurst. Here the gardens were replanted about fifty years ago, but they must have been laid out at a much earlier date. It vividly recalls the mediæval pleasaunce, although differing from it in certain details. There are embattled stone walls surrounding the main enclosure; a bower or banqueting house, also of stone, on one of the terraces near the castle or palace; a flowery orchard, a large oblong fish-pond, high clipped hedges, and a garden of pleasant flowers spreading beneath the palace windows.

DIANA'S POOL : PENSHURST

The orchard is exceptionally delightful; its alleys are bordered with flowers, and a profusion of foxglove and other hardy annuals grow beneath the apple and pear trees, which are planted at a regular distance apart.

At the extreme south end of the walk, which extends along the west side of the main garden, there was formerly an open pavilion, which has unfortunately disappeared. Leading from the terrace on the main house level is a yew walk or alley, known as the "winter walk," and built for one of the ladies of the family for winter exercise. Outside the garden walls is an alley of beautiful beeches known as "Clarissa's walk," since it was a favourite spot with the lady to whom the poet Waller gave this name, a member of the Sidney family.

It is difficult to mention another pleasaunce retaining more than one or two mediæval features. At Sudeley Castle a part of the gardens were relaid out on old lines about fifty years ago. There are high yew hedges with birds quaintly clipped on top and covered alleys, but the choice of flowers has not been in keeping with the rest. In other places survivals or reproductions have been even less complete.

CHAPTER FOUR

Tudor Gardens

ARLY in the sixteenth century the Middle Ages were over. The Tudor accession brought the Wars of the Roses to an end and inaugurated a new epoch. Then assurance of internal peace, accompanied by great changes in social and political life, furnished a basis for the renaissance of art. When law and order were firmly established, people no longer—by herding together within the fortified precincts of castle or monastery—sought safety in numbers. Instead of being obliged to live protected by the lord of the manor, or attached to various religious communities, each family now existed as a distinct unit of society and required a separate home. Moderate-sized mansions of brick or stone were therefore constructed, more or less elaborately according to the wealth and social position of their owners, as dwellings for the previous occupants of the massive feudal strongholds. The spirit of feudalism had died out before the close of the fifteenth century; its form also gradually disappeared. Castles were first disused and then dismantled as they ceased to fulfil the altered requirements. In 1540, when John Leland was sent by Henry VIII on a tour of inspection, he reported that most of these ancient fortresses were running to decay,

A TUDOR MANOR HOUSE: EYAM HALL DERBYSHIRE

and barely mentioned in connection with them any semblance of a pleasaunce.

The sites of the new dwellings were not chosen like those of the castles, on account of their inaccessibility. It was no longer essential to consider strength before convenience. Now, instead of seeking a defensible position, people preferred situations that were pleasant and salubrious, where they might live protected from the cold winds, and where gardens and orchards might be cultivated advantageously. Thus, like the earlier monastic edifices, a gentleman's house was built oftener in a valley than on a hilltop. Here there was more room for expansion, and near the house the grounds under cultivation could be extended to answer the increasing demands for various kinds of plantations.

At first both house and gardens still seem to have been protected  not only by walls, but with a moat. Such was the residence of Edward Stafford, Duke of Buckingham, at Thornbury. Before its completion he was beheaded, and a survey of his estate, added to the state papers, is dated May 1521. From this description (which is all that remains of the gardens now) it appears that they were well supplied with galleries and arbours, or, as they are quaintly entitled, "roosting-places."

Terrace, Haddon Hall. Photograph by R. Keene.

"On the south side of the inner ward is a proper, garden, and about the same a goodly gallery conveying above and beneath from the principal lodgings both to the chapel and parrish church. The utter part of the said gallery being of stone embattled, and the inner part of timber covered with slate. On the east side of the said castle or manor, is a goodly garden to walk in, closed with high walls embattled. The conveyance thither is by the gallery above and beneath and by other privy ways. Besides the same privy garden is a large and goodly orchard full of young graffes well-laden with fruit, many roses, and other pleasures. And in the same garden are many goodly alleys to walk in openly. And round about the same orcharde is conveyed on a good height other goodly alleys with roosting-places covered thoroughly with white thorne and hasel. And without the same on the utter part, the said orchard is enclosed with sawin pale, and without that ditches and quickset hedges. . . . From out of the said orchard are divers posterns in sundry places at pleasure to go and enter into a goodly park newly made."

GARDEN·DOOR: CANONS ASHBY

Gradually battlements, moats, and other defensive accessories entirely ceased to be built in connection with the house, and were retained only to secure the gardens from intruders and for the preservation of the trees and plants from severe winds and the depredations of marauders. For, since the garden was no longer under the protection of the castle wall, it needed special defences. Many of the moats have since been condemned as unhealthy, and destroyed from time to time, but others remain, and are still stocked with fish, as at Losely and Hunstanston. At Helmingham the house and garden are each surrounded by a moat, and exist in nearly their original condition.

Cardinal Wolsey's palace and grounds at Hampton Court were among the latest to be made secure by moats as well as walls. It was in these gardens that the cardinal was accustomed to walk at the close of day as he recited even-song. His fondness for this recreation and the beauty of the gardens (which were located near the Pond Garden, and no longer exist) are described by his disciple Cavendish:

"My galleries were fayer both large and long
To walk in them when that it lyked me best.

"My gardens sweet enclosed with walles strong
Embanked with benches to sytt and take my rest.
The knots so enknotted, it cannot be expresst
With arbors and alyes so pleasant and so dulce
To pestilent ayers with flavors to repulse."

There was no abrupt transition from the style of the Middle Ages to that of the Renaissance in English gardens. Many Gothic features

Grass Alley, Elvaston. Photograph by R. Keene.

were long retained, of which remnants are still in evidence—the carved stonework, the conduits, the walks, and arbours. Trelliswork, as used to surround the beds, remained in fashion with but slight variations throughout the reigns of the Tudors.

Among the royal gardens of this time were those already existing and kept up at the Tower of London, Baynardes Castle, Wanstead, and Westminster, those renovated at York Place and Whitehall, and a new one at Nonesuch.

But the finest of the Tudor gardens were at Hampton Court, where Wolsey's work was almost entirely swept away to make room for the improvements designed by Henry VIII. These changes covered part of the space between the palace and the river, and the only portion now remaining is the small enclosure known as the Pond Garden. Of oblong shape, surrounded by an outer wall of brick, the ground is laid out on three different levels, with low retaining walls and copings of stone;

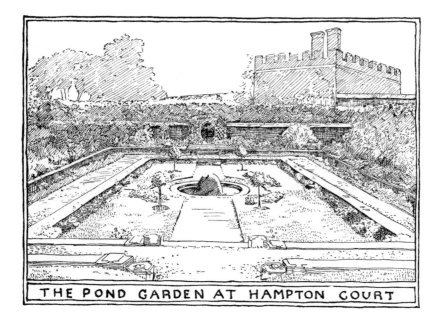

THE POND GARDEN AT HAMPTON COURT

in this stone one can see the holes whereby were fastened the thirty or more heraldic beasts which formerly served to strengthen the wooden railings striped with white and green, the royal colours. Above one corner of the wall appears a battlemented banqueting house built by Henry VII. In the centre of the enclosure is a round fountain, on a line with the entrance at one end and a vine-covered arbour opposite. The present planting is unworthy of special attention; but from the royal accounts we know that among the flowers originally ordered for the garden in Henry VIII's time were "violettes and Primroses, Gilliver-slips, mynts, and other sweet flowers. 100 Roses at 4d the hundred. Sweet Williams at 3d the bushel." It was weeded and watered by women at twopence a day. In this garden young Henry VIII carried on his first flirtations with Anne Boleyn, and here, when overtaken by infirmities, he used to hobble about in his premature old age.

The literature of this period relating to gardens was also slow to develop fresh and individual characteristics. This chiefly consisted of herbals translated from the Latin, as they had been previously by the Anglo-Saxons and by the Anglo-Normans. Beginning with the *Hortus*

The maner of watering with a Pumpe in a tubbe.

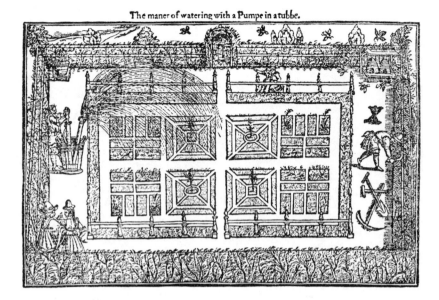

Sanitatus, published in 1485, sprang up a new crop of these books, which were of greater interest to the archæologist than to the practical gardener. Among these the most important was the *Grete Herbal*, printed about 1516, followed by a new translation of a herbal by Macer, a classic writer whose works had been well known in the Middle Ages. But Turner, a scholar of much distinction, was the earliest author of a herbal giving the names of English plants. His books, the *Libellus de Re Herbaria*, the *Names of Herbes*, and a *Herbal*, were published in the second quarter of the sixteenth century, and throw some light upon the gardening as well as upon the botanical researches of his time.

Andrew Borde is the first writer who gave directions in English as to how to plan a house and grounds. Much of his advice was practical, although often he saw fit to drag in a somewhat irrelevant quotation from the Bible, or a passage from some classic author to which we should not attach much importance. He was soon followed by Thomas Tusser with *A Hundredth Pointes of Good Husbandrie*, which has been interestingly edited under the auspices of the English Dialect Society. Hill's *Profitable Arte of Gardening* and his *Gardener's Labyrinth*

DOVE·COT: CRAFTON MANOR

DOVE-COT : MILTON

also add to our information concerning the gardens of this period.

The choice of the site was given careful consideration, and an unexpected importance was attached to the view. "After that a man have chosen a convenient soyle and place . . . he must afore cast in his mind that the prospect to and fro the place be pleasant, fair and good to the eye to behold the woods, the waters, the fields, the dales, the hills as the plain ground." In the opinion of all the early writers the garden and orchard were always to be located as near as possible to the house, and to be considered as an integral part of the same premises.

The approach to the house and gardens was through one or more courtyards, where peacocks sometimes answered the purpose of watch-dogs.

"The peacock is a bird of more beautified feathers than any other that is, he is quickly angry, but he is far off from taking good hold with his feet, he is goodly to behold, very good to eat, and serveth as a watch in the inner court, for that he spying strangers to come into the lodging he faileth not to cry out and advertise them of the house."

Doves too dwelt in the courtyard or in the garden. "A dove-house is also a necessary thing about a mansion place," Borde says. The illustrations show two dove-cotes of Norman types; the earlier form is round.

The confines of the garden still remained rectangular, sometimes forming a perfect square, or an oblong as in the illustration at the top

GARDEN DOORWAY : RISLEY

of page 94. As before, walls, a quickset hedge, or a fence always surrounded the garden. There were several entrances. The principal one
was usually a doorway opening from the house or from the house
court. Ingress for the gardener, and a gate especially for the owner corresponding to the postern of the Middle Ages, were also provided.
Borde says, "The false gate (otherwise called the back or field gate on
that side toward your meadow), made for your own going in and out
alone, shall be set out and garnished with two chevrons set upon one
main timber and no more, and four or five battlements above and shut
with a strong door for that way you shall go into your house privily,
and in like sort go forth again when it seemeth good unto you." Many
of these posterns, often battlemented, continued to be built during the
Renaissance. There are examples at Tissington, Swanopston Hall, etc.

Now we come to the garden itself. As Borde wrote, "It is a commodious thing to a mansion to have an orchard of sundry fruits, but
it is more commodious to have a fayre garden with herbes of aro-
matyke and redolit savoures." The earliest plan giving a good idea of its
chief characteristics is reproduced here from an illustration in the *Gardener's Labyrinth*. As to its main outlines it is not unlike the Pond

 Garden at Hampton Court, which has already been described in this chapter. A square piece of level ground is shown surrounded by a wooden paling, and within it a second enclosure fenced with latticework, strengthened at intervals by wooden posts; also an entrance through a double door protected by a heavy-corniced doorway, but not battlemented as it would have been, almost invariably, at a somewhat earlier period. Opposite to each other, in the middle of two edges of the outer enclosure, are a well and an arched arbour, both of good and simple designs familiar to us beside the old farm-houses in New England. In the centre of the inner enclosure a cluster of beds, intended for flowers, is laid out in geometrical designs. Other beds, oblong in shape and varying in width, form a series of borders for less ornamental plants. The corners of the central border are accented by circular beds. Between the outer paling and the inner latticework is another space filled with oblong beds, probably intended to contain the pot-herbs.

The intermingling of ornamental with useful plants continued to be common. As an innovation, Borde recommended that there should be two divisions separated by a broad-hedged alley. One of these sections was to be devoted to pot-herbs, the other to "quarters and pulse together with a place for bee-hives." Sometimes, too, fruit trees were placed in a special enclosure. Generally in the smaller gardens all sorts of vegetation were included, and herbs, grown for medicinal purposes "to turn up their house and to furnish their pot," were side by side with those cultivated principally for their beauty. By "turning up" the house was meant strewing the floors with sweet-smelling herbs, a prevalent practice before the introduction of carpets and still continued in a few churches.

Among the more ornamental plants grown in the garden were the acanthus, asphodel, auricula, amaranth (flower gentle or flower *amor*), cornflower (or bottle blew, red, and white), cowslip, daffodil, daisy,

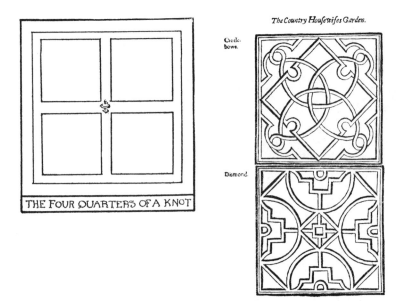

The Country Housewifes Garden.

THE FOUR QUARTERS OF A KNOT

gillyflower (red, white, and carnation), hollyhock (red, white, and carnation), iris (flower *de luce* or the *flos deliciarum* of the Middle Ages), Indian eye, lavender, larkspur (larkes foot), lily of the valley, lily (white and red), double marigold, nigella Romana, pansy or heart's-ease, pink, peony, periwinkle, poppy, primrose, rocket, roses of many sorts, including the sweetbrier or eglantine, snap-dragon (snag dragon), clove gillyflower (sops-in-wine), sweet-william, sweet-john, star of Bethlehem, star of Jerusalem, stock gillyflower, tuft gillyflower, velvet flower (French marigold), violet, wallflower, and besides, sweet-smelling herbs, such as mint and marjoram.

As a matter of decoration, the shape of the flower beds rather than their contents was considered of importance. The four quarters formed by the main alleys, which intersected the middle of the garden, were enclosed by a latticework fence or striped railings fastened to posts or to carved beasts. These quarters were subdivided into knots. The knot was either a geometrical pattern or the outline of some fanciful shape, such as a dragon, kept in place by a coping of wood, brick, stone, or tiles, and edged with box or some other border plant. The design of the knot was known as open or closed, according to whether it

98

was merely outlined with a border plant, and strewn inside the outlines with coloured sands, or was filled with growing flowers.

> "Then we went to the garden glorious,
> Like to a piece of pleasure most solacious
> With Flora painted and wrought curiously
> In divers knottes of marvaylous greteness;
> Rampande Iyons stood up wonderfly
> Made all of herbes with dulcet sweetness,
> With many dragons of marvaylous likeness,
> Of divers floures made ful craftely,
> By Flora couloured with colours sundry."

The more rare and beautiful flowers were planted in the knots, and clipped evergreen shrubs accented the corners of the beds or the centre of the garden.

A maze, or labyrinth, was another favourite ornamental design, and sometimes filled the place of the knots. Occasionally it was planted with hedges high enough to conceal the intricacies of the paths, and to force the uninitiated to wander long upon the outskirts, unable to penetrate within; but often it was merely outlined with lavender or some other lowgrowing plant and served simply as a form of decoration. The central object point was usually an arbour or a clipped tree.

Trelliswork of wood was as much employed as it had been in the Middle Ages. It usually formed a diamond-shaped lozenge, as in the illustration, and was employed to fence in the flower-beds and to cover arbours and galleries. Solid wooden posts, placed at intervals to support the lattice, formed a pleasing contrast.

Every garden contained one or more arbours. In the *Gardener's Labyrinth* two kinds are described in detail. One had a square-topped, the other an arched roof. Both were constructed of willows or osiers "so winded that the branches of

A PLEACHED ALLEY: HATFIELD

YEW CORONET: ELVASTON

the vine, melon, or cucumber running and spreading all over, might shadow and keep both the heat and the sun from the sitters thereunder." Fragrant rosemary, jasmine, and roses of various sorts, especially the sweetbrier or eglantine, were also trained over the trellis, which often rested on a part of the wall. As was remarked by an old writer, "The herbers erected and framed in most gardens are to their much refreshing and delight."

More solid constructions of brick or of stone were useful in winter as well as summer, as they were furnished with chimneys. Such a one, on a large scale, is still to be seen at Hampton Court, and is called the banqueting house. Another, which has now disappeared, was built for Elizabeth of York at Windsor.

Long covered walks formed another important feature in every garden. Sometimes they passed between lines of clipped trees pleached to form an arch, like the hornbeam walk at Hatfield, or the one of witch elm, called Queen Mary's, at Hampton Court. At other times the arches were constructed of woodwork and covered with vines. One of the advantages of these walks was that under their shade it was possible to go from one part of the garden to another without being exposed to the sun.

Beneath the arbours, and in other spots covered or uncovered, were

placed seats and tables convenient for reading and writing, where also refreshments might be served. Most often these were arranged at the ends of the paths or around the fountain. In the illustration is seen a characteristic example from the *Gardener's Labyrinth*.

Another feature developed at this period was the "mount," a mound of earth usually covered with grass and serving as a lookout over the garden wall into the park. Often it was capped by an arbour or a simple seat. There was a very large mount at Hampton Court, constructed in 1533. It was built on a brick foundation covered with earth and planted with twelve hundred quicksets. On the summit was a spacious summer-house.

Carved animals of stone or wood, upholding little weather-vanes, were especially characteristic of this period. At Hampton Court, those erected by Henry VIII included harts, lions, greyhounds, hinds, dragons, bulls, antelopes, griffins, leopards, rams, tigers, and badgers. They were distributed all over the gardens and orchards, and stood at intervals on the posts between the railings, on the stone coping around the terraces and flower-beds, and on top of the mount.

A number of sun-dials were also scattered about, both for use and ornament. Henry VIII apparently ordered them by the dozen. Sun-dials had existed in England before the Roman invasion, but interest in

 them seems to have been especially keen during the sixteenth century. A German protege of Henry VIII, named Kratzer (whose portrait by Holbein, now in the Louvre, shows him with a small sun-dial in hand), wrote a book on sun-dials and designed two to be placed at Oxford, where he was a lecturer on astronomy and mathematics. The first book in English devoted to dialling was published in 1533, and was largely a translation from Witkendus. At this period the actual dial was more fanciful than at a later date and often formed an armillary sphere.

A water supply was considered a very important adjunct to the garden. A central feature was often a well or fountain fed by a spring, or a cistern "well mortarred to receive and keep rain-water." Cisterns were also made of lead and decorated in such a way as to make them very ornamental. Borde advises that there should be also a "pool or two for fish, if the pool be clean kept." Such pools were usually lined with stone, and square or oblong in shape. Good examples of them exist at Drayton and Brickwall.

Various games were played in the garden or its vicinity. Bowling-alleys and greens for archery were common. "And among other things a payre of buttes (targets for archery) is a decent thing about a mansion, otherwise for a great many necessary it is to pass his time with bowls in an alley." No dimensions are given. All that was required was a stretch of good, firm turf or gravel. Tennis was another favourite game. Henry VIII was passionately fond of tennis. Sometimes he used to play in the walled court for "close tennys play" at Hampton Court, which is the oldest one in England, and has since served as a model for many others. A crowd of spectators always watched the king playing. Giustiniani describes him as "extremely fond of tennis, at which game it is the prettiest thing in the world to see him play, his fair skin glowing through a shirt of finest texture." Lawn tennis, or "open tennis play," was another favourite diversion.

Briefly, the garden was now a homely enclosure, like the living-room in a simple house containing few, but good-sized, apartments. Sometimes one large enclosure answered many purposes. First of all it contained the medicinal herbs, for primarily gardening was considered a profitable art because it was "so chayned and linked to the noble arts both of physic and surgery as by no means possible it may be to separate the one from the others, but rather as a daily handmaiden continually serveth them both." Then it answered the purpose of the pleasaunce, providing alleys and arbours for people to walk on and sit under, besides ground for games. Finally, it supplied a mixture of vegetables and flowers for use and ornament. The flower-garden proper, however, was not commonly to be seen until the reign of Queen Elizabeth.

The orchard, if not actually a part of the garden, was placed near it and similarly ornamented. Sun-dials and beasts carved of wood are mentioned in the royal accounts as having been ordered for Henry VIII's New Orchard, at Hampton Court, in 1530. Leland, in his *Itinerary* written in the middle of the sixteenth century, speaks of topiary work as lining the walks and decorating other parts of orchards. He relates that "at Uskeele village about a mile from Tewton is a goodly orchard with walks, opere topiaris," and at Wreshill Castle he describes another where there were "mounts opere topiaris writher about in degrees like turnings of cokil shells to come to the top without payee." Novelties in the orchard at this period were raspberries and gooseberries, which, with strawberries, were abundantly grown. Tusser says that in September,

> "The Barbary, Respis, and Gooseberry too
> Look now to be planted as other things doo.
> The Gooseberry, Respis, and Roses al three
> With Strawberries under them trimly agree."
> — *Five Hundred Points of Good Husbandry.*

Among existing private pleasure gardens, the one most resembling those described as belonging to the early Tudor period is at Longleat. Symmetrical without being monotonous in its plan, formal without

The Garden, Longleat.

being rigid in its planting, cosey without being cramped in its dimensions, it might be cited as the perfection of a small out-of-door dwelling-place for plants and people. The plan could have been designed only by one possessing a knowledge of architecture, although, with the exception of the fountain and conservatory, it might be carried out without "invegetate ornamentation."

PAVILION : LONGLEAT

The house at Longleat is a large and somewhat elaborate edifice in the style of the late Renaissance. Formerly, stiff pleasure grounds laid out by London and Wise in the reign of William and Mary surrounded three sides of this mansion, or rather palace, while on the fourth side it opened into a spacious forecourt. But this extensive arrangement, forecourt and all, was swept away by "Capability" Brown, who substituted the picturesque planting now seen, as the residence is approached, with no visible separation, except the driveway, between the front door and the park. In order to compose well with a house of such magnificence, if closely connected with it, the gardens must necessarily have been carried out on a scale of grandeur making them only suitable as a parade-ground for a large number of people. It is not surprising, therefore, that when a garden-loving ancestress of the Marquess of Bath, the present owner, designed a new pleasaunce, it was detached from the mansion, although near by. This is often the best arrangement when, in order to coincide with the buildings, gardens would be required entailing greater expense or elaboration than seems desirable or practicable.

Although laid out only half a century ago, in general effect and detail there is much to suggest that this is a reproduction of a Tudor flower-garden and was uninfluenced by foreign fashions. The ground plan is an almost perfect square, as was always recommended by the early authorities, while the iron arches covered by Virginia creepers, clematis, wisteria, China roses, and other climbing plants produce much the same effect as the arched wooden trellis or arbour, common in the sixteenth and seventeenth centuries, and existing at an earlier date. Besides many minor points of resemblance, there are here to be found the three fundamental characteristics of an old garden: an outer enclosure, clearly defined subdivisions, and differences of level.

The enclosure is formed by a boundary hedge, one hundred and eighty feet long and about ten feet high, extending along three sides, while a wall of stucco and the conservatory form the fourth. On one side the hedge is of clipped yew, while the other two are of rhododendrons allowed to grow freely. Along each of these three sides runs a walk about eight feet wide, supported by a stone retaining wall and raised three steps above the level of the parterre; opening from this walk are vine-covered arbours shading wooden benches commanding the whole enclosure. Two of these arbours are semicircular in plan with arched tops, while two are rectangular and flat-topped. The garden sides are left open so that "the owner's friends sitting in the same may the freelier see and behold the beauty of the garden to their great delight."

The main body of this garden is divided by the two principal cross paths into quarters, subdivided into knots, while outside runs a border

CONSERVATORY

SEAT

SEAT

FOUNTAIN

PASSAGE

ARBOR

HERBACEOUS BORDER

PATH TO HOUSE

THE FLOWER GARDEN
LONGLEAT · WILTS
MARQUESS OF BATH

SCALE

Conservatory, Longleat.

laid out in elaborate geometrical patterns. But it must be remembered
that any stiffness of effect is far less apparent in reality than in the plan,
since actually the garden is never seen from a bird's-eye point of view.
Flowing lines give freedom and variety to borders which if severely
rectangular might appear set and uninteresting; and miniature hedges,
enclosing the different arrangements of flowers in distinct divisions,
make it possible to mass the colours more or less separately. The subdivisions are marked by borders of *Berberis Darwinii, Cotoreaster Hooker-
iana,* or of common yew or box. The paths, slightly bevelled to shed
water, are of clay mixed with small pieces of flint, pounded and rolled
until so hard and compact that the surface affords no foothold for
weeds. The outer border is treated like a series of closed knots; that is,
the patterns, outlined with yew or box, are closed or filled with flowers.
Among these are eight beds planted with gladioli and white stock,
eight with tiger-lilies and white snap-dragon, and eight with salpiglos-
sis. The three beds forming a quarter of a circle at each corner are filled

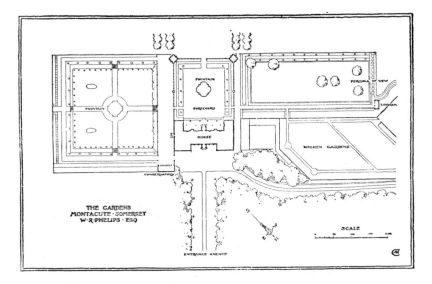

with salvia. Inside the border the earth is raised above the level of the path nearly as high as the top of the yew edging. Each corner is accented by a cone-shaped yew on the outer and a trim rose-bush on the inner angle.

Next, and separated from the border only by a path and a flat band of grass, come the quarters. These are divided into open knots of variegated holly and yew, the golden foliage of one contrasting with the dark green of the other. A basket-shaped vase of flowers marks each corner with a bright spot of colour rising above the masses of closely clipped foliage forming the knots.

Encircling the fountain is a curved bed divided into four sections by the cross paths and planted with pink pentstemon. Crimson rambler roses are trained over the arches of iron tubing, and the Isaac Perrier rose covers the chains suspended between them over the beds. These numerous rose garlands give finishing touches to the unusually festive appearance of the garden. In the herbaceous border next the outer hedge, and running like it around three sides of the enclosure, are growing some sixty or seventy different kinds of plants. Among them are monkshood, asters of many sorts, canterbury bells, coreopsis, helianthus, helenium, pyrethrum, phlox, etc.

The only purely architectural feature is the orangery, a very good example of a seventeenth-century conservatory, intended rather for displaying plants when they have reached perfection, than for rearing and fostering them as in a modern greenhouse. It serves also as a meeting-place for games and conversation, like a casino. The style of architecture resembles that of the house, but it was built at a later period.

In the centre of the garden is its sole piece of sculpture, a marble fountain, with a fluted cup around which three children hand in hand are dancing in a basin of water. This is, of course, more in the style of the late Renaissance than in that of the early Tudor period. A jet of water spouts from the bottom of the cup and overflows into the basin below. Such an arrangement is suggested by Worlidge, who says, "In the centre of your garden is a fountain of spring water always flowing, serving not only to refresh the spirits of such that delight in the sight of it, but is necessary in dry and hot seasons to preserve your choicest plants from injury."

The principal ideas in this small garden might easily be reproduced and could be simplified by making the fretwork of the beds less elaborate. Although the hedges and borders entail a good deal of labour in trimming, they play quite as important a part as the flowers in producing the general effect.

One of the last of the Tudor or first of the Elizabethan gardens is at Montacute. As shown in the plan opposite, the pleasure grounds are contained in three enclosures. At two corners of the smallest are quaint pavilions called "gazebos."

CHAPTER FIVE

The Elizabethan Flower-Garden

HE fruitful age of Queen Elizabeth brought both the planning and the planting of the loveliest English gardens very nearly to perfection. When the other arts of the Renaissance had reached their maturity and were on the verge of decline, garden making began to develop rapidly. Most of the finest houses in England were built at this period. After their erection an attempt to give them fit surroundings was a natural sequence. All conditions were ripe for the evolution of delightful pleasure gardens, which for form without formality have never been surpassed. Both the art and craft of their construction were understood as certainly never before, and perhaps never afterward. Like the gardens described in Sidney's *Arcadia*, these were places "not fairer in natural ornaments than artificial inventions."

As an art this garden making was imbued with the creative as well as the imitative spirit of the Renaissance. Men's eyes were opened, as if for the first time, to the charming aspects of life old and new, past and present. A delight in the beauty of nature as well as in that of artistic invention seemed to develop spontaneously. Its practical outcome was the creation of a style of decoration known as that of the early English Renaissance, which was applied to every branch of design, and finally clothed the garden in fanciful array.

The Hall, Bradford-on-Avon. Photograph by Dotesio and Todd.

 Past records, especially of classic Greece and Italy, were searched for information concerning the growth and arrangement of plants and the garden's architectural features. The early books on horticulture, such as Hill's *Arte of Gardening*, teem with quotations from Columella, Cato, and other ancient husbandmen who were considered great authorities. Gerard, in his herbal published in 1597, says, for instance:

"Besides these and other causes there are many examples of those that have honoured this science; for to pass by a multitude of philosophers, it may please your Honour to call to remembrance that which you know of some noble Princes that have joyned this studie with their most important matters of state: Mithridates the Great was famous for his knowledge herein as Plutarch noteth; Euan, also, King of Arabia, the happy garden of the world for principal simplex, wrote of this argument as Plinie sheweth; Diocletian might he have his praise, had he

GARDEN GATES : PENSHURST

GATE-WAY : PACKWOOD/

not drowned all his honour in the blood of his persecution. To conclude this point, the example of Salomon is before the rest and greater, whose wisdom and knowledge was such, that he was able to set out the nature of all plants from the highest cedar to the lowest moss."

Early in the Renaissance the advice of these classic writers was offered by Thomas Hill and other English authors, apparently on the supposition that it would be followed literally, without considering that the passage of centuries and the difference between Italian and English customs and climate might destroy a part of its usefulness. But the Elizabethan age continued after the death of Elizabeth, and in the seventeenth century the growth of individuality made slavish imitation impossible. Precedent was followed only when suitable, and useless traditions were cast aside. Then systems of horticulture were evolved, adapted to a particular age, climate, and country. Each nation had its own garden literature. In this direction the French took the lead, and in the *Maison Rustique*, translated by Markham, it was first pointed out that "The frame and toil used on our, French Country Farms be not altogether like that of former and ancient days."

Sir Hugh Platt in *Floraes Paradise*, Markham in his books on gardening, and Lawson in *A New Orchard and Garden* show the development of a style of gardens particularly appropriate to England. The descriptions given by Markham and Lawson are especially interesting.

Cautiously the idea was introduced at this time that a thing of beauty might be an excuse in itself, and, this led to the garden of pleasure, or flower-garden. But orchards, herbaries, and kitchen gardens were not done away with, and at the outset even the pleasure garden was excused as having a useful side. For instance, in the *Maison Rustique*, the author concludes his statement that "the most pleasant and delectable thing in our French gardens is the flower garden as well in respect as it serveth the chief lord whose inheritance it is to solace himself therein," by adding, "as also in respect to their service to set beehives in." Gerard also points out that most gardens were of practical service as well as pleasure-giving, in fact, useful ornaments.

"For if delight may provoke men's labour, what greater delight is there than to behold the earth apparelled with plants, as with a robe of embroidered worke, set with orient pearls, and garnished with great diversitie of rare and costlie jewels? If this varietie and perfection of colours may affect the eie, it is such in herbes and flowers that no Apelles, no Zeuxis ever could by any art expresse the like; if odours or if taste may work satisfaction, they are both so soveraigne in plants, and so comfortable that no confection of the Apothecaries can equal their excellent vertue. But these delights are in the outward senses: the principal delight is in the mince, singularly enriched with the knowledge of these visible things, setting forth to us the invisible wisdom and admirable workmanship of Almighty God. The delight is great, but the use greater and joyned often with necessitie."

The discovery of the New World largely increased the range of horticulture. When England joined in the great maritime movement carried on by other nations from the middle of the fourteenth century, her explorers returned with ship-loads of "outlandish commodities." Among these imports was an abundance of plants. Just as the art of gardening had been developed by the fresh appreciation of the beauty of classic design, so the desire to naturalize these exotics stimulated gardening as a craft.

A good comparison between the decadent condition of gardens in the past, compared with their prosperity in his day, is prefaced by Harrison to the second edition of Holinshed's *Chronicles*, published in 1580.

Topiary Gardens, Levens.

"Such herbs, roots, and fruits as grow yearly out of the ground have been very plentiful in the time of the first Edward and after his days; but in the process of time they also grew to be neglected, so that from Henry the Fourth until the latter end of Henry the Seventh and the beginning of Henry the Eighth there was little or no use of them in England, but they remained either unknown or supposed as food more meet for hogs and savage beasts than mankind."

After relating at length how good husbandry had become almost a lost art, he begins to expatiate upon its reestablishment.

"If you look into our gardens annexed to our houses, how wonderfully is their beauty increased not only with flowers, which Columella calleth 'Terrena Sidera,' saying 'Pinget in varios terrestria sidera flores,' and variety of curious and costlie workmanship, but also with rare and medicinable herbs sought up in the land within these forty years, so that in comparison with this present the ancient gardens were but dung-hills and laistowes to such as did possess them. How art also helpeth nature in the daily colouring, doubling and enlarging the proportion of our flowers, it is incredible to report; for so curious and cunning are our gardeners now in these days that they presume to do in manner what they list with nature and moderate her course in things as if they were her superiors.

"It is a world also to see how many strange herbs, plants, and annual fruits are daily brought unto us from the Indies, Americans, Taprobane, Canary Isles, and all parts of the world. . . . There is not almost one noble gentleman or merchant that hath not great store of these flowers, which now also begin to wax so well acquainted with our soils that we may almost account of them as parcel of our own commodities. They have no less regard for medicinable herbs fetched out of other countries nearer hand: insomuch that I have seen in some one garden to the number of three or four hundred of them if not more, the half of whose names within forty years past we had no manner of knowledge."

In conclusion he states with just pride, although with questionable authority, "I am persuaded that albeit the gardens of the Hesperides were so greatly accounted of because of their delicacy, yet if it were possible to have such an equal judge . . . I doubt not he would give the prize unto the garden of our days."

To appreciate the number of new plants introduced at this period, we have only to compare the Elizabethan herbals with those of earlier dates. Gerard's list of plants grown in his own garden, and his herbal imitated from the Dutch work of Dodoens, but containing much original material, are the most valuable sources of information.

The reconstruction of Elizabethan gardens is comparatively simple. Not only herbals giving the lists of plants they contained, treatises on horticulture advising how they should be cultivated, and books showing how they were to be planned and ornamented have been handed down to us, but many of the actual gardens remain with their architectural features unaltered, and only slightly injured by changes in the style of planting. The gardens described were oftenest on a small scale, for, as Markham suggests, "Great cages make the bird never a whit the better."

A CIRCULAR DOVE-COT : HARLESTON

The house might be placed practically wherever the owner pleased. One writer advised that it should be located "on the edge of some great hill, upon some small hill, or the top of the hill if the country be tempestuous and full of mountains," while another considered the lowlands more desirable. Evidently it was a matter of taste, for actually there are Elizabethan gardens still to be seen in every variety of location—on hillsides, as at St. Catherine's Court; on hilltops, as at Hatfield; and on level ground, as at Montacute.

At the entrance to the house was often a forecourt. This was a rectangular enclosure surrounding a grass plot divided by a path leading to the house and sometimes containing fish-ponds and a dove-house. "Near unto the same you shall make your ground dove-house if the law will permit you such a one, in fashion like a round turret in the midst of your court."

Many forecourts have been done away with, but there are, fortunately, a few remaining. Of these, good examples are at Levens in Westmoreland, at Sandywell and King's Weston in Gloucestershire, at Mount Morris, and at Charleston manor-house.

The number and character of the gardens depended of course on the taste and affluence of the owner. If he were poor, he might not be able to afford more than one enclosure, containing, like the early Tudor gardens, all sorts of plants. But if he were rich enough to follow the fashion, he would separate his plantations into three or four divisions, in each of which a certain kind of vegetation predominated. De Serres recommended four divisions—the kitchen garden, the nosegay garden, the medicinal and the fruit garden. Markham was satisfied with two —one for the "household garden" the other the "garden for flowers and sweet smells." But all were more or less intended for profit as well as pleasure. Ornamental features were then included, and are still often retained, in the English kitchen garden, herbary, and orchard; while even such a princely pleasure garden as Bacon describes, contained certain homely herbs and vegetables. In the "garden for flowers and sweet smells" Markham suggests that "about the hedge we shall set for to make pottage withal, pease, beans, citrons, cucumbers, and such like."

Pleasure gardens were always connected as closely as possible with the house, to form a prolongation of the living rooms. If practicable, the drawing-room opened into the parterre of flowers; if not, a terrace formed the means of intercommunication. As Surflet says in his translation of a portion of the *Maison Rustique*: "It is a commendable and seemly thing to behold out at a window many acres of ground well tilled and husbanded, whether it be a meadow, a plot for planting of willows, or arable ground as we have stood upon heretofore; but yet it is much more to behold fair and comely proportions, handsome and pleasant arbours, and as it were closets, delightful borders of lavender, rosemary, box, and other such like, to hear the ravishing music of an infinite number of pretty small birds which continually, day and night, do chatter and chant their proper and natural branchsongs upon the hedges and trees of the garden; and to smell so sweet a nosegay so near at hand, seeing that this so fragrant a smell cannot but refresh the Lord of the Farm exceedingly, when going out of his bedchamber in the morning after the sun-rise and whiles as yet the clear and pearl-like dew doth perch unto the grass, he giveth himself to hear the melodious music of the bees, which busying themselves in gathering of the same, do also fill the air with a most acceptable sweet and pleasant harmony; besides the borders and continued rows of soveraigne, thyme, balm, rosemary, marjoram, cypers, sothernwood, and other fragrant herbs, the sight and view whereof cannot but give great contentment unto the beholder."

The outline of the garden was carefully designed to suit its particular location and to be on the right scale. "You are very much to consider the form and proportions of the same," writes Markham, "wherein, according to the opinion of Serres and Vinet, you must be much ruled by the nature of the soil."

Terraces, St. Catherine's Court.

Each portion of the garden was made almost perfectly level, though parts of it might be raised above the remainder. Raised walks, as at Brickwall and Longleat, often ran around the outer edge above the parterre.

On a hillside a garden was frequently laid out in a series of terraces. "You may also, if your ground be naturally so seated, or if your industry please so to bring it to pass, make your garden rise and mount by several degrees, one level ascending above another, which is exceeding beautiful to the eye and very beneficial to your flowers and fruit trees, especially if such ascents have the benefit of the sun rising upon them."

At St. Catherine's Court is one of the most interesting series of terraced gardens in England. Instead of descending, the terraces ascend above the house. It is unfortunate that the clipped trees at the entrance to the gardens have grown entirely out of scale; otherwise from the house, as the illustration shows, the effect produced would be altogether charming.

TERRACE STEPS : SHRUBLANDS

GARDEN GATEWAY : BRAMSHILL©

The form of the outer enclosure, as in the Middle Ages, usually remained rectangular. Round, oval, and diamond shapes are also mentioned as correct for the "Verge and Girdle of your Garden," but square or oblong was evidently customary.

The most characteristic boundary of an Elizabethan garden was a sort of openwork stone balustrading, either placed directly on the ground or surmounting a wall of stone or brick. Such balustrading is to be seen at Montacute, Bramshill, Claverton Manor, and many other houses. Several good examples are shown in the illustrations [above].

"An earthen wall, if coped with glue and mortar and planted with wall flowers," was recommended by Markham where neither stone nor wood was to be had, and was a favourite resort of bees. Hedges, elaborately planted with a variety of trees and shrubs, wooden palings, differing but little from those described in the last chapter, and brick walls, brought to a greater perfection in the Stuart period, sometimes formed the outer boundary line. Moats are mentioned by Markham, but they had become almost obsolete except as ornaments or preserves for fish.

The entrance was an important and salient feature. The most elaborate was guarded on each side by a gatehouse. Ordinary gateways were either flanked by stone piers or arched over with stonework. Ornaments, such as balls, obelisks, or heraldic beasts, were placed on top of the piers, as shown in the accompanying illustrations [page 120]. Covered gateways were also surmounted with ornaments. Interesting examples are to be seen in many places.

GATEWAY·OUNDLE·NORTHANTS

TERRACE & BOWLING GREEN : BRAMSHILL

A terrace was usually intimately connected with the house, on a vantage ground at least three feet above the level of the garden. Its extent varied according to the size of the neighbouring buildings and the exigencies of the location, and the width depended upon the length. The edge was protected by a parapet ornamented by stone balustrades or openwork. The surface of the ground might be covered either with grass or gravel and was sometimes bordered with flowers. Such a terrace added much to the dignity of a mansion, and often furnished a most attractive view of the garden and the surrounding country. At Haddon Hall is a very beautiful and familiar terrace shaded by some fine old trees. Another well-known example is at the Hall, Bradford-on-Avon. At Bramshill the terrace serves as a bowling-green, and is furnished with seats in niches at each end. In connection with every Elizabethan house a terrace was the rule rather than the exception. Its advantages are charmingly described in the account of Queen Elizabeth's visit to Kenilworth.

The relation between the garden and the terrace is also well pointed out by Sir Henry Wotton. "First, I must note a certain contrariety between building and gardening; for as Fabricks should be regular so Gardens should be irregular, or at least cast into a very wild Regularity. To exemplifie my conceit, I have seen a Garden, for the manner perchance incomparable, into which the first Access was a high Walk like a Tarrace, from whence might be taken a general view of the whole Plot below, but rather in a delightful confusion, than with any plain distinction of the pieces. From this the Beholder, descending many steps,

Grass Steps, St. Catherine's Court.

was afterwards conveyed again by several mountings and valings to various entertainments and of his scent and sight, which I shall not need to describe, for that were poetical, let me only note this, that every one of these diversities was as if he had been magically transported into a new Garden."

As an opportunity for taking exercise was one of the objects in having a garden, the enclosure was intersected by numerous foot-paths. At Hampton Court Queen Elizabeth used "to catche her heat in the colde mornings with a brisk walk," though, at times when conscious of observation, "she was the very image of majesty and magnificence, went slowly and marched with leisure and with a certain grandity rather than gravity"; Hentzner mentions that at Oxford, "As soon as Grace was said after every meal every one is at liberty either to retire to his own chambers, or to walk in the College garden, there being none that has not a delightful one."

COVERED WALK SHRUBLANDS

No rules about the proportions of paths were given, but as a general thing they were rather narrower than at present. Markham considers six feet sufficient for wide walks. Ordinarily, they were strewn with fine sand, or paved with tiles or with squares of stone like the flagging in front of St. Catherine's Court. Fine yellow gravel mixed with pebbles and coal dust was recommended as destructive to weeds, but otherwise considered undesirable. Grass walks seem to have been less common than in the next century.

Alleys, as the broader paths were called, were often shaded by trees, their branches pleached in an arch. Hornbeam, witch-elm, and yew were used for this purpose. Such pleached alleys often surrounded the garden, and exist to-day at Hatfield, Shrublands, and many other places.

Wooden galleries, answering the same purpose as covered alleys of pleached trees, were usually constructed in all the larger gardens. The roof was almost invariably arched and covered with vines. On the side toward the garden were apertures for viewing its arrangement. Turrets of latticework accented the corners and sometimes the middle of the

IONICA

Garden, from Vredeman's Hortorum Viridariorumque.

——

gallery. A great variety of different forms are shown in Vredeman's *Hortorum Viridariorumque*, published at Antwerp in 1583, in the engravings by Crispin de Passe illustrating the "Hortus Floridus," and in many contemporaneous pictures. Such galleries corresponded to the classic portico and the monastic cloisters, and were a survival from the mediæval pleasaunce. The construction of the simpler forms was minutely described in the *Jardinier Hollandais*, by J. van der Groen, in the middle of the seventeenth century.

There were also arbours, garden-houses, and banqueting houses in similar styles and of more or less elaborate forms. Green arbours, Markham says, were covered with the wild vine, hops, jasmine, Mary's seal, muskroses, woodbine, gourds, cucumber, and sweetbrier, and might shade a wooden bench or a bank of camomile. Often they were built in the shape of a round turret. Clipped cypress, bay, cedar, and box trees, planted in the ground, in flower-pots or in wooden cases, were used to mark the entrance to the arbour.

Garden-houses were placed in all the more ambitious gardens. The plan was usually either square or octagonal. The building was composed of one or two stories, and seldom contained more than one room on a floor. Sometimes the side toward the garden was left open, as in the little wooden pavilion in the old gardens at Whitehall. Others were substantially built of stone, like the well-known gazebos at Montacute. Usually they were located in the corners of the garden or in the centre

of the wall, at the end of the main path. Two views of one at Packwood are shown in the illustrations [opposite]. An elaborate and fanciful garden-house is at Chipping Camden, Gloucestershire, while the triangular lodge at Rushton is even more quaintly designed.

Mounts continued to be raised in the centres or the corners of gardens. Mandelso mentions one at Theobalds, called the Mount of Venus, "which is placed in the midst of a labyrinth, and is, upon the whole, one of the most beautiful spots in the world." In the garden at Whitehall stood a "Parnassus Mount, on top of which was the Pegasus, a golden horse with wings, and divers statues, one of black marble representing the river Thames, beneath which is this Latin distich in letters of gold:

> "'Me pones imperium, emporium sunt classis et artes,
> Et schola bene floxens, florida prata rigo.'

"It far surpasses the Parnassus Mount in the Pratolino near Florence." Less pretentious mounts were capped with arbours or summer-houses.

Lawson favoured a mount built of stone or wood "curiously wrought within and without," or of earth covered with fruit trees. On such a mount, he says, "you might sit and angle a peckled trout, or a sleighte Eele, or some other fish" in the old moat outside the wall, or in a stream meandering close by. Or if the mount overlooked the park, there was "nothing to prevent your taking an occasional shot at a buck."

For the inner enclosure or "inward proportions," as they were called, "You may draw your garden into what form soever you please, not respecting that shape soever the outer verge carrieth: for you may make the garden which is square without to be round within, and that which is round without, either square or oval; that which is oval either of the former, and that which is diamond any shape at all, and yet all exceedingly comely." This enclosure might be formed by a railed fence or by a low hedge of cypress, box, or juniper.

The intersection of the paths and counterpaths usually divided the garden into four quarters. "These inward quarters wherein you place the knots or other devices may be bound as well with fine envious hedges made battlementwise in sundry forms, according to invention, or carrying the proportions of pilasters, flowers, shapes of beasts, birds, creeping things, ships, trees, and suchlike." These hedges were considered advantageous, because they did not take up much room and could be set with a variety of different shrubs. The frame of the design was constructed either of wood or wire.

In *Floraes Paradise*, Sir Hugh Platt says, "Instead of privie hedges about a quarter I commend a fence made of lath or sticks thinly placed and after graced with dwarf apple and plomme trees, spread abroad upon the stick." This is one of the earliest mentions of trees grown to form an espalier. As the gardens were infested with rabbits, it was evidently necessary to have some form of protection for the beds.

The beds were raised from one to two feet above the level of the paths and laid out in the beautiful designs called knots. Markham says that the pattern of the design could not be decided by rule, but depended upon the gardener and the pleasure of his master, "The one whereof is led by the hops and skips, turning and windings of his brain; the other by the pleasing of his eye according to his best fantasia." In looking at the patterns of the knots it must be remembered that they were intended to be laid out on a large scale, each knot occupying a piece of ground from twenty-five to one hundred feet square. The knot

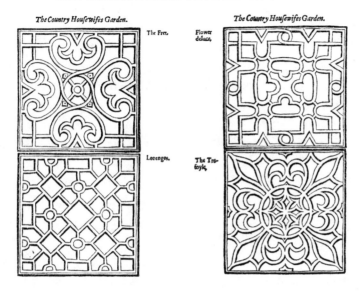

was outlined in box, lavender, or sometimes with an edging of pinks and daisies.

The flowers commonly planted in the pleasure garden were those considered as most appropriate for nosegays and garlands. In the *Country Farm*, among those mentioned to be cultivated for this purpose are "March violets, Provence Gillo-flowers, and Indian Gillo-flowers, small Paunces, Daisies, yellow and white Gillo-flowers, Marigolds, Lilly-convally, Daffodils, Canterburie-bells, Purple velvet flowre, Anemones, Corn-flag, Mugwort, Lillies, and other such like." Besides are mentioned "All sorts of strange flowers as is the Crown Imperiall, the Dulippos of sundrie kinds, Narcissus, Hyacinthus, Emeryes Hellitropiano, and a world of others of like nature, whose colours being glorious and different make such a brave checkered mixture that it is both wondrous pleasant and delectable to behold." Lawson was especially fond of the gillyflower, which he considered "the king of the flowers except the rose"; and he dwells upon its fragrance and its beauty. Double marigolds as big as roses were among the showiest ornaments.

Bacon held that "in the royal Ordering of *Gardens* there ought to be *Gardens* for all the *Months* in the Year; in which, severally, Things of

Beauty may be then in Season. For *December* and *January*, and the Latter Part of *November*, you must take such Things as are Green all Winter; Holly, Ivy, Bays, Juniper, Cypress Trees, Yew, Pine-apple Trees,[1] Fir Trees, Rosemary, Lavender; Periwinkle, the white, the purple, and the blue; Germander, Flags, Orange Trees, Lemon Trees, and Myrtles, if they be stoved; and Sweet Marjoram warm set. There followeth, for the latter part of *January*, and *February*, the Mezereon Tree, which then blossoms; Crocus vernus, both the yellow, and the gray; Primroses, Anemonies, the early Tulipa, Hyacinthus Orientalis, Chamairis, Fritellaria. For *March* there come Violets, specially the single blue, which are the earliest; the Yellow Daffodil, the Daisy, the Almond Tree in blossom, the Peach Tree in blossom, the Cornelian Tree in blossom, Sweet Briar. In *April* follow the double white Violet, the Wall-flower, the Stock Gilliflower, the Cowslip, Flower de Luces, and Lilies of all natures, Rosemary Flowers, the Tulipa, the Double Peony, the pale Daffodil, the French Honeysuckle, the Cherry Tree in blossom, the Damascene and Plum Trees in blossom, the Whitehorn in leaf, the Lilac Tree. In *May*, and *June* come Pinks of all sorts, specially the Blush Pink; Roses of all kinds, except the Musk, which comes later; Honeysuckles, Strawberries, Bugloss, Columbine, the French Marygold, Flos Africanus, Cherry Tree in Fruit, Ribes, Figs in Fruit, Rasps, Vine Flowers, Lavender in Flowers, the Sweet Satyrian, with the White Flower; Herba Muscaria, Lilium Convallium, the Apple Tree in blossom. In *July* come Gilliflowers of all varieties, Musk Roses, the Lime Tree in blossom, early Pears, and Plums in Fruit, Gennitings,[2] Quodlins. In *August*, come Plums of all sorts in fruit, Pears, Apricoks, Barberries, Filberds, Musk-Melons, Monks Hoods of all colours. In *September* come Grapes, Apples, Poppies of all colours, Peaches, Melo-Cotones, Nectarines, Cornelians,[3] Wardens, Quinces. In *October* and the beginning of *November* come Services, Medlars, Bullaces, Roses cut or removed to come late, Hollyoaks, and such like. These particulars are for the

---

1. *I.e.*, The Pine, of which several sorts were then cultivated.

2. Gennitings, an early apple, its true name June eating. Quodlins, *i.e.*, Codlings, a boiling apple.

3. Melo-cotone, a kind of quince. Cornelians, the Cornel or Cornelian cherry tree. Wardens, a keeping pear, by the French called *Poire de garde*.

climate of London: but my meaning is perceived that you may have *Verperpetuum,* as the place affords.[1]

"And because the *Breath* of Flowers is far sweeter in the Air (where it comes and goes, like the Warbling of Musick) than in the Hand, therefore nothing is more fit for that delight than to know what be the *Flowers* and *Plants* that do best perfume the Air. Roses, Damask and Red, are fast Flowers of their Smells[2]; so that you may walk by a whole row of them, and find nothing of their Sweetness; yea though it be in a Morning's Dew. Bays, likewise, yield no Smell as they grow; Rosemary little, nor Sweet Marjoram: that which, above all others, yields the *Sweetest Smell* in the *Air,* is the Violet, specially the White double Violet, which comes twice a year, about the middle of *April,* and about *Bartholomewtide.* Next to that is the Musk Rose; then the Strawberry-Leaves dying, with a most excellent Cordial Smell; then the Flower of the Vines; it is a little dust, like the dust of a Bent, which grows upon the Cluster in the first coming forth; then Sweet Briar; then Wallflowers which are very delightful to set under a Parlour or lower Chamber Window; then Pinks, specially the Matted Pink, and Clove Gilliflower; then the Flowers of the Lime-Tree; then the Honeysuckles, so they be somewhat afar off. Of Bean Flowers I speak not, because they are Field Flowers. But those which *Perfume* the Air most delightfully, not passed by as the rest, but being *Trodden Upon* and *Crushed,* are three; that is Burnet, Wild Thyme, and Water-mints. Therefore, you are to set whole Alleys of them, to have the Pleasure, when you walk or tread."

Topiary work added much to the variety of the parterre. The firm foliage of the dark evergreens, clipped sometimes into a simple straight hedge, sometimes into the most fantastic shapes, formed a background in charming contrast to the waving masses of brilliantly coloured flowers. In the old gardens at Levens are many delightfully quaint figures, among them Queen Elizabeth and her maids of honour represented as

---

1. In Mr. Montague's edition this passage has been, I know not on what authority, altered in the following manner: "Thus if you will, you may have the Golden Age again, and a Spring all year long." The allusion is probably to Virg. Geor. II, 149.

2. "Fast flowers of their smells," *i.e.,* do not give them out any distance. Comp. *The History of Life and Death,* 1638, 12 mo., pp. 294–295

A BUTTRESS OF CLIPPED YEW : ARLEY

wearing the fullest of hoop-skirts. At Packwood is simulated the Ser-
mon on the Mount, while at Cleeve Prior Manor the twelve apostles
hand in hand stand six on one side and six on the other along the path-
way from the road to the house. There are fine collections of topiary
work at Elvaston and at Ascott. "Your Gardiner," writes Lawson, in
1618, "can frame your lesser wood to the shape of men armed in the
field, ready to give battell: or swift running Grey Hounds to chase the
Deere, or hunt the Hare. This kind of hunting shall not waste your
corne nor much your coyne." Bacon despised images cut out in juniper
or other garden stuff as only fit to amuse children, but when in suitable
surroundings, they certainly have a distinct charm. For, above all, a garden should furnish food for the imagination, and these fantastic forms
are indeed made of such stuff as dreams. In the sunshine their shapes
are vaguely outlined behind the gayly hued flowers; but as the light
grows dim, shadows lengthen, and colour becomes indistinguishable,
the quaint images of men and beasts, moving darkly forward from the
background, have a mysterious fascination and transform the garden
into a new and strange wonderland.

In the water-works were given frequent opportunities for fanciful
devices. Every garden seems to have had a fountain, usually a round
basin with a statue in the centre, combined with a jet of water. At
Nonesuch, Hentzner describes "two fountains that spout water, one
round, the other like a pyramid, upon which are perched small birds

Cleeve Prior Manor. Photograph by E. A. Rowe.

that stream water out of their bills. In the grove of Diana is a very agreeable fountain, with Actœon turned into a stag as he was sprinkled by the goddess and her nymphs."

Cunning schemes were also contrived to surprise the visitors to the garden with a sudden shower bath. Hentzner mentions having seen at Nonesuch "a pyramid of marble full of concealed pipes which spurt upon all those who come within their reach." At Whitehall, he says that "in a garden joining to this palace, there is a jet d'eau, with a sun-

FOUNTAIN TRINITY COLLEGE

dial, which, while strangers are looking at it, a quantity of water forced by a wheel which the gardener turns at a distance through a number of little pipes, plentifully sprinkles those that are standing round." The Duke of Wirtemberg remarked upon one of Queen Elizabeth's few erections at Hampton Court, "a splendid high and messy fountain, with a water-work by which you can, if you like, make the water play upon the ladies and others who are standing by, and give them a thorough wetting." It was evidently considered highly amusing to victimize unfortunates with such practical jokes. Our sense of humour has apparently changed far more than our sense of beauty since the days of the virgin queen.

Bathing pools are mentioned by Bacon in his essay "On Gardens." He describes a *"faire Receipt* of *Water* of some Thirty or Forty Foot Square, but without Fish or Slime or Mud," with sides and bottom paved with stone, and water flowing in and out perpetually. It was to be encompassed with "fine Railes of low Statuas," and embellished with coloured glass. A square pool at Penshurst may have been intended for bathing. It is placed at a secluded end of the gardens, and surrounded by a hedge. The illustration shows a corner with steps conveniently placed for a bather leading into the water.

Many gardens contained fish-ponds, usually built of brick or stone, and of square or oblong shape. In Sir Philip Sidney's *Arcadia* is described a "fair Pond whose shaking Crystal was a perfect Mirror to all the other Beauties." Ducks and swans as well as fish were often admitted to the water. In a plan showing the lay-out of the ground surrounding Holdenby House in Northamptonshire, as it existed in 1587, there are seven ponds varying in size, but all oblong.

Quaint conceits were devised for ornaments. Sir Hugh Platt sug-

SUN·DIAL: SHRUBLANDS

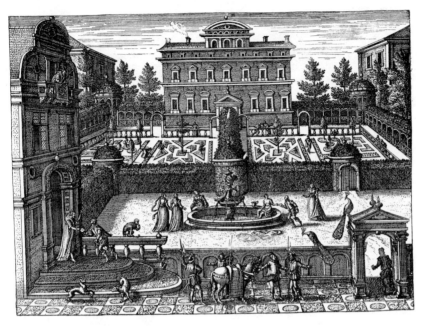

Garden, from Vredeman's Hortorum Viridariorumque.

gests procuring flower-pots twice the usual size, perforated with holes an inch apart and an inch circumference. A lily or a carnation was planted in the middle of the pot, and in the holes thyme or hyssop kept evenly clipped. "Set these pots upon faire pillars in your garden to make a beautiful shew." The design of flower-pots was often elaborate. Pyramids, lozenges, circles, pentagons, or any form of beast or fowl, in wood, stone, or burnt clay, with similar holes planted with rosemary or another herb, formed an attractive feature. Other ornaments were gilded wooden images and round balls of coloured glass to catch the sunlight, and sun-dials. Statuary was considered by Bacon an innovation adding to the state and magnificence, but nothing to the true pleasure of a garden.

Tennis was still a favourite amusement, and the tennis-court an adjunct to the garden. It was when Queen Elizabeth was seated in the gallery of a tennis-court watching a game between the Duke of Norfolk and the Earl of Leicester that "my Lord Robert being verie hotte

Garden, from Vredeman's Hortorum Viridariorumque.

and swettinge, took the Queens napken oute of her hande, and wyped his face, which the Duke seeinge, saide that he was too sawsie, and swore that he wolde laye his racket upon his face. Hereupon rose a great troble, and the Queen offended sore with the Duke." It will be remembered that Sir Philip Sidney's famous quarrel with the Earl of Oxford also took place in a tennis-court.

Greens for archery and bowling continued to be laid out in connection with the garden. Mazes afforded a form of amusement not too childish for grown people, who retained a fondness for all such quips and cranks.

In contrast to the prim regularity of the parterre a few gardens contained a "wilderness," which was a more ordinary feature at a later period. Bacon's account of the wilderness in his essay on gardens shows that it was then a piece of enclosed ground, comprising thickets of sweetbrier, honeysuckle, and grape-vines, and mounds of earth, covered with various cultivated flowers. It was a tangle not planted in any

The Country Housewifes Garden.

BOWLING ALLEY : BROCKENHURST

order, and not containing trees like the later wildernesses, which were developed by Le Nôtre into the famous bosquets at Versailles.

The kitchen garden in its way was also made beautiful. "Though your garden for flowers doth in a sort peculiarly challenge itself, a profit and Exquisite form to the eyes, yet you may not altogether neglect this where your herbs for the pot do grow. And, therefore, some here make comely borders with the herbs aforesaid. The rather, because roses and lavender yield much profit. The beds need not here be raised. You place your herbs of biggest growth by walls, or in borders, and the lowest in the midst."

As yet the distinction between an orchard and a garden was not very marked. Lawson describes them collectively in his *Orchard and Garden*, which was written in the Elizabethan spirit although it did not appear until 1618. It is full of practical directions as well as charming sentiments.

"The very works of and in an Orchard and Garden are better than the ease and rest of and from other labours. When God had made man after his own Image in a perfect state, and would have him represent himself in authority, tranquility and pleasure upon the Earth, He placed him in Paradise. What was Paradise? But a Garden and Orchard of trees and herbs, full of all pleasure, and nothing there but delights.

The gods of the Earth resembling the great God of heaven in authority, Majesty and abundance of all things, wherein is their most delight? And whither do they withdraw themselves from the troublesome affairs of their estate, being tired with the hearings and judgings of litigious Controversies? choked (as it were) with the close aire of their sumptuous buildings, their stomachs cloyed with variety of banquets, their ears filled and over-burthened with tedious discoursings. Whither? but into their Orchards made and prepared dressed and destinated for that purpose to renew and refresh their senses, and to call home their overwearied spirits. Nay, it is (no doubt) a comfort to them, to set open their casements into a most delicate Garden and Orchard, whereby they may not only see that, wherein they are so much delighted, but also to give fresh, sweet and pleasant air to their Galleries and Chambers.

"What can your eye desire to see, your ears to hear, your mouth to taste, or your nose to smell, that is not to be had in an Orchard? with abundance and variety? What more delightsome than an infinite variety of sweet smelling flowers? decking with sundry colours the green mantle of the Earth, the universal Mother of us all, so by them bespotted, so dyed, that all the world cannot sample them, and wherein it is more fit to admire the Dyer than imitate his workmanship. Colouring not only the earth, but decking the air, and sweetening every breath and spirit."

In concluding his description Lawson says: "One chief grace that adorns an Orchard I cannot let slip. A brood of Nightingales, who with their several notes and tunes, with a strong delightsome voice out of a weak body will bear you company night and day"; and he goes on to name some of the other birds whose presence might be desired. Then he adds: "What shall I say? 1000 of delights are in an Orchard and sooner shall I be weary, than I can reckon the least part of that pleasure, which one, that hath and loves an Orchard may find therein. What is there, of all these few that I have reckoned, which doth not please the eye, the ear, the smell and taste? and by these senses, as Organs, Pipes and Windows, these delights are carried to refresh the gentle, generous and noble mind."

The ancient custom of receiving important visitors in the garden was followed by Queen Elizabeth. At Hampton Court she afforded in her private garden a clandestine interview to one of the first suitors for her hand, the Earl of Arran. Here, too, occurred some of her amusing meetings with the Queen of Scots' agent, Lord Melville.

The royal gardens at Whitehall, Windsor, Nonesuch, and Hampton Court, according to the account of foreign visitors, were well kept up at the close of the century, but we do not hear that the queen added much to them, except the terrace at Windsor Castle. Of Nonesuch Hentzner has left us a description; in part he says:

"The palace itself is so encompassed with parks full of deer, delicious gardens, groves ornamented with trelliswork, cabinets of verdure, and walks so embowered by trees, that it seems to be a place pitched upon by Pleasure herself to dwell in along with Health." The Duke of Wirtemberg, who travelled through England in 1592, speaks of Hampton Court as comprising many beautiful gardens both for pleasure and ornament; some planted with nothing but rosemary, others laid out with various other plants, which are "trained, intertwined, and trimmed in so wonderful a manner and in such extraordinary shapes that the like could not easily be found."

Directly, Queen Elizabeth did very little for the gardens of her day, but indirectly they owed much to her influence. She encouraged her nobles to live on their country estates and to build fine houses and gardens where they might have the honour of receiving her as a guest. Their efforts were stimulated by her progresses, which included visits to almost every part of her kingdom. Among the gardens where Elizabeth stopped were those at Helmingham, Kenilworth and Wilton, where there was a celebrated grotto. Lord Burleigh entertained her magnificently at Theobalds in 1591. Here a masque written for the occasion by George Peele was recited, describing the dificulties of constructing the garden and comparing its beauties to the queen's virtues. It began with a speech by a mole-catcher, who said, "I cannot discourse of knots and mazes; sure I am that the ground was so knotty that the gardener was amazed at it, and as easy had it been to make a shaft of a cammock as a garden of that craft."

Theobalds was one of the finest gardens seen by the German traveller Hentzner. He describes it as it existed at the close of the sixteenth century. "The first was Theobalds, belonging to Lord Burleigh, the treasurer: in the gallery was painted the genealogy of the Kings of England; from this place one goes into the garden, encompassed with a ditch full of water, large enough for one to have the pleasure of going in a boat, and rowing between the shrubs; here are great variety of trees and plants; labyrinths made with a great deal of labour, a jet d'eau, with its bason of white marble; and columns and pyramids of wood and other material up and down the garden. After seeing these, we were led by the gardiner into the summer-house, in the lower part of which, built semi-circularly, are the twelve Roman emperors in white marble, and a table of touchstone: the upper part of it is set around with cisterns of lead into which the water is conveyed through pipes, so that fish may be kept there, and in summer-time they are very convenient for bathing: in another room for entertainment very near this and joined to it by a little bridge, was an oval table of red marble."

A small garden, but one of the most delightful, must have been that laid out by Leicester at Kenilworth. His secretary's description of its charms is too vivid not to be given at length, and will serve as a last word as to the appearance of an actual Elizabethan garden.

"Unto this, his Honor's exquisite appointment of a beautiful garden, an acre or more in quantity, that lieth on the north there; Whereon hard all along by the Castle wall is reared a pleasant terrace ten feet high, and twelve feet broad, even under foot and fresh of fine grass, as is also the side thereof: In which, by sundry equal distances, with obelisks and spheres, and white bears, all of stone upon their curious bases, by goodly shew were set; To these, two fine arbours redolent by sweet trees and flowers, at each end one, the garden plot under that, with fair alleys green by grass, even voided from the borders on both sides, and some (for change) with sand, not light, or too soft, or soily by dust, but smooth and firm, pleasant to walk on, as a sea-shore when the water is availed. Then, much gracified by due proportion of four even quarters; in the midst of each, upon a base of two feet square and

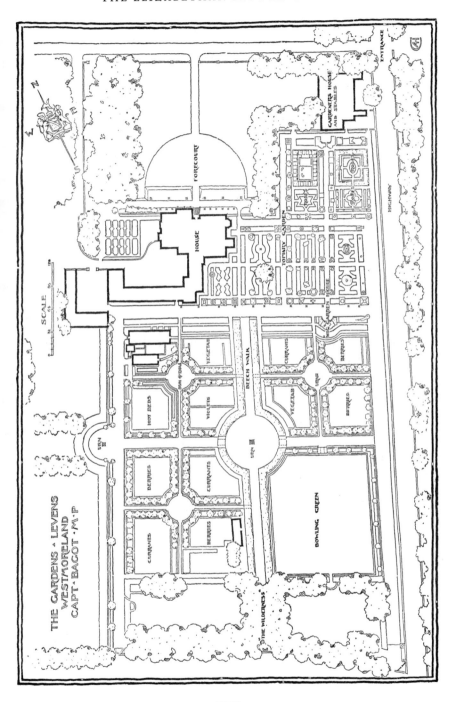

THE GARDENS AT LEVENS
WESTMORELAND
CAPT. BAGOT. M.P.

high, seemly bordered of itself, a square pilaster rising pyramidically fifteen feet high. Symmetrically pierced through from a foot beneath to two feet of the top: whereupon, for a Capitol, an orb of ten inches thick; everyone of these with its base, from the ground to the top, of one whole piece; hewn out of hard porphyry, and with great art and heed (think me) thither conveyed and there erected. Where, further also, by great cast and cost, the sweetness and savour on all sides, made so respirant from the redolent plants, and fragrant herbs and flowers, in form, colour and quantity so deliciously variant; and fruit trees bedecked with apples, pears, and ripe cherries. . . .

"A garden then so appointed, as wherein aloft upon sweet shadowed walk of terrace, in heat of summer to feel the pleasant frisking wind above, or delectable coolness of the fountain-spring beneath; to taste of delicious strawberries, cherries, and other fruits, even from their stalks; to smell such fragrancy of sweet odours, breathing from the plants, herbs, and flowers; to hear such natural melodious music and tunes of birds; to have in eye for mirth sometime these underspringing streams; then, the woods, the waters, (for both pool and chase were hard at hand in sight) the deer, the people (that out of the East arbour in the base Court, also at hand in view), the fruit trees, the plants, the herbs, the flowers, the change in colours, the birds flittering, the fountain streaming, the fish swimming, all in such delectable variety, order, and dignity; whereby at one moment, in one place, at hand, without travel, to have so full fruition of so many God's blessings, by entire delight unto all senses (if all can take) at once; for etymon of the word worthy to be called Paradise: and though not so goodly as Paradise, for want of the fair rivers, yet better a great deal by the lack of so unhappy a tree. Argument most certain of a right noble mind, that in this sort could have thus all contrived."

The gardens at Levens give perhaps the best idea of Elizabethan planting, while at Bramshill and Montacute are good examples of the architectural features of this period. There are many similar places in all parts of England and Scotland.

· CHAPTER SIX ·

Gardens of the Stuarts

N the days of the Stuarts the Elizabethan gardens underwent certain modifications according to the predominance of French, Italian, or Dutch fashions. In architecture classic traditions prevailed, but in garden design suggestions were less welcomed from the ancient Greeks and Romans than from contemporary horticulturists. Evelyn, a great authority on gardens at the height of this period, considered the writings of Tusser, Markham, Hartlib, and Walter Blith, with the *Philosophical Transactions*, *The Maison Rustique*, and other books of a similar description, as filled with much more valuable information than could be found in Cato, Varro, Columella, Palladio, or the Greek Geoponics. He also thought that in floriculture, the gardeners of his day were far ahead of the ancients, and that the number of plants then known was infinitely greater than ever in the past.

Changes at this period were introduced gradually. Garden architecture altered, like the rest of domestic architecture, from the Elizabethan to the later styles without any abrupt transition. The tendency was to give additional breadth to the gravel walks and minor importance to the flower-beds, producing a feeling of space which may be

The Parterre, Drayton House.

attributed to French influence. Beautiful wrought-iron gates and pal-isades were an importation from France or Holland. Leaden statues and vases, first designed in France, were often executed by Dutch workmen in England. Dwarf fruit trees were probably a Dutch fashion adapted to the miniature gardens in Holland, but seem to have become an important feature in every English garden toward the close of the seventeenth century. These innovations may be traced as far back as the reign of James I they continued rather in abeyance through the troubled times of Charles I and flourished most extensively after the Restoration. During the reigns of Charles II and of William and Mary, the seventeenth-century garden was at its prime.

In the reign of James I the most striking novelty was the cultivation of numerous collections of exotics. Various private botanical gardens were founded and the study of botany, with a fondness for the classifi-cation of new specimens, became common. Herbals and horticultural treatises were examined eagerly and herbalists attained great fame. Parkinson, an apothecary to the king, wrote the *Theatrum Botanicum*,

GATEWAY HIGHLOW HALL Nᵉ HATHERSAGE

FISHING LODGE BECKETT BERKS⊙

one of the best-known works on botany. The Tradescants, father and son, were distinguished as importers of exotics from Holland and America. Their epitaph is characteristic:

> "Know, stranger, ere thou pass, beneath this stone
> Lye John Tradescant, grandsire, father, son.
> The last died in his spring;—the other two
> Liv'd till they had travell'd Art and Nature through;
> As by their choice collections may appear
> Of what is rare, in land, in sea, in air.
> Whilst they (as Homer's Illiad in a nut)
> A world of wonders in one closet shut.
> These famous Antiquarians that had been
> Both gardeners to the Rose and Lily Queen
> Transplanted now themselves, sleep here, and when
> Angels shall with their trumpets waken men
> And fire shall purge the world, these hence shall rise,
> And change this garden for a Paradise."

The first public botanical garden in England, however, was not laid out until the reign of Charles I. It was founded and endowed by Henry, Earl of Danby, in 1632, at the University of Oxford. Five acres of land were contained within its enclosure. Some of the beds were simple oblongs for long rows of plants, while others formed elaborate knots

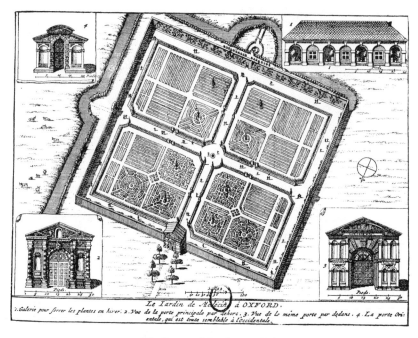

The Botanical Garden, Oxford.

accented by cone-shaped trees. By 1648 there already flourished sixteen hundred varieties of plants, including twenty sorts of roses, four of foxglove, ten of lychnis, nine of clematis, and rare exotics such as nicotiana or English tobacco, and yucca or Indian bread. Entrance gateways were designed by Inigo Jones, and among other architectural features were several greenhouses, an orangery, and a house for the gardener. The illustration shows the original orangery, gateways, and plan. At the close of the seventeenth century, Celia Fiennes wrote that these gardens "afforded great diversion and pleasure; the variety of flowers and plants would have entertained one a week."

The garden literature of the seventeenth century, apart from herbals, illustrates a variety of phases. The earlier books by such English writers as Markham and Lawson practically referred to Elizabethan gardens. Then, as the influence of Le Nôtre became paramount, a French school of gardeners was founded in England. Of these and their works more will be said later. Dutch authorities were also consulted, as shown by Hartlib's *Discourse of Husbandrie used in Brabant and Flanders.* But Parkinson, Evelyn, Rea, and Worlidge, the best English writers of this period, although they took note of foreign fashions, did their utmost to uphold English traditions.

At Hatfield there are a series of gardens especially interesting as showing the transition from the simple Elizabethan flower-garden to the more formal pleasure grounds of the Stuarts. On three sides of the present house, built for the first Lord Salisbury by John Thorpe of Padua, are gardens belonging, roughly speaking, to three different periods—those of Elizabeth, of James I, and of Charles II. Each is a very good example of its kind. Perhaps the planting has been more or less altered, but the design remains practically as it was in the beginning.

The earliest portions near the site of an ancient palace (of which the remains have been turned into a stable) lie west of the present mansion. But of the three divisions located there, only one was surely laid out in the time of Elizabeth. This is the enclosure surrounded by pleached limes, known as the Privy Garden. Here Queen Elizabeth herself must have often walked, shaded beneath the broad brim of a garden hat still preserved at Hatfield. This precious relic was a gift

PAVILION AT HATFIELD

PAVILION : HATFIELD

Old-fashioned Garden, Hatfield.

from the queen to her Lord Treasurer Burleigh, whose youngest son, the first Earl of Salisbury, afterward gave Theobalds to James I in exchange for Hatfield.

After the first Lord Salisbury came into possession of the estate and had built the present magnificent house on an axis with the old gardens, which he retained on one side, he laid out the remaining portion of the ground. The gardens west and south of the house therefore belong to the time of James I and of his son Charles I, when grass work was beginning to come into fashion, and the planting of flower-beds grew more formal. The garden-houses with their tiled roofs and terracotta balustrading are very good examples of Jacobean architecture on a small scale.

Below the rather stiff parterre, on the east side of the house, are a series of terraces. The first, covered with turf, is now used as a croquet-

Parterre, Hatfield House.

ground and was formerly a bowling-green. Next comes a maze out-lined with yew. The lowest terrace contains a charming oblong garden enclosing a circle of beds planted entirely with sweet-scented spikes of lavender. Celia Fiennes describes a garden similarly filled with nothing but lavender. Near the pond is an Elizabethan pavilion.

For descriptions of gardens in the time of Charles I the parliamen-tary surveys of his confiscated property are most complete. Of the royal estates at Wimbledon and Theobalds, among others, we can thus form an exceptionally good idea. Part and parcel, the beauties they con-tain as well as their money value were carefully noted down in the in-ventories made for the benefit of the Commonwealth.

At Wimbledon, the favourite country-seat of Henrietta Maria, the three principal enclosures contained the vineyard, the orange garden, and the great garden, all intimately connected with the dwelling-house,

SIDE DOOR TO A GARDEN

and covering between fifteen and twenty acres. The kitchen, pheasant, and "hartichoke" gardens, as rather for use than for ornament, were kept more in the background. High brick walls shut out the park and formed the main boundaries, while wooden palings served for the partitions of minor importance. The plan was intended to seclude the gardens from the rest of the grounds, while permitting them to appear to the greatest advantage from the house. To assist in this arrangement both the house and main gardens were placed on the same axis.

Each part of the garden was laid out symmetrically with knots of choice flowers, bordered with box, grass-plots, fountains, and statues. Several wooden pavilions varying in size were placed at the ends of the paths. Usually their roofs were covered with blue slate, and their floors paved with stone, brick, or tiles.

Next the mansion came a broad gravel walk, 170 yards long and 25 feet wide, running from east to west. At one end of this walk stood a "garden-house, part of boards, part of rails, covered with blue slate, and ridged and "uttered with lead, paved with square stone, having one door going into the end alley, leading into the said upper level, and one other door opening into the Hartichoke Garden." Two similar "garden, summer, or shadow houses" were placed, one on the north side of the gravel alley, the other in the middle of the east wall.

A quaint feature in a little grass-court near the house was an elaborate bird-cage. It was described as having "three open turrets very well wrought for the sitting and perching of birds; and also having standing in it one very fair and handsome fountain, with three cisterns of lead belonging to it, and many several small pipes of lead, gilded, which, when they flow and fall into the cisterns, make a pleasant noise. The turrets, fountain, and little court are all covered with strong iron wire and lie directly under the windows of the two rooms of the said Manor House called the Balcony Room, and the Lord's Chamber; from which Balcony Room one pavement of black and white marble containing 104 foot, railed with rails of wood on each side thereof, extends itself into the said alley over the middle of the said bird-cage. This bird-cage is a great ornament both to the House and Garden." Such aviaries were very popular in the seventeenth century. They were sometimes intended to contain people as well as birds. It will be remembered how during the reign of Charles II, Lady Castlemain used to receive her admirers in an aviary, and was playfully entitled the "bird of passage." The "Bird-cage" at Melbourne was practically an arbour intended entirely for people.

An account of the maze and the wilderness is especially interesting. "The Maze consists of young trees, wood, and sprays of good growth and height, cut into several meanders, circles, semi-circles, windings, and intricate turnings, the walks or intervals whereof are all grass-plots. This Maze, as it is now ordered, adds very much to the worth of the Upper Level. The Wilderness (a work of vast expence to the maker thereof) consists of many young trees, woods, and sprays of good growth and height, cut and formed into several ovals, squares, and angles, very well ordered; in most of the angular points whereof, as also in the centre of every oval, stands one Lime tree or Elm. All the alleys of this Wilderness, being in number eighteen, are of a gravelled earth very well ordered and maintained; the whole work being compiled with such order and decency, as that it is not one of the least of the ornaments of the said Manor or Mansion House."

A simple garden-house was placed at the west end of the turfed terrace. Opposite stood a much more elaborate construction. "One fair banqueting house, most of wood; the model thereof containing a fair round in the middle of four angles, covered with blue slate, and ridged and "uttered with lead, wainscoted round from the bottom to the roof, varnished with green within and without, benched in the angles, having sixteen windows or covers of the same wainscot to open or shut at pleasure, having also sixteen half rounds of glass to enlighten the room when those covers are shut up; the floor paved with painted tile in the angles and with squared stone in the middle; in one of which angles stands a table of artificial stone very well polished; and in every of the said angles, besides the said benches, there stands one wainscot chair. There are to the said banqueting house two double leaved doors, the one pair of which doors opens in the very middle of the said tarras, the outside thereof being gilt, with several coats of arms; the other of the said leaved doors opens into a fair walk within the Park, planted with Elms and Lime trees, extending itself from the said banqueting house in a direct line eastward, to the very Park pale. The round of the said banqueting house is handsomely arched; within which thirteen heads or statues, gilded, stand in circular form, adding very much to the beauty of the whole room."

A quaint feature was the private walk, where, unobserved, many important interviews took place. It was enclosed by a high thorn hedge.

At Theobalds, the general idea of the gardens was much the same as at Wimbledon. But there are one or two additional and characteristic features. Among them a knot "compassed aboute with a Quadrangle or square squadron Quicksett hedge of white thorn and privets of nine foot in height, cutt into a compleate fashion with fower round arbors with seats in them in each corner, with two Doore wayes betweene each arbour, in all the fower sides and betweene the two doore wayes in each side runs out a Roman T: made of the same sort of hedginge and of the same height." Two figures of wainscot well carved were in the middle of two of the knots, and there were covered alleys where "one might walk two myle in the walkes before he came to their ends."

The gardens at Richmond Court are less fully described and contained nothing especially original. Yew trees marked the centres of the box-bordered flower-beds, the brick walls twelve feet high were covered with fruit trees, and the water supply was contained in a lead cistern. The great orchard was symmetrically laid out with 223 trees. Here was a handsome bird-cage for turtle doves.

After the Restoration the seventeenth-century gardens became more numerous. Worlidge, writing about the year 1675, says:

THE TERRACE : BRYMPTON

"Neither is there a noble or pleasant seat in England but hath its gardens for pleasure and delight, scarce an ingenious citizen that by his confinement to a shop being denied the privilege of a real garden but hath his boxes, pots, and other receptacles for flowers, plants, etc.

"So that we may without vanity conclude that a garden of pleasant avenues, walks and fruits, flowers and other branches springing from it well composed, is the only permanent inanimate object of delight, the world affords.

"Such is its pre-excellency that scarce a cottage of the southern parts of England but hath its proportionate garden."

In many respects the garden remained the same as in the time of Queen Elizabeth. It formed an adjunct to the dwelling-house, which was entered through a forecourt and possibly a house court; it was to be square in form, enclosed by walls, a hedge, or a fence, and often adjoined by a terrace. But the fantastic spirit of the early Renaissance had been broken by Puritanical common-sense. Quaint figures in clipped box, elaborate wooden galleries, and luxurious masses of flowers began to seem superfluous. Despite protests, carefully raked gravel paths, smooth squares of grass, and a few specimens of rare exotics were now the centres of admiration.

In Pepys' *Diary* he records a conversation with the architect Hugh May about the gardens of this period, laid out in the height of the style, which evidently met with their approval:

"22nd Lord's Day. Walked to Whitehall, where saw nobody almost, but walked up and down with Hugh May, who is a very ingenious man. Among other things, discoursing of our present fashion of gardens to make them plain that we have the best walks of gravell in the world, France having none nor Italy; and our green of our bowling allies is better than any they have. So our business here being ayre, this is the best way only with a little mixture of statues or pots, which may be handsome, and so filled with another pot of such or such a flower or greene, as the season of the year will bear. And then for the flowers, they are best seen in a little plat by themselves; beside their borders spoil the walks of another garden; and then for fruit, the best way is to have walls built circularly one within another, to the south, on purpose for fruit, and leave the walking Garden only for that use."

Flowers began to be considered of less and less importance, and were planted in pots rather than directly in the soil. This gave a somewhat cold and forbidding aspect to the garden, which Rea protests was rarely "found well furnished out of the hands of an affectionate florist," and he goes on to explain:

"Love was the Inventor and is still the Maintainer of every noble science. It is chiefly that which has made my flowers and trees to flourish, though planted in a barren desert, and hath brought me to the knowledge I now have in plants and planting.

"I have seen many gardens of the new model in the hands of unskilful persons with good walls, walks and grass plots; but in the most essential adornments so deficient, that a green meadow is a more delightful object. And as noble fountains, grottoes, statues, etc., are excellent ornaments and marks of magnificence; so all such dead works in gardens ill done are little better than blocks in the way to interrupt the sight.

"A choice collection of living beauties, rare plants, flowers and fruits, are indeed the wealth and glory and delight of a garden.

"The new mode of gravel walks and grass plots is fit only for such houses or palaces as are situated in cities and great towns, although they are now become precedents for many stately Country residencies,

A LEADEN STATUE

where they have banished out of their gardens flowers, the miracles of nature, and the best ornaments that ever were discovered to make a seat pleasant. But it is hoped that this new, useless, and unpleasant mode will, like many other varieties, still go out of fashion." In Plot's *Staffordshire* there is a picture of the house and grounds at Ingestre. The gardens consist of squares and ovals of grass, ornamented with statues, but do not appear to contain a single flower.

Of the many books describing how gardens were to be laid out at this period, the best by English writers were *Flora, Ceres, and Pomona* by John Rea and the *Systema Horticulturæ, or Art of Gardening*, by John Worlidge. The first of these publications appeared in 1676, the second in 1677, both in London.

The situation of the garden in relation to the house is taken for granted by Worlidge. One reason for his premise was the advantage of having the principal entrance into the garden from the best room in the house to make the walks convenient for exercise after meals.

"It may seem needless to say anything of the situation of a Garden, it being so absolute a concomitant to your habitation that a garden remote or by itself, is neither pleasant or useful. Therefore where ever your house is, near it must be your garden."

Circular Garden, from the Systema Horticultura.

If, however, the house was not already built, in choosing its location, a site with good soil for a garden was selected, with a southern or southeastern exposure, a water supply, and a pleasant view. At some distance, a belt of tall trees was planted to break the wind in winter and spring, and furnish shade in the warm weather.

Both Rea and Worlidge considered the "most graceful grounds an entire level." If the site were a hillside, then the gardens were naturally laid out in terraces, if possible below the house. "For it is much more pleasant to view a garden under the eye than above it, and to descend into a garden and ascend into a house than on the contrary."

In speaking of the form, Worlidge says: "The round is very pleasant and some curious gardens there are of that form in foreign parts. The walls about such a garden are very good for fruit, the wind not being as severe against a round as against a straight wall. The walk also that circumdates the garden is not unpleasant, for there you may walk as long as you please in it, always forwards without any short turning; some straight walks there may be that tend from the circumference to the centre. The several quadrants may be subdivided and planted with fruits, the borders of the round walks and the cross walks being sufficient for flowers and plants of beauty and delight. At the centre of this Garden may be planted a fountain, or in defect of water a banqueting house or house of pleasure.

"A rude draught of such a form is here presented to your view, the inner parts of the grass plots planted with fine trees, and the quadrants within the lesser circle planted with a variety of fruit trees, and the principal walks, round and straight, bordered with flowers and delightful shrubs and plants.

"Encompassed with a palisade in the centre of your garden is a fountain of spring water always flowing, serving not only to refresh the spirits of such that delight in the sight of it, but is necessary in dry and hot seasons to preserve your choicest plants from injury."

A rectangular garden, however, was considered decidedly preferable. "The square is the most perfect and pleasant form that you can lay your garden into where your ground will afford it; every walk that is in it being straight and every plant and tree standing in a direct line, represents it to your eye very pleasing. The delight you take in walking in it being much the more as you are less careful: for when you walk in a round circle you are more subject to trespass on the borders without continual thought and observation of the ground.

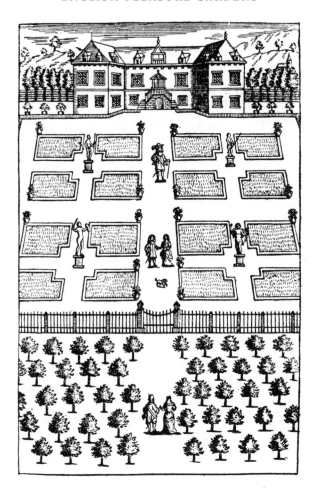

"You may divide your square into three parts by palisades, the long way beginning at your house, the middle part containing a large gravel walk adorned on each side with a border of your most select plants, shrubs, and flowers between those borders and the palisades, green walks with borders next the palisades, on which you may plant perennial greens and your more ordinary plants and flowers.

"The other two partitions of your square you may convert the one of them into an orchard the other into a kitchen garden, which will be no small ornament to your middle garden of pleasure.

"But if you are willing to celebrate so fair a spot of ground as the whole square to the delights of flora, make of them grass-plots leaving only borders on their confines for your variety of plants.

＊　＊　＊　＊　＊

"A draught of the square garden I have given here, which may be varied as the designer pleaseth, each principal walk is bordered with flowers, each principal corner with flower pots and the middle of the quarter-square with statues. The farther end fenced with a palisade that the prospect of the adjacent orchard may not be lost where now the statues stand, if water be to be obtained, fountains would be placed with more delight."

GATE-WAY CHICHESTER

After the shape of the garden had been determined the method of enclosure was taken into consideration: "When you have discovered the best Land and pleased yourself with the compleatest Form you can imagine for your garden; yet without a good Fence to preserve it from severall evils that usually annoy it your labour is but lost." This protection might be afforded by hedges, wooden palings, wooden or iron palisades, or walls of earth, brick, or stone.

Brick walls were considered best. Usually they were strengthened at regular intervals by pilasters, and coped with bricks set on edge and sometimes slightly projecting. The dark purplish red of the seventeenth-century brick was often a beautiful colour, and a most becoming background to the peach and plum trees trained in fan shapes to cover its surface. Niches containing seats were often built at the end of paths and were among the pleasantest places to sit and view the garden. The foundation of the wall according to Rea might be of stone as high as a foot above the level of the ground, but the upper part should be always of brick. The height of an outside wall was about nine feet. Lesser

Terrace, Annesley.

Gateway, Hampton Court.

walls, dividing, for example, the fruit from the flower garden, rose only to five or six feet. White marble trimmings made an attractive contrast to the red brick. At Hampton Court there are several fine brick walls ornamented with niches and alcoves and pilasters. A portion is shown in the above illustration. Another very beautiful and unusual brick wall separates the terrace from the garden at Annesley; it can hardly be seen in the illustration that the top curves downward between the pilasters. At Ham House there are some simple but good brick garden walls. One defining the forecourt is more elaborate, and contains twelve lead busts of the Roman emperors, placed in oval niches.

Palisades of wood, or more often iron, were a characteristic innovation. They were used when a barrier which would not shut out the view was required, and were fastened to the tops of walls built breast high. Numerous examples are to be seen of enclosed forecourts, as at Ham House and Levens.

Gateways with beautiful wrought-iron gates were also introduced at this period. At Hampton Court, Packwood, Kew, and Drayton are some of those shown in the illustrations. No feature gives more style to a garden.

Walks, arbours, and places of repose in a garden did not cease to be considered of importance.

AN ALCOVE AT ARLEY

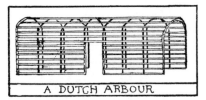

A DUTCH ARBOUR

"It is not the least part of the pleasures of a garden to walk and re-fresh yourself either with your friends or acquaintances or else alone, retired from the cares of the world, or apart from company that some-times may prove burdensome to you, and when your own lassitude or the heat, rain, or scorching beams of the sun render the open walks un-pleasant, to repose yourself under some pleasant tree or some covert or shade until you are willing to try the air again."

A new method of making walks in three divisions was recom-mended by Worlidge. "The best for winter and wet seasons are those paved with stone, about the breadth of five feet, in the midst of a gravel walk of about five or six foot, gravel on each side of the stone or of grass, which you please. For on these flat stones may you walk securely under foot in all weathers." Walks of fine-screened gravel were consid-

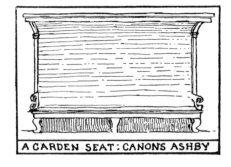

A GARDEN SEAT: CANONS ASHBY

Sun-dial, Hampton Court.   *Pleached Alley, Melbourne.*

ered as next best and very ornamental; they might be bordered with grass "for your use in hot weather." In summer the pleasantest walks underfoot and overhead were those of grass arched over with a cradle alley of pleached trees.

As there were few verandas of any description in connection with English houses, it was particularly important to have arbours and other shady nooks in the garden. High-backed wooden seats afforded

protection from the wind, like the interesting example existing at Canons Ashby, where there is a pretty, though small garden, which was laid out in 1700. Such benches were painted white or green. Sometimes the seat was round and placed in a corner of the wall; then it might be covered with a circular roof half supported on the top of the wall, half on wooden posts or stone columns. "Having several of these seats facing

AN OCTAGONAL GARDEN-HOUSE

SUN·DIAL : PACKWOOD

SUN·DIAL·.TRINITY COLLEGE

to each coast," Worlidge says, "be the wind or sun either way, you have a place to defend yourself from it."

Even such celebrated architects as Inigo Jones and Sir Christopher Wren gave attention to the design of summer-houses. Their appearance always had a touch of quaintness. Either the eaves were made very broad, as in the illustration of the fishing-lodge, or the pitch of the roof was remarkably steep, or the ground-plan was octagonal. In the Parliamentary Surveys accounts of a number of these pavilions are described, with all their details.

In the middle of one side of the garden Rea advises locating a "handsome octagonal summer-house roofed every way and finely painted with landskips, furnished with seats about and a table in the middle, serving both for delight and use, a place wherein to store bulbs, etc." The charming little summer-house at Iford Manor near Bradford-on-

Avon seems to answer almost exactly to this description, and a similar one at Bramshill is shown in the illustration on page 161.

There are attractive pavilions at Nun Moncton, near York, and the Cedars, Beckington, Somersetshire, containing single rooms, one twelve feet square and the other ten. Large ones are at Charlton, Kent, and Drayton, in Hamptonshire. Sometimes they were two stories high, as at Severn End, near Worcester.

Greenhouses were an important adjunct to gardens which contained many exotics too tender to be left out of doors in the winter. Here also gillyflowers, carnations, and orange trees were forced into bloom. The latter were numerous, and sometimes when the greenhouse was particularly devoted to their use, it was called an orangery. At Wimbledon, as early as the time of James I, there was an orangery with walls of brick and the roof covered with blue slate. Here were sheltered forty-two orange, one lemon, one pomecitron, and six pomegranate trees.

In the late seventeenth century, garden statues, obelisks, dials, and other "unvegetative" ornaments seemed to take the place of flowers. The best position for a statue was supposed to be in the midst of a fountain or at the termination of a shady walk, rather than on the naked surface of the earth or the centre of a grass-plot. Obelisks, either plain or supporting sun-dials, were considered more appropriate for an

Fountains, from the Systema Horticultura.

GARDEN-HOUSE : PACKWOOD

open space of ground. Sun-dials were as numerous as ever, and constantly appearing in new forms. In New College Garden at Oxford was one planted in box. Flower-pots painted blue or white and placed on pedestals or directly on the ground, lined the paths or surrounded the basins of the fountains.

The importance of water could never be overlooked by reason both of its use and its ornament. If there were none at hand, it might be sought according to the precepts of Rapinus, an author much admired by Evelyn and quoted by Worlidge.

"Where small declining Hillocks you perceive
Or any soil where flags and rushes live,
Where the flat ground shiny moisture yields
There hidden springs with confidence expect
For Sedgy Places still do Springs direct."

Every garden was supposed to have one or more fountains, generally constructed of marble or some other stone. The illustrations from Worlidge show a variety of different designs. Celia Fiennes mentions a clock "which by water-work is moved and strikes the hours and chinnes the quarters, and when they please play lilibolaro on the chimes."

Bowling had now become the favourite outdoor game to the exclusion of tennis. At Norton Conyers in Yorkshire there is a historic bowling-green where Charles I, while waiting for supplies, is said to have played for five consecutive days. At Levens are some old seventeenth-

GARDEN-HOUSE: PACKWOOD

WROUGHT IRON GRILLE: DRAYTON

century bowls bearing the Bellingham crests. A garden with any pre-
tensions was always supplemented by a bowling-green, usually shaded
by trees and varying in its proportions.

The most celebrated gardens in England were visited by two travellers, John Evelyn and Celia Fiennes, toward the close of the seventeenth century. Each has left descriptions of these gardens, which add
much to our existing store of information, and have been already
quoted in this chapter.

Evelyn was particularly interested in gardens and proposed to write
a book about them, so his observations are deserving of especial attention. Of Althorpe and Cassiobury he speaks with admiration, but does
not describe in such detail as the gardens at Swallowfield. These were
"as elegant as 'tis possible to make a flat by art and industry and no
mean expense, my Lady being extraordinarily skilled in the flowery
part, and my Lord in diligence of planting, so that I have hardly seen a
seate which shews more tokens of it than what is to be found here, not
only in the delicious and rarest fruite of a garden, but in those innumerable timber trees in the ground aboute the seate to the greatest ornament and benefit of the place. There is one orchard of one thousand
golden and other cider pippens, walks and groves of elms, limes, oaks,
and other trees. The garden so beset with all manner of sweete shrubbs

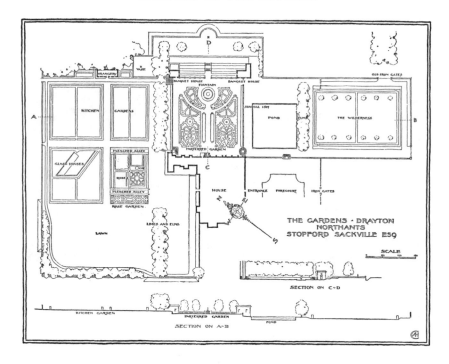

that it perfumes the aire. The distribution also of the quarters, walks, and parterres is excellent; the nurseries, kitchen garden, full of the most desirable plants; two very noble orangeries, well furnished; but above all, the canall and fishponds, the one fed with a white the other with a black running water, fed by a quick and swift river, so well and plentifully stor'd with fish that for pike, carp, breame, and tench I never saw anything approaching. . . . The waters are flagged about with Calamus Aromaticus, with which my Lady has hung a closet that retains the smell very perfectly. There is also a certaine sweete smelling willow and other exotics, also a very fine bowling greene, meadow, pasture, and wood; in a word all that can render a country seat beautiful and delightful."

At Drayton, in Northamptonshire, is perhaps the most perfect specimen of a seventeenth-century garden now in existence. The pleached alleys, the parterre with its gravel walks edged with grass, the banqueting houses, beautiful wrought-iron gates, and orangery are all

167

The Parterre, Drayton House.

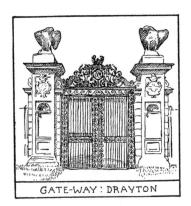

in keeping. The Elizabethan wing, added to the original house of Drayton, bears the date 1584 and has been attributed to John Thorpe, who was much employed in the neighbourhood. The owner and builder was Lewis, third Lord Mordaunt, who succeeded his father in 1572 and died in 1601. His wife was Elizabeth D'Arcy, and their arms occur on the sun-dial, still existing on the low wall between the formal garden and the wilderness. The formal garden is evidently made to conform to the shape of the enlarged house.

168

SUN-DIAL: BRYMPTON

GATE·WAY : KEW· GARDENS

The banqueting houses bear an earl's coronet and the arms of Henry, second Earl of Peterborough, 1642-1699. The iron gates were put up about 1699 by Mary, Baroness Mordaunt, who succeeded to the estate on her father's death in 1697. She married first Henry, seventh Duke of Norfolk, and second Sir John Germain, who is thought by some to have been a half brother of King William III, and who is alluded to by Horace Walpole as bringing "the garden from Holland; pyramidal yews, treillages, and square cradle walks with windows clipped in them."

CHAPTER SEVEN

French Fashions

 DISTINCTIVE style of garden planning and planting developed in France and spread thence all over Europe in the latter half of the seventeenth century. Previously, although the French had excelled in many kinds of horticulture, their gardens had developed no especial characteristics to distinguish them from those laid out at the same time in neighbouring countries. Contemporary designs were decidedly inferior to those of the Italian Renaissance. But when Louis XIV came into power, French society underwent a revolution which had a far-reaching effect upon the outward expression of literature and art. A new policy was inaugurated by the young king, the reverse of that adopted by his predecessors.

Henry IV, whose example was followed by Louis XIII, had kept the peace by insisting that the great noblemen should disperse from Paris and live practically isolated on their country estates. His own tastes were simple, and he did not encourage others to indulge themselves with needless luxuries. The gardens attached to the royal palaces and to those of the aristocracy, as we see them depicted by Du Cerceau and described by Mollet, the head gardener of both Henry IV and Louis

A French Renaissance Garden.

XIII, were neither extensive nor elaborate compared to those of Louis XIV. To be sure, the former contained most of the component parts of the later gardens; Mollet, in 1582, had already planted parterres and *compartements* of *broderie*, according to the designs of the Sieur du Perac, the king's architect, which were illustrated by De Serres. Both Du Perac and De Serres were evidently well acquainted with ornamental avenues of trees, parterres, bosquets, labyrinths, high and low palisades, trelliswork, alleys whose vistas were terminated by statues, fountains or perspectives painted on canvas, grottoes, terraces, canals, and other water-works. There was, however, a lack of freedom and continuity in the contours, which gave the design a cramped appearance.

Louis XIV with his passion for power, splendour, and centralization, began his reign by concentrating the aristocracy in the neighbourhood of Paris, to shine as rays emanating from the sun which he typified in his own person. To meet the requirements of the king and this brilliant court, remarkable constructions were not only attempted but completed on a scale of grandeur scarcely rivalled since the time of

Gardening, from an Old Manuscript.

Hadrian. Royal palaces were built large enough to contain a numerous assemblage of courtiers under the same roof as the king. Magnificent gardens were constructed outside these palaces, where not only Louis and his court, but thousands of his guests—including finally the public at large—were provided with suitable parade-grounds. At Versailles, Marly, and St. Cloud, the most celebrated of these gardens were rapidly laid out under the king's personal supervision.

"A un roi majestueux il fallait un décor en conséquence," states M. Georges Riat in *L'Art des Jardins*, continuing as follows: "The personality of Louis XIV explains the horticulture as well as the art and letters of his time. Just as the little gardens of the Middle Ages had failed to suit the Medici and other great Italian noblemen who found them too restricted for the display of their court, so the king desired vast parks symbolizing the immensity of his sway, where courtiers and visitors of distinction would be impressed with the new sovereignty. And as the writers and artists sought inspiration in the masterpieces of antiquity, gardeners also were inspired by these models. Extraordinarily well-chosen they were to accomplish the desired ends. The pomp of a magnificent court could conveniently display itself in the broad and endless alleys among the parterres, where the beauty of the flowers and statues was only intended to bring into prominence the charms of the ladies, where nature, submissive to man, lent itself to every sort of theatrical fancy."

The credit for all these marvellous works of art was given to the king. While Le Nôtre planned the arrangement of the bosquets and parterres, Le Brun designed the fountains and statuary, and Francini engineered the stupendous water-works, their ideas were said to be the king's. In the words of a contemporary poem:

> "Au roi de toute chose on doit l'invention
> De toutes les beautés de toutes les merveilles
> Qui charment les esprits, les yeux et les oreilles."

After making liberal allowances for poetical exaggeration, the fact remains that without Louis' active interest as well as his pecuniary assistance, such gardens could never have come into existence. Everywhere it was his delight to appear to do the impossible. The triumphs of man over nature were strikingly evident. Arid plains were diversified by a series of terraces, parterres of flowers, and marble fountains; wildernesses of trees were pierced with avenues, irrigated by canals, and divided into beautiful groves ornamented with architecture and sculpture. Only the king's imagination and revenues could have sufficed for such transformations.

Le Nôtre, however, was the actual creator of most of the famous pleasure grounds of Louis' reign and the originator of the new style. He was born in Paris early in the seventeenth century. At first he studied painting under Vouet in the studio with Mignard, Le Brun, and Lesueur; then he decided to adopt his father's profession and to succeed him as superintendent of the king's gardens. To fit himself for this position he travelled through Italy and carefully studied the magnifi-

French Engravings of Gardens.

cent villa gardens of the late Renaissance. The villas Pamphili and Lu-
dovisi especially impressed him. But while these may have been his
point of departure in the Italian style, the great garden architect soon
developed a system of his own as different as France from Italy, as
French from Italian society, and as the seventeenth from the sixteenth
century. The garden of Louis XIV and of Le Nôtre was as distinct a

creation as the architecture of Mansart or the literature of Racine. The superstructure may have been built on a classic foundation, but it developed decidedly individual characteristics.

The style of Le Nôtre can be studied in the existing gardens he laid out, in engravings from his plans, and in numerous descriptions of their arrangement. These show that he understood the laws of balance, variety, and contrast, as well as those of symmetry. But in looking at the plans it must be remembered that the gardens were never actually seen from a bird's-eye point of view, that perspective would give the straight paths the appearance of converging, that trees and shrubs of varying height filled the geometric outlines of the bosquets, that light and shadow played in and out of the scene. Such gardens were far from rigidly formal or monotonous when executed in the right spirit. Each feature had its object. The broad paths were to afford sufficient space for the enormous hoop-skirts of the ladies, the covered alleys gave opportunity for private conversation, the bosquets were "salons" for royal entertainments. Even the ornamentation had its distinct purpose, and was not carelessly distributed.

The most celebrated of these great gardens now remaining is Versailles, though in their day Marly and St. Cloud were considered equally fine. During the life of Louis XIV, Versailles underwent constant changes. At first the palace was a hunting-lodge and the grounds insignificant. In the middle of the seventeenth century, Louis took up his abode there, and alteration succeeded alteration, until, when the grounds were completely laid out, he destroyed his own creations in order to replace them by new marvels. The vast enclosure of the park was a parallelogram divided into halves by a wide opening between groves of trees, affording space for the canals, and a vista stretching far away to the horizon. Near the palace were the magnificent terraces ornamented with parterres of flowers, fountains, and statues. Beyond were the plantations of trees pierced with avenues and divided into fourteen bosquets, not to mention several acres of untouched woodland.

From the palace the visitor passed out, then as now, on a broad terrace extending the whole length of the building, and flanked on each

The Bosquet des Dômes, Versailles.

side by *parterres de broderie*. Directly in front was the superb vista, stretching as far as the eye could reach through the centre of the park, ornamented by the Grand Canal, 1560 metres long by 120 wide, forming at its extremity a piece of water 195 metres square. Innumerable marble seats, groups of statuary and fountains, added to the sumptuous appearance.

Below the left-hand parterre was the orangery, a building consisting of a central gallery 155 metres long, by 1290 wide, and two lateral galleries each 115 metres long. It was constructed by Mansart on the site of a former building by Le Vau. The scale and proportions are remarkably good, and the two staircases leading to it have been considered the finest pieces of architecture at Versailles. When Louis brought the Siamese ambassadors to look at this building, they exclaimed that it was good enough to house a king. Behind the glass doors hundreds of Louis' favourite orange trees were protected during the winter, and thence distributed over the grounds in summertime. In front of the orangery was a parterre designed by La Quintinie.

The bosquets occupied by far the greater portion of the park. Most of them still exist, although the wrought-iron gates which shut them in have often disappeared, and the trees are kept less trim than formerly. They were constructed by Le Nôtre, after the symmetrical avenues, intersecting the old hunting forest of Louis XIII, had been completed. Each bosquet was a grove of trees arranged to outline some geometrical pattern, and containing an ornamental feature in its centre. The first was the Labyrinth, designed about 1615; the last, the Colonnade, was finished in 1686. But each portion was remodelled again and again. The Palatine writes that "there is not a place at Versailles, which has not been done over ten times, often only to be worse for the change in the end." Among the most celebrated of these ornamental groves were the Labyrinth, the Theatre d'Eau, the Salle de Bal, the Marais, the Bosquet des Dômes, the Isle d'Amour, and the Quincunx du Midi.

The Bosquet des Dômes is perhaps the most interesting of those now remaining. On its site was originally placed the Grotto of Thetis, where La Fontaine read aloud the *Amours de Psyche* to Boileau, Racine, and Molière. This was supplanted by the Fountain of Fame, by the Baths of Apollo, and finally by nearly the present arrangement. The central fountain, enclosed by double rows of balustrades, remains the same, but formerly in the middle stood a gilded lead figure of Fame. On each side of the fountains were placed marble pavilions designed by Mansart, which, with eight statues placed in niches of trelliswork, have disappeared, but the other features have been recently restored. As a whole in fact the Bosquet has perhaps never been as perfect as now. The engraving by Israel Silvestre gives a good idea of its appearance in 1612.

The other bosquets were equally if not more elaborate. In the Labyrinth were lead animals coloured to make them as lifelike as possible, and considered to be among the greatest marvels. The Marais was a very conventional swamp designed by Mme. de Montespan and ornamented by a formal island, bearing a bronze tree which spouted water from each of its iron leaves. On two opposite sides were the celebrated buffets, gigantic sideboards of white and red marble. From the

The Labyrinth, Versailles.

shelves water spouted in the shape of glasses, carafes, and vases, which looked as though they were made of rock crystal. In the Théâtre d'Eau was a stage framed and ornamented by numerous and various water-works. Spouts of water took the place of footlights and fell from dozens of fountains or rose from others. While music sounded, twelve different combinations of water, forming aigrettes, lances, chandeliers, etc., played upon the stage. The Salle de Bal was an elliptical bosquet, enclosing an arena surrounded by several rows of seats. In the centre of the arena the dancers assembled, and sometimes the king himself took part in the ballet.

The statuary was mostly inspired from the antique, if not an exact copy of some well-known work of art, such as the Venus of Medici or the Venus of Richelieu. It was profusely scattered throughout the gardens and park, to terminate a perspective, embellish a fountain, or adorn the centre of a parterre.

More originality was shown in the vases of marble, bronze, or lead.

They were also of classic design, but more modern in sentiment. Blondel edited a book called
*Profils et ornements de vases, executez en marbre,
bronze et plombs dans les Jardins de Versailles, Trianon, et Marly.* The urn shown in the illustration
is French in character.

LEADEN URN·PENSHURST

The French style exerted a marked influence
in England. On account of its expense, however,
it was seldom reproduced except in the larger
gardens, principally in those belonging to the king. Charles II desired
to emulate Louis XIV, and for this purpose he endeavoured to per-
suade Le Nôtre, among other French garden architects, to enter his
service. It is not absolutely certain whether Le Nôtre ever came to England, but it is generally supposed that he designed the plan of St. James'
Park and important alterations at Hampton Court. Other English gardens which have been attributed to him are those at Chatsworth,
Bramham, and Holme Lacey. At any rate these have much in common
with the French style. Beaumont, who called himself a pupil of Le

Garden-house, Holme Lacey.

179

CUPID : MELBOURNE

Nôtre, remodelled part of the gardens at Levens, and also assisted at Hampton Court. La Quintinie gave Charles various suggestions, but could not be persuaded to remain in his employ. Finally John Rose, a protégé of the Earl of Essex, who had been sent by him to study the arrangement of Versailles, was appointed royal gardener. Rose, with his pupil and successor, London, then became the leaders of the Anglo-French school.

The natural beauties of Hampton Court were greater than those of Versailles on account of the proximity of the river Thames, but there was less opportunity for obtaining a view of the surrounding country. When Charles II began his improvements, the stretch of ground behind the palace was apparently devoid of interest. His gardeners (inspired by Le Nôtre, if not under his actual guidance) laid out the three avenues of limes converging in a goose-foot at the west of the palace. On the line of the principal axis of the palace beyond the goose-foot, is a canal of water three quarters of a mile long and one hundred and twenty-six feet wide, fed by the Longford River. Five hundred acres came within the scope of the design which was afterward completed by

GATE BY TIJOU: HAMPTON COURT

SUN-DIAL: HAMPTON COURT

Trees and Water, Bramham. Photograph by T. Maffet.

William III. In Knyff and Kip's *Britannia Illustrata* is a bird's-eye view of the palace and its surroundings as they appeared early in the eighteenth century, with the Pond Garden, the banqueting house, and other Tudor features much as they were when first laid out, and the new gardens begun under Charles II and completed in the two following reigns. Later Kent swept away the parterres of embroidery and many other curious features, substituting for them the present lawns of grass. Enough remains, however, to form one of the most delightful series of gardens in England.

At Bramham in Yorkshire is the most extensive and in certain respects the finest specimen of the French style in England. The park containing hundreds of acres is covered with a forest of magnificent trees pierced with broad avenues. As the ground is hilly there are opportunities for beautiful vistas, which in some cases are terminated with handsome vases. The water-works are extensive; a long canal reflects the foliage on its surface like a mirror. The spirit of Versailles has never been more delightfully reproduced.

THE BIRDCAGE: MELBOURNE

Another very charming garden in the French style is at Melbourne. Sir John Coke, secretary of state under Charles I, acquired the estate in 1628. The present gardens were laid out for Thomas Coke, afterward chamberlain to George I, by London's partner, Wise, between 1704 and 1711. Near the house are some grass terraces badly cut up with poorly designed flower-beds, but the rest of the gardens were planned with great skill and have been kept up almost to perfection. The scale of the walks, the square basin of water, the fountains and statuary are excellent. In the middle of one side of the pond is the bird-cage arbour, a splendid piece of wrought-iron work which would look better if not painted white.

The gardens at Wrest Park were laid out by Henry, Duke of Kent, early in the eighteenth century and are in the French style. They are particularly noticeable for their beautiful avenues of elms. One of them

SUN·DIAL AT LEVENS

GATE·WAY: KEW GARDENS:

forms a perspective through the middle of the park ornamented with a long canal. Another of the avenues was laid out to commemorate the landing of William III. Other gardens showing Le Nôtre's influence are at Holme Lacey, where there is a charming garden-house and some grass alleys bordered with fine yew hedges, and at Levens, where a part of the gardens was designed by Beaumont, who was a pupil of Le Nôtre, also employed at Hampton Court.

Gardens in the French style, many of which have disappeared, are shown in Kip's *Britannia Illustrata*, published in 1709, in the third volume of *Vitruvius Britannicus*, issued by Campbell in 1725, in *Les Delices de la Grande Bretagne*, and in Badeslades *Views*. All contain numerous bird's-eye views of elaborate schemes, showing that almost every great house at this period was surrounded by magnificent gardens extending into the park with long avenues of trees. Among the finest were those at Badminton, Brome Hall, Cassiobury, Boughton, Hinchinbrooke Wollaton, and Longleat.

The works of contemporaneous French writers on gardens were well known in England during the seventeenth and eighteenth centuries and are frequently quoted by English authors. Among others the writings of Sieur Legendre and of La Quintinie were popularly translated, the latter first by Evelyn in 1658, under the name of the *Compleat Gardner*, and again by London and Wise in 1699. *The Retired Gardner*, from the French of Louis Liger, and the *Solitary or Carthusian Gardener*, from the French of François Le Gentil, were translations by London and Wise.

Park, Melbourne. Photograph by R. Keene.

The best of these, or in fact of any similar books written before or afterward, is *The Theory and Practice of Gardening*, by A. Le Blond, attributed to D'Argenville, translated by John James and published in 1703. It explains Le Nôtre's theories, as applied to gardens of ordinary dimensions, planned to be laid out and kept up at moderate expense. Le Blond's precepts are so valuable to every one interested in this subject that they have been quoted almost verbatim in the following pages. It would be impossible to improve on either the matter or the manner.

In the first place it was assumed that the garden architect should be a man of parts. He must be proficient in the practice of the arts of architecture, drawing, and ornamental design, and in the sciences of geometry and horticulture. Starting with a natural sense of beauty, he should acquire good judgment from actual experience and from the contemplation of the finest examples of art and nature. Garden architecture was a profession necessitating unusual intelligence strengthened by varied attainments not to be acquired without great difficulty.

The garden was to correspond to the building in its neighbourhood. But the house was to be sacrificed to the garden rather than the garden to the house. "By reason a Country-house ought to differ from one in Town, where the Extent of the Buildings is more necessary than that of Gardens, on account of being the more usual place of Dwelling and of Land bearing a higher Value. The country we court chiefly to have our Gardens in it more spacious and magnificent."

These fundamental maxims were to be observed in laying out a garden. "First to make Art give place to Nature; secondly, never to cloud and darken a garden too much. Thirdly, not to lay it too open; and fourthly, to always make it look bigger than it really is." In detail these maxims are explained as follows: "In Planting a Garden we ought to have more regard to Nature than Art, making use of the latter only to set off the beauties of the former. In some Gardens we see nothing but what is uncommon, forced, and preternatural, everything done by Dint of Money; such as high Walls to terraces, Great Stairs of stone like as many Quarries, Fountains cluttered with Ornaments, and abundance of Arbours, Cabinets, and Porticoes of Lattice work filled with Figures, Vases, and so forth, which shew more manual Art than anything else.

"Gardens should not be made dull and gloomy by clouding them with Thickets and too much Cover. Fine openings should be preserved about the Building and in other places where the Prospect of the Country can be seen to advantage: for which reason we never set anything upon Parterres, Terraces, Bowling-Greens, Slopes, etc., but small Yews and Flowering Shrubs which taking up little room in the Air, we have the free Prospect of everything about us.

"We now often fall into the contrary Extreme and lay our Gardens too open under the pretence of making the Parts large; there are twenty considerable Gardens about Paris spoiled by this very thing, and where it is needless to go into them to see them; you discover the whole at one view from the Vestibule of the House without troubling yourself to walk in them. This is certainly very wrong. The pleasure of a Garden is to have the View stop in certain places, that you may be led on with Delight to see the more agreeable Parts of it, as fine Groves or Woodwork, Green Halls adorned with Fountains and Figures, etc. Those great flat Parts and the Walks about them rob us, as I may say, of the room where the Wood and raised Works should grow, which make the Contrariety and Change in a garden, and which make all the rest valuable; when the shade of these, which is so necessary, is wanting there is no walking in summer without being roasted, which is one of the greatest Inconveniences and Faults that can be.

"Gardens that lie thus open, have commonly indeed a fine and extensive Prospect, the Walls being under Terraces, and nothing intervening to shut out the sight any way: but that is what makes them look half as little again as they truly are; for comparing them with the neighbouring Country, with which they are blended, in the view, they appear, as it were, no bigger than one's Hand, contrary to that fundamental Maxim of making a Garden always look bigger than it really is, either by artfully stopping the Eye with Hedges, Walks of Trees, or Woods judiciously placed and kept to a proper height, or making Blinds of Wood against the Walls to amuse the Eye with a considerable Extent where the Bounds of the Inclosure would otherwise appear."

The general proportion of a garden was to be one-third longer than its width, or the length might be once and a half the breadth; "that the

Evergreen Arches, Brockenhurst. Photographs by E. A. Rowe.

parts by being longer than they are wide, may be more pleasing to the Eye: but to make it twice or thrice its breadth makes the place look disagreeable and no more than a Gut."

The other general rules that were to be observed in the disposition and distribution of gardens were these:

"There should always be a Descent from the Building to the Garden, of three steps at least; this renders the Fabrick more dry and wholesome; and from the Head of these Steps you have a general View of the Garden, or of the great Part of it, which yields a most agreeable Prospect.

"A Parterre is the first thing that should present itself to Sight, and possess the Ground next the Fabrick, whether in Front or on the Sides; as well on account of the opening it affords the Building as for the Beauty and Richness where it constantly entertains the Eye, when seen from every Window of the House. The Sides of a Parterre should be furnished with such Works as may improve and set it off; for this being low and flat, necessarily requires something raised as Groves and

Hedges. But herein, Regard should be had to the Situation of the Place; and it should be observed, before you plant, whether the Prospect that way be agreeable; for then the sides of the Parterre should be kept entirely open, making use of Quarters of Grass, and other flat Works to make the best of the View, and taking care not to shut it up with Groves, unless they be planted in Quincunce, or in open lines, with low Hedges, which hinder not the Eye from looking between the trees, and discovering the Beauties of the Prospect on every side.

"If there be no Prospect, but, on the contrary, you have a Mountain, Hill, Forest, or Wood, that by their Vicinity deprive you of that Pleasure, or some Village too near adjoining, the Houses of which make no agreeable Sight; you may then edge the Parterre with Hedges and Groves, to hide those ill-favoured Objects; for by this means you lose nothing, nor have anything to regret in Time to come. . . .

"Groves make the chief Beauty of a Garden, and are a great Ornament to all the other Parts; so that one can never plant too many of them, provided the places designed them take not up those of the Kitchen and Fruit-Gardens, which are Things very useful and necessary for a great House, and which should be constantly placed near the Bass-Courts, that the Slovenliness, which is unavoidable in these Places, may lie all together, and be separated by a Wall from the other Parts of the Garden.

"To accompany Parterres we make Choice of those Designs of Wood-work that are most delicate, as Groves opened in Compartiments, Quincunces, Verdant-halls, with Bowling-greens, Arbourwork, and Fountains in the middle. These small Groves are so much the more agreeable near a House, in that you presently find shade, without going far to seek it; besides, they communicate a coolness to the Apartments, which is very much courted in hot Weather.

"It would be of use to plant some small Groves of Evergreens, that you might have the Pleasure of seeing a Wood always verdant in the very coldest Seasons. They would look very well when seen from the Building; and I earnestly recommend the planting of some Squares of them in a handsome Garden, to make a Diversity from the other Wood; which having lost its leaves appears quite naked all the Winter.

"The Head of a Parterre is usually adorned with Basins or Waterworks; and beyond, with a circular line of Palisades, or Woodwork cut into a Goose-foot, which leads into the great Walks; and the Space between the Basin and the Palisade is filled with small Pieces of Embroidery, or Grass-work, set out with Yews, Cases, and Flower-Pots.

"In gardens that have Terrasses, whether Sideways, or in Front of the Building, where there is a delightful Prospect, as you cannot shut up the Head of the Parterre by a circular Palisade, you must, to continue the View, lay several Compartiments of a Parterre together, such as Embroidery, Green-plots after the English Manner, or Cut-work which should be divided at convenient Distances by Cross-walks; taking care that the Parterres of Embroidery be always next the Building, as being the richest and most magnificent.

"The principal Walk should be made in Front of the Building, and another large one to cross it at right Angles, provided they be double, and very wide. At the end of these Walks, the Walls may be pierced with Grills, or have Openings with Ditches at the Foot of them to continue the view; and these Grills and Openings may be made to serve several Walks by disposing them into Goose-feet, Stars, etc.

"If you have any Part of your Ground naturally low and marshy, that you would not be at the Expense of filling up, you may employ it in Bowling-greens, Waterworks, and even in Groves, raising the Alleys only to the Level of those that are near, and lead to them.

"After you have laid out the great Walks and chief Lines and have disposed the Parterres and Works about the Sides and Head of them as is most suitable to the Ground, you may furnish the upper part and the rest of the Garden with several different Designs as tall Groves, Quincunces, Close-Walks, Galleries, and Halls of Verdure, Green-Arbours, Labyrinths, Bowling-greens, and Amphitheatres adorned with Fountains, Canals, Figures, etc. All these Works distinguish a Garden very much from what is common, and contribute not a little to make it magnificent.

"You should observe, in placing and distributing the several Parts of a Garden, always to oppose them one to the other. For example: A Wood to a Parterre or a Bowling-green, and not to put all the Parterres on one side, and all the Wood on the other; not to set a Bowling-green against a Basin, which would be one Gap against another: this must be constantly avoided by setting the Full against the Void and Flat Works against the Raised to make a Contrariety.

"And this Diversity should be kept not only in the general Design of a Garden, but likewise in each distinct Piece; as, if two Groves are upon the Side of a Parterre, though their outward Form and Dimensions are equal, you should not, for that reason, repeat the same Design in both, but make them different within. For it would be very disagreeable to find the same thing on both sides; and when a man has seen one to have nothing to invite his Curiosity to see the other; which makes a Garden so repeated justly reckoned as no more than half a Design. This Fault was formerly very common; but it is not so of late, every one being now convinced that the greatest Beauty of Gardens is Variety. The several Parts of each Piece should also be diversified as, if a Basin be circular, the Walk that surrounds it should be octangular, and so of Bowling-greens and Grass-plots that are in the midst of Groves.

"The same Works should never be repeated on both sides, but in the open Places, where the Eye by comparing them together, may judge of their conformity, as in Parterres, Bowling-greens, Groves opened in Compartiments and Quincunces. But in Groves formed of Hedges and tall Trees, the Designs and Out-parts should be always varied; which though different, ought, however, to have such Relation and Agreement with each other in their Lines and Ranges as to make the Openings, Glades, and Vistas regular and agreeable.

"In the Business of Designs, you should studiously avoid the Manner that is mean and pitiful and always aim at that which is great and noble; not making little Cabinets and Mazes, Basins like Bowl-dishes and Alleys so narrow that two Persons can scarce go abreast in them. 'Twere infinitely better to have but two or three things somewhat large than a dozen small ones which are no more than very Trifles.

Gateway, Brockenhurst. Photograph by E. A. Rowe.

"Before the Design of a garden be put in Execution, you should consider what it will be in twenty or thirty years to come; very often a Design which looks handsome and of good proportion when it is first planted, in process of time becomes so small and ridiculous that one is obliged to alter it or to destroy it entirely, and plant another in room of it.

"Care should be taken in the general Distribution of a Garden to place the Trees so at the Ends of all the Walks, that they may not offend the Eye, to which End the Corners and the Angles of every part of a Garden should be sloped, or cut hollow, which would make the Cross-walks more agreeable to the Eye, and more convenient for walking, than to find Points and Corners advancing, which look ill upon the Ground and are very inconvenient."

There are many other rules besides these, relating to the proportion, conformity, and place of the different parts and ornaments of gardens, which are treated of in ensuing chapters, and are of great value to the student.

After all these general rules, the several sorts of gardens in use are distinguished under three heads: gardens on a perfect level, gardens on an easy ascent, and gardens whose ground and level are separated and interrupted by falls of terraces, slopes, banks, flights of steps, etc.

"Gardens on a perfect level are certainly the best as a well for convenience of walking as for that their long Alleys and Glades having no risings nor failings, are less chargeable to keep than others.

"Grounds on a gentle Ascent are not altogether agreeable and convenient; though the Shelving be imperceptible nevertheless it fatigues and tires one extremely to be always going up Hill or down Hill without finding scarcely any resting place. These sloping Grounds are also very liable to be spoiled by the Torrents and require a constant Charge to maintain them.

"Gardens in Terrasses have their peculiar Worth and Beauty, in that from the Height of one Terrass you discover all the lower Part of the garden: and the compartments of the other Terrasses, which form so many several gardens one under another, and present you with very agreeable Views and different Scenes of Things provided the Terrasses are not too frequent and there be good Lengths of Level between them. These Gardens lie very advantageously also for Water, which may be repeated from one to another, but they are a great Charge to keep up, and cost a great deal the Making."

"'Tis to these different Situations that the general Disposition of a

Steps and Gateway, Brockenhurst. Photograph by E. A. Rowe.

Garden and the Distribution of its parts ought ever to be accommo-dated: This is so evident, that an excellent Design, which would be very proper for a Garden flat and upon a perfect Level, would be good for nothing in a Ground cut asunder by divers terrases which break off both the Level and the Continuity."

A series of divisions, called parterres, from the Latin word *partire* (to divide), was usually placed on some level spot near the house. These compartments, surrounded by borders, were laid in more or less elaborate geometrical designs edged with box. In common use there were four styles of parterres, laid out in embroidery, in compartment, in cutwork, or after the English manner.

The parterre of embroidery was considered the finest, and therefore placed nearest the house. The design was an imitation of embroidery outlined in box. The interior of the knots was filled with dark earth or iron filings, and sand was placed on the narrow paths to bring out the pattern in relief. Similar to these were the compartment parterres.

In cut-work, the divisions of the parterre were filled with flowers and surrounded by sand paths. These paths were wider than those in the parterres of embroidery and compartment and were broad enough to walk on.

The parterre after the English manner was considered the least ornamental. It consisted of a large grass-plot, surrounded by a border of flowers. The grass was separated from the border by a sanded path two or three feet wide. A *boulingrin*, or bowling-green, was a sunken *parterre á l'Anglaise*.

The border was an important feature, and might be given several forms. The most common continuously surrounded the parterre, was edged with box, daisies, sea-thrift, or some other plant, and planted with flowers and shrubs. Others were of grass or sand and ornamented with yews, orange trees, or flowering shrubs, in vases, flower-pots, or boxes, or with lines of clipped and pleached trees planted in the ground.

Walks were carefully laid out, their breadth proportioned to their length. The principal ones leading to the house, or to some important object point, were left open, while covered walks were placed where they would not obstruct the view, therefore not on the main axes of the garden. Some paths were single; others were in threes, the central one twice the width of those on each side. Lines of detached trees bordered these paths. Three feet was allowed each person, enabling two people

Fountains and Statuary, Brockenhurst. Photographs by E. A. Rowe.

to walk abreast on a path six feet wide, four on one twelve, etc. The surface was covered with pit or river sand.

"Hedges," Le Blond says, "by the agreeableness of their Verdure, are
of the greatest Service in Gardens, to cover the Walls that inclose the
Ground, to shut up and stop the sight in many places, that the Extent
of the Garden be not discovered at one View, and to correct and redress
the Bevelings and Elbows of Walls. They serve also to inclose and border the Squares of Wood, to divide them from the other Parts of the
Garden, and to prevent their being entered but by the Walks made for
that purpose.

"The most usual form of Hedges is a great Length and even Height,
making, as it were, a Wall or green Tapestry; all the Beauty of which
consists in being well filled up from the very bottom, of no great Thickness, and handsomely clipped on both sides as perpendicularly as possible. They are usually cut into Fans, Curtains, and low Hedges,
according to the Nature of the Place.

"Those we call Fans and Curtains are no other than great and very
tall Hedges which serve to stop the View, to shut out Places that are
disagreeable, or to hide the Divisions of a Garden, whence they have

their name; Their Height should be two thirds of the Breadth of the Walk. The Hedges that are higher than this Proportion make the Walks look pitiful and disagreeable to the Eye, which is too much confined by them.

"However, if you would raise Hedges very high, as fifty or sixty Foot, you should plant tall trees in the line of the Hedge itself, and keep them clipped perpendicularly forwards and backwards, so that the Hedge may fill up to about twenty Foot and the Trees make good the rest. And as it would be difficult to cut the tops of these high Trees they may be left with their Tufts with no ill effect. It happens sometimes that these Hedges are unfurnished at Foot, which is remedied by filling up the lower part with Box or Yew, supported by a small trellis of five or six Foot high as may be seen in many Gardens.

"As for the Banquettes, they are low Hedges breast high, seldom exceeding three or four Foot: they serve on the Sides of double Walks, where being also kept under, they are no hindrances to the enjoying a pleasant View between the Trees: they become disagreeable when they are so low as two Foot and a half, and at four Foot they are too high; their true measure is three Foot and a half. There are some of these Hedges adorned at certain Spaces with small Balls rising out of the Hedge itself, to keep Place with the Trees that are planted in the others: these sorts of Hedges with Balls, are set in Places where one cannot plant large Trees, and where there must be scarcely anything to accompany them because of the View.

"You may likewise at proper Distances make Niches and Sinkings in the Hedges for placing of Seats, Figures, Vases, and Fountains, as in Groves and at the ends of Walks, which is the greatest good of Hedges; for then their Verdure, serving as a Ground to these Figures, Fountains, etc., infinitely enhances their Beauty by making them look detached, and mightily improves their Worth by the Opposition it produces: but in such particular Places as the Cloisters, Galleries, and Halls, which are made in Squares of Wood, Hedges are usually cut into Arches and Porticos of different forms, and these make even a better Effect than the others. These are all the Forms of Hedges that are

LEADEN BUSTS AT ELVASTON

most beautiful, and of the greatest Variety I could think of, without running from a good taste and into an impossibility of Execution. I was not willing to run the hazard of offering any pieces of invention only, lest they should appear too extraordinary to some People and even impossible; but chose rather to collect Examples already executed in the Royal Gardens and those of the greatest Reputation, which are inserted in a particular Plate and expressly named; that they who please may go and see them upon the spot for the cure of their Incredulity, and for forming a Judgment of their beautiful Execution. . . .

"These Decorations in Green compose a kind of Order of Field Architecture . . . most proper for great Gardens where the conformity of the Hedges tires the Sight unless relieved by these extraordinary Verdures.

"This is what may be done agreeable to the Taste in the matter of Hedges, and is at the same time the richest and most distinguished in the whole Business of Gardening. Heretofore they gave them a thousand extravagant Forms, which are yet much in use in the Gardens of

A Surprise Fountain.

The Cedars of Lebanon, Wilton.

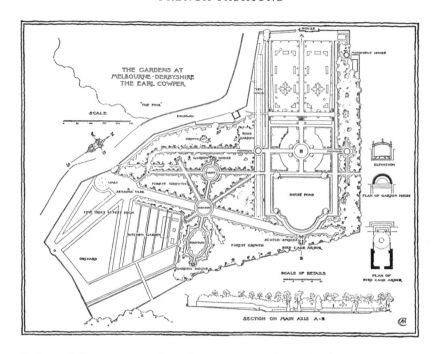

Italy and Spain: some shaped out Men on horse-back, Boars, Stags, Dogs; in short an entire Hunting-piece. Others cut them into Pyramids, Obelisks, Balls, and Scrolls; instances of which are to be seen in some old Gardens about Paris. This practice still continues in Holland and Flanders, where these whimsical Designs are more in vogue than in any other Country. And this particular taste prevails not only in their Hedges, but their Groves, Parterres, Fountains, and other parts of their Gardens have a great deal of it. The English and Swedes fall more into our manner of Gardening; having their Designs sent over to them from hence, which are well enough performed, and have also had French Architects and Gardeners in their country, who have left their Productions behind them. At present no one gives in to these Trifles in French. They chuse rather a plain regularity less cluttered and confused, which indeed looks much more noble and great."

Porticoes, arbours, and cabinets of latticework had begun to go out of fashion when Le Blond's book was written, and green arbours formed by interweaving the branches of trees were perhaps more common. Greenhouses or orangeries were frequently built. In winter they served to protect the numerous tender plants, and in summer they served as a gallery to walk in when it rained. They were usually built with an arched façade. Other little pleasure houses, like the pavilion at Holme Lacy, were common. Belvederes or pavilions of Aurora were similar constructions placed where they could command a view of the surrounding country.

Statues and vases contributed very much to the "Embellishment and Magnificence of Gardens" and their natural beauties. They were made of several forms and different materials; the richest were those of bronze, lead gilt, and marble; the ordinary sort were of iron, stone, or stucco. Statues either singly or in groups generally represented mythological characters.

CUPID:MELBOURNE

"The usual places for Figures and Vases are along the Hedges, in the Front and upon the Sides of a Parterre; in the Niches and Sinkings of Hornbeam, or of Lattice-work made for that purpose. In Groves they are placed in the Centre of a Star or St. Andrew's Cross; in the Spaces between the Walks of a Goosefoot, in the middle of Halls and Cabinets among the Trees and Arches of a Green Gallery, and at the Head of a row of Trees or detached Hedges. They are also placed at the lower End of Walks and Vistas to set them off the better; in Porticos and Arbours of Trellis-work; in Basins, Cascades, etc. In general they do well everywhere, and you can scarce have too many of them in a Garden. But as in the Business of Sculpture, it should be excellent, as well as in Painting and Poesy. I think it would be more advisable for a private Gentleman to be content without Figures than to take up with such as are indifferent which do but create a continual Longing after this Perfection, the Expense of which is only for Princes and Ministers of State."

· CHAPTER EIGHT ·

Italian Villa Gardens

ROM the time of the Renaissance, Italy has been the fountain-head of inspiration for garden-lovers. Its climate is especially adapted to horticulture, its soil is a mine of garden ornaments, and it has maintained the traditions of the finest gardens of antiquity. For their design and ornamentation, the statuary, fountains, and pavilions of Italian gardens are unsurpassed. Their fame has been noted in England since the seventeenth century, and reproductions of all their phases have been abundant.

A rapid survey of gardens as they exist or have existed in Italy will help us to understand these reproductions. In describing them no mention will be made of the collections of botanical specimens and of strange animals which were initiated by the scientists early in the Renaissance, for these collections, though interesting as the forerunners of all modern botanical gardens and zoological parks, do not, strictly speaking, come under the head of pleasure gardens. During the fifteenth century there were, indeed, no gardens constructed, except for more or less practical purposes.

The transition from the mediæval garden of the fifteenth to the architectural one of the sixteenth century was largely brought about by

FOUNTAIN BY VERROCCHIO

A VENETIAN GARDEN PAVILION

the influence of Humanists like Æneas Silvias Piccolomini and Gio-
vanni Colonna. In the *Hypnerotomachia Poliphili* (a novel by Colonna,
containing a mixture of love, philosophy, science, and archæology) we
read of topiary work, statues and columns, temples to the Graces and
to Venus, not as existing in Colonna's time but as long before described
by Pliny, and later to develop in the typical villas of the Renaissance.

In Italy the best gardens were laid out during the middle period of

Fountain, Villa Petraja.

the Renaissance, beginning in the sixteenth century. A spontaneous delight in the beauty of nature, a sincere love of art, and keen interest in archæology combined to create the formal garden in a nearly perfect style. Almost without exception these gardens were attached to the

GARDEN DOOR: VILLA MADAMA

DOORWAY : CAMBRIDGE

villas near Rome belonging to the cardinal princes of the Church. Many have been preserved in practically their original condition and may still be studied to advantage.

Chronologically, the villa gardens can be classed in three divisions. Of the first period (1500 to 1540), the Villa Madama, by Raphael, is the best example now extant. In the second (1540 to 1580), the greatest perfection was reached in garden architecture. Among the country-seats built at that time are the Villa Caprarola at Caprarola, the Villa Lante at Bagnaja, and the Villa Papa Giulio at Rome, all three designed by Vignola. The Villa d'Este at Tivoli by Ligorio, the Villa Giusti at Verona, partly attributed to Sammicheli, and a number of others near Genoa also belong to the middle period. Finally, after 1580, came the third or Barocco period, in which may be included the villas Aldobrandini, Pamphili-Doria, Borghese, and Albani, near Rome, with most of those at Frascati.

The earliest, and the one which would have been the most magnificent if its plans had been completely carried out, was the Villa Madama, designed by Raphael for Cardinal Giulio Medici, later Clement VII. Raphael was not an inexperienced architect, for—then twenty-six years old—he had built the Farnesina, a charming country house, and had afterward constructed several churches and palaces.

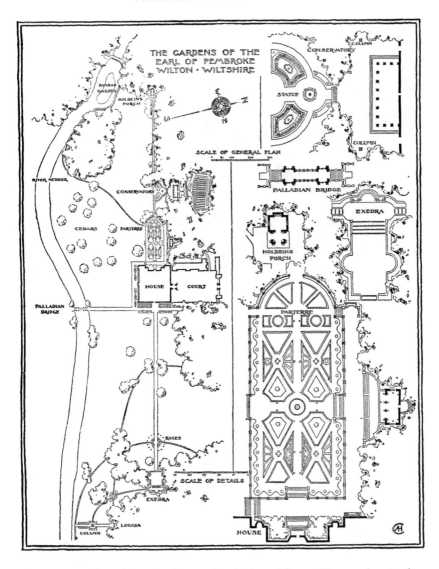

Bramante, when dying, had accredited him with excelling no less in the art of building than in that of painting. At the time he designed the Villa Madama he was architect-in-chief of St. Peter's. As Clement VII was an antiquarian and Raphael shared his interest in archæology, it is supposed that together they attempted to reproduce a classic villa. But the site, on the abrupt slope of Monte Mario, was so peculiar that the

Italian Garden, Castle Ashby.

general arrangement of Clement's villa must have been original. Pliny's description of his own villa perhaps suggested some of the details—the hippodrome, the swimming bath, the terraces, and the casino—but in Raphael's hands these underwent a transformation. As, however, he died before the villa was much more than begun, his plans were modified by his pupil, Ginlio Romano, though owing to the precarious position of Clement VII, the building was delayed, and before its completion sacked by the Pope's enemies. The general scheme was reconstructed by Percier and Fontaine in *Villas près de Rome*. At the entrance was a spacious forecourt leading up to a sort of loggia which ran under the house and connected it with the rear courtyard, an enclosure divided into four quarters, intended for flowers, but now overgrown with grass and weeds. One of several interesting details in this enclosure is the doorway, flanked by colossal statues, shown in the illustration [page 204]. The whole lay-out of this villa must have given more or less direct inspiration to later garden architects.

The Villa d'Este, the masterpiece of Piero Ligorio, is one of those said to have been inspired by the Villa Madama. According to Percier

and Fontaine, it was originally begun by the Bishop of Cordova; afterward it belonged to a succession of Cardinals d'Este, and a recent occupant was the late Cardinal Hohenlohe. The large quantity of water employed to adorn the grounds and the great variety shown in its treatment seem to indicate a reminiscence of the Moorish gardens in Spain.

Architecturally, this villa is especially interesting on account of the ingenious construction of the terraces and ramps connecting the palace with the gardens far below. The ornamental details are excellent in scale and proportion and merit especial attention. But the peculiar charm of these gardens is in their atmosphere, a charm none the less real because indefinable. The mass of the grounds is in shadow; the trees have grown to a great height, the once trim hedges are no longer clipped, and the parterres contain no cultivated flowers. In fact, the garden has become an unkempt wilderness; but gleams of sunshine, the songs of birds, and the sound of trickling water lighten the gloom and give to the desolation an agreeable melancholy. Looking from the ter-

CARYATIDES: VILLA FARNESE: CAPRAROLA

races and belvederes, through the firm, dark foliage of the cypresses, there are wonderful views of the Campagna, which, stretching boundless as the ocean, fades into the sky on the distant horizon.

At Caprarola, forty miles or so north of Rome, the octagonal fortress-like castle constructed by Vignola still stands intact. As the garden, however, is not kept up, it is

The Villa Lante.

Garden Scene, from a Tapestry.

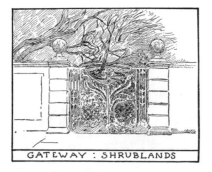

GATEWAY : SHRUBLANDS

GATEWAY : CASTLE ASHBY

chiefly interesting on account of its charming casino, its weird hermæ, fauns, and caryatides ranged along the terraces, and the stone stairway bordered by dolphins spouting water into basins.

The Villa Lante is another of Vignola's creations. In excellent condition, both as to house and gardens, it is perhaps the most perfect example of a seventeenth-century villa. "In narrow-room, nature's whole wealth, nay, more-a heaven on earth." The beautiful motives which nature carelessly scatters over the landscape are here in harmonious contrast with art and logically concentrated near the chief dwellings or casinos. For instance, the mass of water gushes from a formal cliff backing the highest terrace, falls into an *abreuvoir* or trough, rises in a spouting fountain, descends in a rippling stream, tumbles in a noisy cascade, and makes a final appearance in the central fountain which feeds the miniature lake in the middle of the flower-garden below the house. The river-gods on each side of the cascade were added in the seventeenth century. In the older fountains like the one at Castello, an absence of water would have detracted but little from their beauty, as was fitting at Florence where pure drinking water was supplied only on Sundays, and at Bologna which furnished none at all in public places. At Rome, however, the water-supply was abundant, and in the fountains originated by Bernini and his school, water was the dominant and sculpture the subordinate feature.

The Boboli Gardens of Florence, surrounding the Pitti Palace, were designed by Tribolo about 1550. The greater part of the grounds bears more resemblance to a park than to a garden, but there are several en-

Casino, Wilton.

closures intended for flowers. One of these is connected with a charming spot ornamented by Parigi, known as the Isola Bella. This artificial island is in the centre of a geometrically designed lake resembling the one at the Villa Lante.

The barocco period is demonstrated in the villas Medici, Albani, Aldobrandini, Pamphili-Doria, and in many others in the neighbourhood of Rome as well as scattered all over Italy. At this time the palace was enriched by heavy ornamentation, the garden became correspondingly pompous, and the general effect was rather too magnificent. The Villa Pamphili-Doria is one of the most elaborate examples in this style. Below the handsome palace is a broad terrace, covered with a typical parterre, large and well kept up. The ground is planted with an intricate tracery of box accented by shrubs grown in decorative flower-pots. This kind of parterre has been frequently copied in England, but seldom with much success. The Italian gardens of an earlier period are better adapted for reproduction in northern countries.

One of the oldest Italian designs was carried out at Wilton, for the Earl of Pembroke, by Isaac de Caux, in the first half of the seventeenth century. In 1640 there was published a book which contained illustra-

TREES AND A SEAT : WILTON

VASE : WILTON

tions of Wilton and the following description of its plan:"The Garden within the enclosure of the New Wall is a Thousand foote long and about Foure hundred in breadth divided in its length into three very long Squares or Paralellograms; the first of which divisions next the building hath ffoure Platts embroydered; in the midst of which are ffoure ffountaynes with Statues of marble in theire midle, and on the sides of those Platts are the Platts of fflowers, and beyond them is the little Terrass rased for the more advantage of beholding those Platts; this for the first division. In the second are two Groves or woods cut with diverse walkes and through those Groves passeth the river Nader having a breadth in this place 44 foote upon which is built the bridge of the breadth of the grease walk, in the midst of the aforesayd groves

THE COLUMN AT WILTON

are two great Statues of white marble of eight ffoote height, the one of Bacchus and the other Flora, and on the sides ranging with the Platts of fflowers are two covered Arbors of 300 ffoote long and diverse allies att the beginning of the third and last division are on either side of the great walke, two ponds with ffountaynes and two Columnes in the midle casting water all their heigth which causeth the moving and turning of two Crownes att the top of the

Garden, Wilton.

same and beyond is a compartiment of greene with divers walkes planted with cherrie trees and in the midle is the great Ovall with the gladiator of brass, the most famous Statue of all that Antiquity hath left, on the sydes of this compartiment and answering the platts of flowers and long arbours are three arbours of either side with turning Gallaryes communicating themselves one unto another; at the end of

AN EXEDRA WILTON

HOLBEIN PAVILION : WILTON

the grease walke is a Portico of stone cutt and adorned with Pilasters and Nyches within which are 4 ffigures of white marble of 5 ffoote high, on either side of the sayd portico is an assent leading up to the terrasse upon the steps whereof instead of pillasters are Sea Monsters casting water from one to the other, from the top to the bottome and above the sayd portico is a great reserve of water for the Grotto." A celebrated feature was this elaborate grotto, which was always particularly admired by visitors to Wilton.

At present nothing remains of the pleasure grounds designed by De Caux except a few scattered ornaments. A comparatively new garden near the house has, however, been laid out. It is about 110 feet long by 50 feet wide. Here the contrast of light and shade produces a charming effect. The dense foliage of clipped elm, yew, and ilex, forming a high boundary wall on the northwest side of the parterre, is a perfect foil for the gay colours of the flowers glowing in their full exposure to the sunshine. All the architectural features of the parterre are designed with great refinement. The fountain, suggested perhaps by that of G. de Bologna at Petraja, with the balustrading surmounted by amorini, the

THE PALLADIAN BRIDGE : WILTON

VASE : SHRUBLANDS

Palladian Bridge, Wilton.

leaden urns, designed by Inigo Jones, the seats, and even the stone copings of the flower-beds show excellent taste. Above the garden is a
triple-arched casino, called the sculpture gallery, in accord with the
prevalent Italian style. Through the high clipped hedge a vista is gained
along a straight path extending, on a line with the main axis of the garden, through a plantation of trees for several hundred feet, and terminated by the pavilion known as the Holbein porch. This was designed
by Holbein for an entrance to the original house, afterward partly destroyed.

Indirectly the beauty of the lawn, which covers over fifty acres between the formal surroundings of the house and the pretty, though
sluggish, river Nader, contributes to the loveliness of the parterre. It is
restful for the eye to glance from the brilliant flower-beds over the cool
stretches of closely shaven turf, relieved from monotony by the occasional interposition of shrubbery and groups of trees. Among the latter are some remarkably fine cedars of Lebanon.

The Palladian Bridge, spanning the Nader, forms another delightful

STONE SEAT: SHRUBLANDS ·

ARCH-WAY: CASTLE ASHBY

pavilion. This was formerly attributed to Inigo Jones, but is now said to be the work of a later architect, named Morris. The illustrations show its excellent proportions.

Various other interesting architectural features are scattered through the pleasure grounds. An orangery, an exedra suggesting one of those at Pompeii, a column surmounted by a statue, and a quaint Tudor summer-house, built of stone curiously carved and ornamented, may be noted as especially worthy of attention.

It is evident that the Villa d'Este furnished many of the ideas so successfully carried out at Shrubland Park. Here is one of the best-planned Italian gardens in England. All the architectural features are good in scale and proportion. There are terraces, pavilions, vases, and statuary of charming design, as can be seen from the illustrations. The

VASE AT CASTLE ASHBY

ROSARY WITH PERGOLA: CASTLE ASHBY

Italian Garden, Shrublands. Photograph by J. Palmer Clarke.

The Terrace, Bowood. Photograph by R. F. Houlston.

RUSTIC PERGOLA: CASTLE ASHBY

staircases connecting the terraces near the house with the pleasure grounds on the level ground far below are managed with great skill.

At Harewood, the style of architecture is similar to that of Shrubland, as both houses were built by Sir Charles Barry. Below the house is a magnificent terrace, where the planting and ornamentation are exceptionally fine and in the best of keeping with the surroundings. Beside the retaining wall is a herbaceous border of well-selected annuals and perennials.

Another fine terrace is at Bowood. The architecture is interesting in spite of being rather heavy; for both the house and its surroundings are sombre if not gloomy in character.

Castle Ashby, although Elizabethan, shows Italian influence to good advantage in a series of gardens in different styles, extending toward the west. The so-called Italian garden is diversified by having the family coat-of-arms and various rococo designs, outlined in box and filled in with many-coloured pebbles and coal-, slate-, or granite-dust; the idea is the same as that of the Villa Albani near Rome. The archway connecting this with an adjoining garden is shown in the illustration.

Near the house are several parterres ornamented with fountains and well accented by cone-shaped yews, laurels, and bay trees. Compact yew hedges mark the subdivisions, and the outer enclosure is framed by a curious balustrading in which letters, taking the place of

STATUARY AT LONGFORD CASTLE

VASE : LONGFORD CASTLE

the ordinary balusters, spell out biblical texts. This scheme is attractive more from a sentimental than an architectural point of view. The rosary is very prettily arranged; in the centre is a rustic summer-house, and a simple, rose-covered arbour, ornamented at intervals with statuary, surrounds the outside.

The grounds around Longford Castle are, for some distance, perfectly level. The parterre is sunk below the castle and engirdled by terraces. It is well laid out in the formal Italian style, partly bedded out and partly planted with hardy annuals and perennials. The architectural features are charming. A figure under a canopy supported by four

PERGOLA AT LONGFORD CASTLE

columns, near the end of the main path, is especially interesting. The vases surrounded by flint pavement in the centre of each section of the parterre and the terminal figures around the semicircle are also well placed and well designed. In general effect the parterre is formal without being too stiff or monotonous for juxtaposition with the castle.

Other so-called Italian gardens are numerous in England, but few are worthy of the name. Marble statues and geometrical designs bedded out with geraniums and other showy plants form but a travesty of the real villa gardens.

CHAPTER NINE

Eighteenth-Century Extremes

XTREMES met in the eighteenth century. English gardens (no longer original creations or even clever adaptations) had degenerated into meaningless repetitions of French and Dutch fashions. Conventional plans were mimicked or exaggerated until the formal manner became merely an affected mannerism. Finally, nothing remaining but the defects of the old system, a reaction resulted in its entire destruction. On the ruins was created the Landscape Garden, in the strict meaning of the word no garden at all, but a stretch of cultivated scenery. Throughout Europe this revolution accorded with the spirit of the times. Every sentimentalist, republican philosopher, or romance writer, rebelling against rigid law and order of any kind, delighted in this so-called return to the freedom of nature. Soon, however, nature pure and simple came to be considered insipid,

AN 18ᵗʰ CENTURY DIAL

A DUTCH ARBOUR

A DUTCH ARBOUR

and its tameness was relieved by picturesque pieces of architecture and other features designed to give the scene a more sensational appearance. A love of the romantic was partially inspired by the Chinese, whose gardens were designed to appeal to the emotions. Eventually this landscape or picturesque style, a too studied and over-sentimental struggle for effect, lost all spontaneity, and in its turn fell into decay.

At the close of the first quarter of the century, French and Dutch influences became paramount in England. Both styles were distinguished by a mathematical precision attributable rather to the geometrician than to the architect. Scale and proportion were considered of no special importance. The ideal was regularity. If the garden appeared spick and span, with paths absolutely straight and smooth, and grass-plots exactly square and even, nothing was lacking, except an occasional statue or dwarf tree, to complete its perfection. The larger the garden, the larger the number of grass-plots all alike and of enclosures similar if not exactly the same. Symmetry was carried out on a pointlessly large scale, for the corresponding objects were often too widely separated to come within the same line of vision. It seemed as though the proprietor was principally desirous of showing the extent of his property, and the gardener his knowledge of geometry, while neither displayed a ray of originality, or evinced any fondness for the real pleasures of a garden.

VASE AT ELVASTON

The French style, without the guidance of Le Nôtre, had even in France degenerated to a mere display of magnificent dimensions, oppressive but seldom impressive. "A false taste for grandeur which is not made for man, spoils his pleasures," Rousseau remarks in this connection, continuing: "The grand air is always melancholy; it makes us think of the miseries of the man who affects it. Amid his parterres and endless alleys his littleness does but increase, a tree twenty feet high shelters him as well as one of sixty. He can never occupy more than his three feet of space, and is lost like a worm in his immense possessions." This description reproduces the impression received upon looking at pictures of English gardens in the same style. Ineffective symmetry, endlessly long, straight avenues with no apparent object point, and a succession of prim enclosures are wearisome in their meaningless rigidity.

The Dutch garden is said to have been brought to England by William III, though some of its characteristics might have been discovered there before his day. It was an adaptation of the French and Barocco styles, hardly to be called original, but comprising certain features at least individual. This individuality was due to the limited extent of terra-firma and to the abundance of water in Holland. An ordinary plan became extraordinary because laid out on such a surprisingly small scale. A scheme covering dozens of acres in France was to be seen reproduced on a fewer number of feet in Holland. The parterres of Versailles might almost as well have been reduced to serve as embroidery for a pocket handkerchief. In a Dutch garden no tree could be admitted until its growth had been stunted, and no flower larger than a tulip could be allowed to engross the space without danger of spoiling the composition. Shell-work took the place of marble, and glass balls or other trivial objects were often substituted for statues, as ornamentation. Miniature canals were more usual than fountains; for the supply of water, though large, had not the force to rise to a height.

A favourite architectural feature was a grotto, answering the purpose of both an arbour and a summer-house. This niche of shell-work, sometimes encasing paintings of mythological subjects and sheltering a spout of water, was far less attractive than similar niches at Pompeii, where the barocco ornamentation appeared more appropriate.

The diminutive size of the Dutch gardens is well brought out by De Amicis in his account of Broek.

"The gardens are not less odd than the houses. They seem made for dwarfs. The paths are scarcely wide enough for the feet, the arbours can only contain two very small people standing close together, the box borders would not reach the knee of a child four years old. Between the arbours and the tiny flower-beds there are little canals apparently made for toy boats, which are spanned here and there by superfluous bridges with little painted railings and columns. Basins about as large as a wash-bowl contain a Lilliputian boat tied by a red cord to a sky-blue post; tiny steps, paths, gates, and lattices abound, each of which can be measured with the hand, or knocked down with a blow of the fist, or jumped over with ease. Around houses and gardens stand trees cut in the shape of fans, plumes, disks, etc., with their trunks painted white and blue, and here and there appears a little wooden house for a domestic animal, painted, gilded, and carved like a house in a puppet show."

The bizarre effects suggested in the preceding description are still more evident in accounts of the mineralogical gardens in Holland. Here vegetation was barely allowed to subsist on a few narrow strips of ground. Walls were ornamented with shell-work, parterres with variegated pebbles and statues made of cockle-shells.

Evidences of Dutch taste were shown in England by the frequent introduction of dwarf trees, choice tulips, and canals of water. Although the dampness of the climate made grottoes peculiarly unattractive, they also were favourite accessions. Travellers early in the seventeenth century often described the famous grotto at Wilton, but this was rather in the Italian than the Dutch style. Evelyn designed one at Albury with a "crypta through the mountain thirty perches in

Pavilion, Audley End.

length." Defoe mentions gardens at Richmond and Sutton Court where besides canals there were several grottoes, and others are described by various contemporaneous writers. Inconsistently such an example of laboured artificiality was the pride of Pope, as he was among the first to ridicule many lesser absurdities.

"I have put my last hand to my works of this kind, in happily finishing the subterraneous way and grotto. I there found a spring of the clearest water, which falls in a perpetual rill, that echoes through the cavern day and night. From the river Thames you see through my arch up a walk of the wilderness to a kind of open temple, wholly composed of shells in the rustic manner; and from that distance under the temple, you look down through a sloping arcade of trees, and see the sails on the river passing suddenly and vanishing as through a perspective glass. When you shut the doors of this grotto it becomes on the instant, from a luminous room, a *camera obscura*, on the walls of which all the objects of the river, hills, woods, and boats are forming a moving picture in their visible radiations; and when you have a mind to light it up, it affords you a very different scene. It is finished with shells interspersed with pieces of looking-glass in angular forms; and in the ceiling is a star of the same material, at which, when a lamp of an orbicular figure of thin alabaster is hung in the middle, a thousand different rays glitter and are reflected over the place.

"There are connected to this grotto by a narrow passage two porches with niches and seats—one towards the river of smooth stones, full of light, and open; the other towards the arch of trees, rough with shells, flints, and iron-ore. The bottom is paved with simple pebble as the adjoining walk up the Wilderness to the temple is to be cockle-shells, in the natural taste, agreeing not ill with the little dripping murmur and the aquatic idea of the whole place. It wants nothing to complete it but a good Statue with an inscription like that beautiful antique one which you know I am so fond of:

> 'Nymph of the Grot, those sacred springs steep,
> And to the murmur of these waters sleep.
> Ah, spare my slumbers, gently tread the cave!
> And drink in silence or in silence lave.'"

The English—perhaps because they had most abused the conventional system—were the first to raise an outcry against formal gardening. Formality could certainly be carried to no greater excess; it was

logical to seek beauty in a contrary extreme. Freedom from every restraint was the gospel of the new school. Kent, its leader according to
Walpole, was the first to jump outside the fence and insist that the garden should be "set free from its prim regularity, and the gentle stream
taught to serpentize." His method, as described by Lord Kames, was,
"to paint a field with beautiful objects, natural and artificial, disposed
like colours upon a canvas. It requires indeed more genius to paint in
the gardening way: in forming a landscape upon a canvas, no more is
required but to adjust the figures to each other: an artist who lays out
grounds in Kent's way, has an additional task: he ought to adjust the
figures to the several varieties of the field.

Kent was an unsuccessful painter, whose idea was to make the garden a reproduction of the pictorial effects in nature, as seen in the compositions of Claude Lorraine, Poussin, and Salvator Rosa. "He felt the
delicious contrast of hill and valley changing imperceptibly into each
other, tasted the beauties of the gentle swell or concave scoop, and remarked how loose groves crowned an easy eminence with a happy ornament, and while they were called in the distant view between their
graceful stems, removed and extended the perspective by delusive comparison.

"Thus the pencil of his imagination bestowed all the arts of landscape on all the scenes he handled. The great principles on which he
worked were perspective and light and shade. Groups of trees broke
too uniform or too extensive a lawn; evergreens and woods were op-
posed to the glare of the champain, and where the view was less fortunate, or so much exposed as to be beheld at once, he blotted out some
parts by thick shades, to divide it into variety or to make the richest
scene more enchanting by reserving it to a farther advance of the spectator's steps. Thus selecting favourite objects, and veiling deformities
by screens of plantation; sometimes allowing the rudest waste to add
its foil to the richest theatre, he realized the compositions of the greatest masters in painting. Where objects were wanting to animate his
horizon, his taste as an architect could bestow immediate termination.
His buildings, his seats, his temples, were more the works of his pen-

cil than of his compass. We owe the restoration of Greece and the diffusion of architecture to his skill in landscape."

In plain words, nothing remained of the old style in the new gardens. These latter consisted of smooth lawns of grass, diversified by clumps of trees, and intersected by curved paths or irregular pieces of water. Nature was said to abhor a straight line; hence walks and brooks were always laid out in "serpentine meanders."

Marks of decay are often to be seen in nature; Kent reproduced this effect by planting dead trees and stumps. These attempts to make a beautiful wilderness often resulted in nothing but a confused mass of disorder, and were received with ridicule even by the sentimentalists.

Among Kent's successors was "Capability" Brown, so nicknamed because he invariably discovered that every piece of ground had capabilities of being improved by his methods. He is said to have had supreme control over the art of modern gardening for nearly half a century. He and his admirers increased the dimensions of the naked lawn, multiplied the number of belts of trees and shrubbery, but unfortunately destroyed many of the beautiful old gardens to make way for their improvements.

The best exponent of the landscape school was Repton. In spite of certain weak points, his book, *Observations on Landscape Gardening*, 1803, is of great assistance. He condemned the prevalent custom of substituting everywhere sunken fences or ha-has for hedges, and the location of a palace or villa on a field of grass, while approving of straight avenues as a means of approach to the dwelling and of other similar heresies. Many beautiful estates in England have been developed according to his ideas, and bear witness to his good taste.

Intercourse with China strengthened the influence of the naturalistic school, while adding to its sentimentality. In China the landscape garden had flourished from 2600 B.C. It was a microcosm of the idealized beauties of the landscape and an arrangement of souvenirs collected from all over the country. The composition was reduced to a system, where balance took the place of symmetry. Mountains, rivers, lakes, all the most striking features to be found in the landscape were reproduced on a small scale and given appropriate surroundings. It was intended not only that the garden should satisfy the sense of beauty, but arouse emotions of gaiety, melancholy, or amazement. The varying moods of nature were reflected and enhanced by artificial scenic effects, and accented by suitable architectural features. Each season, and even each hour of the day, was given a fit accompaniment.

All over Europe results similar to those produced by the Chinese were aimed at with more or less success. "The English have not yet brought the art of gardening to the same perfection as the Chinese," remarks Oliver Goldsmith, "but have lately begun to imitate them; nature is now followed with greater assiduity than formerly; the trees are suffered to shoot out into the utmost luxuriance; the streams, no longer forced from their native beds, are permitted to wind along the valleys; the spontaneous flowers take the place of the finished parterre and the enamelled meadow of shaven green."

One of the earliest descriptions of the Chinese style was a translation of an *Account of the Emperor of China's Gardens near Pekin*, by the Jesuit father, Père Attiret, which was widely circulated in England. After describing the pleasure houses, courts open and closed, porticoes, hills, valleys, streams, lakes, rivers, and cascades, "which, when viewed all together, have an admirable effect on the eye," he continues: "They go from one valley to another, not by formal straight walks as in England, but by various turnings and windings, adorned on the sides by little pavilions and charming Grottoes; and each of these valleys is diversified from all the rest both by their manner of laying out the Ground, and in the Structure and Disposition of its Buildings.

"All the Risings and Hills are sprinkled with Trees and particularly with Flowering Trees which are here very common. The sides of the Canals or lesser Streams are not faced (as they are with us) with smooth stone and in a straight Line; but look rude and rustic with different Pieces of Rock, some of which jut out, and others recede inwards; and are placed with so much Art that you would take it to be the work of Nature. In some Parts the Water is wide, in others narrow; here it serpentizes and there spreads away, as if it were really pushed away by the hills and Rocks. The Banks are sprinkled with flowers, which rise up even through the Hollows in the Rock work, as if they had been produced there naturally. They have a great variety of them for every season in the year."

Another treatise which produced a still more widespread effect was Sir William Chambers' *Dissertations on Oriental Gardening*. He advanced the proposition that the Chinese were not averse to straight lines, and fully explained their methods of appealing to the emotions. His writings are worth quoting more on account of their far-reaching influence than as a literal description of Chinese gardening. In an introduction he states that "The Chinese Gardeners take nature for their pattern and their aim is to imitate all her beautiful irregularities ... yet they are not so attached to her as to exclude all appearance of art. Art must supply the scantiness of nature and not only be employed to produce variety but also novelty and effect: for the simple arrangements of nature are to be met with in every common field to a certain degree of perfection, and are therefore too familiar to excite any strong sensations in the mind of the beholder or to produce any uncommon degree of pleasure.

"The Chinese are no enemies of straight lines, because they are productive of grandeur, which often cannot be obtained without them: nor have they an aversion to regular geometric figures which they say are beautiful in themselves, and well suited to small compositions, where the luxuriant irregularities of nature would fill up and embarrass the parts they should adorn. They likewise think them properest to flower gardens and all other compositions where much art is apparent in the culture, and where it should therefore not be omitted in forms.

"Their regular buildings they generally surround with artificial terraces, slopes, and many flights of steps, the angles of which are adorned with groups of sculpture and vases intermingled with all sorts of artificial waterworks, which, connecting with the architecture, spread the composition, serve to give it consequence and add to the gaiety, splendour, and bustle of the scenery.

"Round the main habitation, and near all the decorated structures the grounds are laid out with great regularity and kept up with great care: no plants are admitted that intercept the view of the buildings, nor any lines but such as accompany the architecture properly, and contribute to the general symmetry and good effect of the whole composition, for they hold it absurd to surround an elegant fabric with disorderly rude vegetation, saying it looks like a diamond set in lead, and always conveys the idea of an unfinished work. When the buildings are rustic the scenery which surrounds them is wild, when they are grand it is gloomy, when gay it is luxuriant: in short the Chinese are scrupulously nice in preserving the same character through every part of the composition; which is one great reason of that surprising variety with which their works abound.

"In their large gardens they contrive different scenes for different times of the day, disposing at the points of view, buildings which from their use point out the proper hour for enjoying the view in its perfections; and in their small ones, where, as has been observed, one arrangement produces many representations, they make use of the same artifice. They have beside scenes for every season of the year: some for winter generally exposed to the southern sun and composed of pines, firs, cedars, evergreen oaks, phyllyrea, hollies, yews, junipers, and many other evergreens, being enriched with laurels of various sorts, laurestinas, arbutus, and other such plants and vegetables as grow or flourish in cold weather: and to give variety and gaiety to these gloomy productions, they plant amongst them in regular forms, divided by walks, all the rare shrubs, flowers, and trees of the torrid zone, which they cover during the winter with frames of glass disposed in the form of temples or other elegant buildings. These they call conservatories: they are warmed by subterraneous fires and afford a comfortable and agreeable retreat when the weather is too cold to walk in the open air. All sorts of melodious birds are let loose within, and they keep there in large porcelain cisterns placed on rocks gold and silver fishes with various kinds of water lilies, they also raise in them a variety of fruit." Other buildings which could be used in winter were menageries, aviaries, decorated dairies and buildings for various games, besides large enclosures in the woods provided for military sports, riding, and archery.

For summer there were all sorts of pavilions provided, some of them built in the trees, others in the form of Persian tents or in various fantastic shapes. On the grounds of one of the imperial palaces there were four hundred pavilions, each in a different style. One cost two hundred thousand pounds and consisted of a hundred rooms. Perhaps Marie Antoinette got the idea of her miniature village at the Petit Trianon from this same garden, where there was a fortified town with everything noteworthy at Pekin on a small scale. In this mimic town the emperors, too much the slaves of their greatness to appear in public, were diverted several times in the year by the eunuchs of the palace, who personated merchants, shopkeepers, artisans, and even thieves and pickpockets. On the appointed day each put on the habit of his profession; the ships arrived at the port, the shops were opened, etc., and the business of life was carried on as if this were a real town.

For autumn there were plantations of oak, beech, and other deciduous trees whose leaves turn to brilliant colours as winter approaches. Amidst these were planted evergreens and fruit trees, where the few flowers which blossom late in the year grew beside "decayed trees and dead stumps of picturesque forms overspread with moss and ivy."

The buildings with which these scenes were decorated were such as indicated decay, being intended as mementos of death to the passer-by. Some were hermitages and almshouses, where the faithful old servants of the family spent the remainder of their lives in peace amidst the tombs of their predecessors. Then there were various sorts of ruins: half-buried triumphal arches and mausoleums with mutilated inscriptions, that once commemorated the heroes of ancient times; sepulchres, catacombs, and cemeteries for favourite domestic animals; or whatever else might serve to indicate the debility, the disappointments, and the dissolution of humanity, which, by cooperating with the dreary aspect of autumnal nature and the temperature of the air, filled the mind with melancholy and inclined it to serious reflections.

As the aim of the Chinese in their gardens was said to be not only to please but to terrify or surprise the spectator, they were accredited with almost inconceivable devices intended to produce these effects. For instance, Sir William Chambers describes scenes of terror in gloomy woods, or dark caverns where everything had been blighted or devastated. Bats, owls, vultures, and other birds of prey dwelt in these groves; wolves, tigers, and jackals howled in the forests; while half-famished animals wandered over the plains where gibbets, crosses, wheels, and every instrument of torture were visible from the thoroughfare. The surprises he describes are even more incredible.

To us it does not seem strange that some people doubted the accuracy of these descriptions, although Sir William declares in the second edition of his book that it was all the exact truth. At any rate many writers followed his suggestions in their theories, and many garden makers put them into practice.

The emotional or sentimental garden found a practical exponent in William Shenstone. He wrote some *Unconnected Thoughts on Gardening*, in which he improved on the Chinese theory, saying that "objects should be less calculated to strike the immediate eye than the judgment or well-informed imagination as in painting," and he believed that the "sublime had generally a deeper effect than the merely beautiful," while he considered that "every scene we see in nature is either tame or insipid."

Shenstone's Sentimental Farm at Leasowes, in Shropshire, was much admired. It was calculated to arouse the emotions by means of urns, trophies, weeping-willows, inscriptions, dragons and serpents in hideous attitudes, and other symbols in harmony with the grand, savage, melancholy, horrid, or beautiful character of the landscape.

Melancholy seems to have been a favourite emotion most appropriately inspired by placing funereal monuments in the garden. The grave of Pope's mother, for instance, was a feature in his pleasure ground, approached by a solemn avenue of cypress trees, while Byron's favourite dog was buried under a conspicuous monument in the garden at Newstead.

Interesting examples of the landscape and of the sentimental styles,

TEMPLE OF THE SUN: KEW

designed by Kent, Brown, Repton, Chambers, and their disciples, can be readily recalled as still existing. Perhaps time and neglect have added to their charm; at any rate some of these pleasure gardens have a restful beauty not to be despised.

Kent designed, among other gardens, those at Stowe, Gunnersbury, and Rousham. The number of temples at Stowe has excited ridicule, but it must be remembered that some of these were added by Sir John Vanbrugh. At Gunnersbury Kent's achievements are seen to great advantage. The stately effect of the classic temple overshadowed by ancient cedars and the Gothic tower above the placid lake, in contrast to the neighbouring woodland, was produced by an expert in the combination of the romantic with the picturesque.

The charming temples in the Royal Botanical Gardens at Kew were many of them designed by Sir William Chambers. Those shown in the accompanying illustrations are known as the temples of the Sun and of Æolus, beside two smaller classic pavilions.

Brown is responsible for the gardens at Blenheim, Nuneham, Trentham, Burghley, and other pretentious places. His treatment of water was often delightful, as is shown in the lily pond at Castle Ashby. Unfortunately his first step was often to undo the work of his predecessors, until he has come to be considered less of a creator than a destroyer of gardens.

Gardens, Gunnersbury.

In Repton's various publications his methods are fully described and illustrated with pictures, showing how the landscape would appear before and after his alterations. The present gardens at Ashridge remain much as he laid them out and were perhaps his favourite design. No less than fifteen different kinds of gardens were proposed in his map, and most of them were afterward constructed. Two of the prettiest are enclosures called the Rosary and the Monks' Garden, both formal in their arrangement. At Beaudesart he restored an old garden that it might be in keeping with the Tudor mansion, and everywhere he showed a respect for the past surprisingly in contrast to Brown's iconoclastic methods. In speaking of temples he mentions the temple at Tivoli as the perfection of its type. This is shown in the illustration at the beginning of this chapter [page 220], drawn from a painting by Claude Lorraine.

The French were quick to adopt the English style. It was heralded by philosophers such as Rousseau, who, as Taine said, "made the dawn visible to people who had never risen till noon, the landscape to eyes that had only rested hitherto upon drawing-rooms and palaces, the natural garden to men who had only walked between tonsured yews and rectilinear flower-borders." It was praised by the poets and exemplified by many owners of fine estates. The Abbé de Lille (entitled "le nouveau Dieu des Jardins" by the Prince de Ligne), whose book called *Les Jardins* went through twenty editions, is loud in admiration of the pictorial side:

> "Moins pompeux qu'élégant moins décoré que beau
> Un jardin à mes yeux est un vaste tableau.
> Les arbres, les rochers, et les eaux et les fleurs
> Ce vent là vos pinceaux, vos toiles, vos couleurs."

The Prince de Ligne, who wrote an essay called the "Coup d'œil sur les jardins," laid out his estate at Beloeil in a style "tout à la fois magnifique et champêtre." His taste was for moderation; he preserved the gardens of the old school designed for his father, while adding pleasure grounds comprising all that was best in the English fashion. He visited many of the gardens in England, and showed his discrimination by objecting to the temple mania at Stowe and to the cheap manufacture of classic ruins and Gothic architecture, "apparently inspired," he says, "by the delirium of a nightmare."

At Ermenonville the Marquis de Girardin laid out some gardens in the height of the new style, which attracted much attention. One of his treasures on a little island was Rousseau's grave. It was overshadowed by tall poplars and marked by a monument of antique design ornamented with bas-reliefs and two inscriptions: *"Ici repose l'homme de la nature et de la vérité"* and *"Vitam impendere vero."* Another tomb, not far away, was that of an unknown young man, who was, fortunately for the marquis, inspired by Rousseau to commit suicide on the island, and thus add to the melancholy interest of this retired spot. "On découvre dans une partie touffue et sauvage du bois, une petite tombe simple et négligée, mais remarquable pour le triste anecdote qui y a donné lieu. Un jeune homme, dont on n'a jamais su le nom ni l'histoire, se tua en ce lieu il y a quelques années et pria, par un écrit qu'il laissa, M. de Girardin de l'y faire enterrer. Il parut qu'une partie de ces chagrins venait d'une passion malheureuse, et que la lecture des ouvrages de J.-J. l'avait depuis longtemps décidé à finir ainsi ses malheurs, auprès de celui qui lui en inspirait le triste courage. Quelques jours après sa mort une jeune femme vînt pleurer près de ce monument et y écrire des vers qui firent juger qu'elle même était la cause du désespoir de l'inconnu."

Besides the temple of philosophy, there was a pyramid dedicated to the same study and inscribed with the names of the *quatre chantres de la campagne*, Theocritus, Virgil, Gessner, and St. Lambert. A grove, impenetrable to the sunlight, sheltering a limpid stream, a Gothic tower, a mill recalling the picturesque loveliness of Italy, and a dreary desert containing a simple hut where, in surroundings as *sauvage* as himself, Rousseau had been accustomed to compose his writings, were features much admired.

Other aspects of Ermenonville were described by the English traveller Arthur Young. "Reach Ermenonville, through another part of the Prince of Conde's forest, which joins the ornamented grounds of the Marquis Girardon. This place, after the residence and death of the persecuted, but immortal, Rousseau, whose tomb every one knows is here, became so famous as to be resorted to very generally. It has been described, and plates published of the chief views; to enter into a particular description would therefore be tiresome. I shall only make one or two observations, which I do not recollect having been touched on by others. It consists of three distinct water scenes; or of two lakes and a river. We were first shown that which is so famous for the small Isle of Poplars, in which reposes all that was mortal of that extraordinary and inimitable writer. This scene is as well imagined and as well executed as could be wished. The water is between forty and fifty acres; hills rise from it on both sides, and it is sufficiently closed in by tall wood at both ends to render it sequestered. The remains of departed genius stamp a melancholy idea, from which decoration would depart too much, and accordingly there is little. We viewed the scene in a still evening. The declining sun threw a lengthened shade on the lake, and silence seemed to repose on its unruffled bosom. . . . The worthies to whom the temple of philosophers is dedicated and whose names are marked on the columns, are Newton, *Lucem.*—Descartes, *Nil in rebus inane.*—Voltaire, *Ridiculum.*—Rousseau, *Naturam.*—And on another unfinished column, *Quis hoc perficiet?* The other lake is larger; it nearly fills the bottom of the vale, around which are some rough, rocky, wild, and barren sand-hills, either broken or spread with heath; in some places wooded and in others thinly scattered with junipers. The character of the scene is that of wild and undecorated nature, in which the hand of art was meant to be concealed as much as was consistent with ease of access."

A morbid fondness for funereal monuments was shown even more frequently in France than in England. The, sentimental garden without a grave could never hope to arouse a powerful sensation of agreeable melancholy. Girardin's possession of Rousseau's remains made him the object of much envy. Coliguy's grave added to the charms of Maupertin, but at Mereville there was only an empty cenotaph to Captain Cook. This memorial, a blue marble column ornamented with rostra and surrounded by weeping willows and other foreign trees, was on the middle of an island. The pedestal was decorated with bas-reliefs of savages, urns, and other mournful trophies. At Morfontaine a black marble monument, erected apparently in memory of no one in partic-

GOTHIC DAIRY, HODDESDON

ular, was placed in the midst of a gloomy grove, and served to enhance its sad and solitary appearance; while Comte d'Artois had to satisfy himself at Bagatelle with the disused tomb of one of the Pharaohs. Further evidence of this funereal taste was seen at Le Plessis, Chamant, and other gardens of this period.

Carmontelle, a garden architect and historian, had a good deal of influence in forming the French taste of his day. His theory was that, as French customs, tastes, and climate differed from the English, their gardens should not be a servile imitation of those across the Channel, but should be composed with regard to these differences. The French were a theatric nation, their gardens should be made *pays d'illusions*, where the change of scene should resemble that on the stage. They should not be wholly occupied with representing the *vie purement champêtre*, since the actual peasantry did not comprise such types as were painted by Boucher or Fontenelle or appeared among the singers at the opera.

Rusticity found its exponents at the Parc Monceau and at Chantilly. Here were rural hamlets, including barns, dairies, mills, inns, and bakeries. One of the barns, however, contained a superb salon, decorated in the most elaborate way, where a ball was given in honour of the king and queen. These miniature villages are said to have inspired Marie Antoinette with a desire for the farm at the Little Trianon.

Etiquette was so burdensome at the French court that the pleasure-loving queen had to create a spot where she could lay it aside. Apparently she was successful, for the Prince de Ligne wrote of the Little Trianon, "Here truly one may breathe the air of happiness and liberty. One might believe oneself a hundred leagues from the court."

The English Garden at the Petit Trianon was planned, directly under Marie Antoinette's supervision, by the Comte de Caraman and carried out by her gardener, Richard, who had visited England. The latter was succeeded by his son, a celebrated horticulturist. Near the chateau were the more formal grounds, containing the pagoda, grotto, and belvedere. A hamlet, inspired by that of the Prince de Condé, at Chantilly, was added to the original plan in 1783. It consisted of two groups of buildings: the first comprising the queen's cottage and a mill connected with a billiard-room; the second, a gardener's lodge, poultry-house, tower, dairy, and farm-house, with its dependencies. Here the queen could play the milkmaid or the shepherdess and indulge in all her frivolous whims.

In Germany the landscape school was upheld by Kant, who classed gardening under the head of painting, saying:"It is nothing else but the decoration of the ground with the same variety (grasses, flowers, bushes, and trees, even waters, hills, and valleys) as nature presents to the sight, only in different combinations and according to certain ideas. But the beautiful juxtaposition of material things is only presented to the eyes as in painting."

All over Germany and Austria gardens were laid out in the English fashion. At Sans Souci Frederick the Great began some gardens in this style, which were finished by Frederick William III. There were *Englischer Gärten* at Hanover, at Woerlich in AnhaltDessau, at Nymphenburg in Bavaria, at Wilhelmshohe near Cassel, at Potsdam, at Weimar, and at various places in Austria. These had the usual funereal monuments, classic temples, Chinese pagodas, and artificial ruins.

Even in Russia there was an English garden in the imperial park of Tsarkoe-Selo, which was begun by the Empress Elizabeth and completed by Catherine II. Here the inscriptions, temples, and votive offerings were so numerous that M. Xavier Marmier remarks, "If the

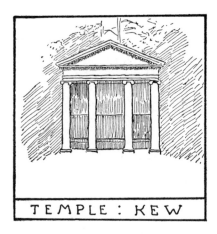

TEMPLE : KEW

austere divinities and the nymphs of the wood and water in that northern region are not satisfied with the ornamentations in their honour,
they must be pretty hard to please."

Everywhere, in fact, the manufacture of the beauties of nature, of
sham temples, artificial ruins, and ornamental farms was wholesale. To
be in keeping with the landscape, ladies masqueraded as goddesses or
milkmaids, according to whether they graced a classic or a rustic scene.
Simplicity was a pose, while nature was a mass of deceitful illusions. At
the close of the century, as Mr. Sedding remarks, "[F]ormality gone
mad was supplanted by informality gone equally mad."

GARDEN-HOUSE AND WALL·THE ORCHARDS ⟡

CHAPTER TEN

Modern Gardens

LL sorts of gardens exist in England to-day. To classify them is almost impossible, but broadly they may still be separated into two divisions—the naturalistic and the formal. Each is an evolution containing motives derived from the different styles described in the preceding chapters, with the addition of certain novel features bringing the garden up to date. These additions are, however, adaptations rather than original creations in their design.

Under the head of naturalistic might be mentioned the many so-called wild, Alpine, rock, bog, water, and subtropical gardens, if the latter name can be applied to a plantation unconfined by apparent boundaries. This style is usually adopted also for botanical gardens. The object in all these plantations is to naturalize exotics in places where they will take care of themselves and gradually grow wild. This practice results from a reaction against the troublesome and expensive custom of bedding out greenhouse plants to the exclusion of the hardy

---

Picturesque Planting, Ascott.

old-fashioned annuals and perennials. The art of the naturalistic garden is an attempt to conceal art and to give nature free play.

The wild garden owes much to its able advocate, Mr. W. Robinson,
who is singularly in touch with many phases of nature and has vigor-
ously protested against bedding out and all elaborate mosaic culture.
He says that what he terms the wild garden has no connection with the
wilderness, though it may happen to be carried out there; and that it
does not necessarily mean the picturesque garden, for picturesqueness
may exist on a cultivated plot of ground. The main object is to make
the plantation look natural and at the same time to group the plants
gracefully. Unfortunately, this is by no means easy, especially for gardeners who have seen nothing outside England. Their conception of
an Alpine garden is about as incongruous with the given surroundings
as would be an English park on the top of Mont Blanc. The most successful wild gardens are those where a demand for exotics is ignored

DOORWAY : SHRUBLANDS

and only English plants are assisted to fulfil a natural bent.

Alpine and rock gardens are substantially one and the same thing. These are adapted to a rocky country where by rights they seem to belong. Artificial rockwork constructed in places where there are no natural cliffs or boulders has seldom a pleasing appearance. The result when these gardens are carried out on an extensive scale, as in the large grounds at Batsford Park, may be very charming, but the effect when they are crowded into a small space and almost crushed under the walls of a suburban mansion is pitiful if not grotesque. A great variety of Alpine plants are successfully grown in England; among them rockfoil, sun roses, maiden pink, soapwort, Alpine linaria, Alpine aster, rock speedwell, erinus silene, violets, arabis, gentians, primula, and even the rare edelweiss.

A bog garden, it need hardly be explained, is a bog where plants, usually exotics, adapted to moist soil are encouraged to thrive. Where there is no natural bog available, an artificial one is constructed as described at length by Mr. Robinson in the *English Flower Garden*. There was an artificial bog at Oxford in the seventeenth century containing about sixteen hundred species and varieties of plants. Among those now considered best adapted for the purpose are trilliums, *iris kæmpferi*, cipripediums, primula japonica, *primula sikkimensis*, marsh marigolds, etc.

The water garden, equally of course, consists of plantations of flowers growing in or beside streams and ponds. Of water-plants, varieties of the nymphea or water-lily, are most effective. The lotus is very beautiful but less easy to supply with right conditions. Where it is possible to combine groups of water-plants with those thriving by the waterside and those requiring only moist ground, the result may prove delightful. A good example is to be seen at Great Tangley Manor, near Guildford.

Another form of wild garden contains only subtropical plants. The bamboo, first discovered to be hardy by Lord de Saumarez at Shrublands, the yucca, tamarix acanthus, and certain palms can be cultivated even in the more northern English counties, while in parts of Cornwall, camellias, and other plants of an almost tropical appearance, flourish in the open air.

Botanists in general seem to prefer the naturalistic method. The best part of the important botanical collections at Kew is thus treated, as are most of the smaller English botanical collections.

On the other hand, advocates of the formal garden are constantly becoming more numerous. One of the first was T. James, who, as early as 1839, had the courage to decry the natural or English style, which had developed into scores of unmeaning flower-beds disfiguring the lawn in the shapes of kidneys, tadpoles, sausages, leeches, and commas. James says: "If I am to have a system at all, give me the good old system of terraces and angled walks and clipt yew edges, against whose dark and rich verdure the bright old-fashioned flowers glittered in the sun. I love the topiary art with its open avowal of its artificial character. It repudiates at the first glance the skulking and cowardly 'celare artem' principle, and in its vegetable sculpture is the properest transition from the architecture of the house to the natural beauties of the grove and paddock."

William Morris also championed the formal garden and declared that it should be contained in a definite enclosure. "Large and small, the garden should look both orderly and rich. It should be fenced from the outer world. It should by no means imitate the wilfulness or wildness of nature, but should look like a thing never seen except near a house."

Several modern garden architects—notably Messrs. John Sedding, T. H. Mawson, R. Blomfield, and F. Inigo Thomas—have published their ideas as to how a garden can be brought to perfection and have also put their theories into practice. According to a consensus of opinion the essentials of their system are balance if not symmetry of design;

Modern Garden, Newstead Abbey.

an outer enclosure providing seclusion for people, and protection, besides a background, for flowers; clearly defined divisions. and subdivisions and ornamental features to accent various centres of interest.
Differences of level in the different sections are added, when possible,
to avoid further danger of stiffness or monotony.

245

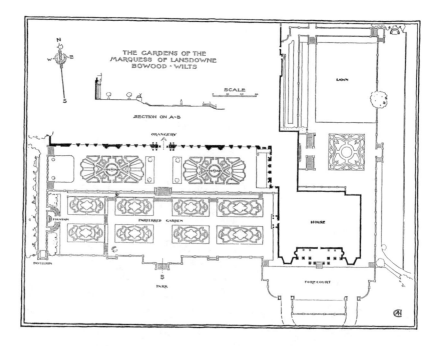

Next the house, when its site is on a slope, a terrace is considered desirable. Sometimes it may be treated merely as a walk. In this case the surface is planted entirely with grass, or with alternate strips of grass and gravel as at Battle Abbey; or with a pavement of tiles, of brick, or of stone flags as at Annesley. Clipped trees or borders of herbaceous plants are often added as ornaments.

Sometimes the terrace is large enough to contain a parterre of flowers, as at Shrubland Park, Harewood or Wollaton Hall. The parterre must then receive a treatment corresponding in style to that of the adjacent house. The scale of the beds and their ornamentation must harmonize to a certain extent with that of the building, and both it and the parterre should be on the same axis.

A terrace is occasionally abutted by a bank of grass, but preferably by a stone retaining wall. Where there is but a slight drop—not more than three feet—from the level of the terrace to that of the ground below, the top of the retaining wall need not rise above the surface of the terrace. If there is a greater descent, the terrace is bounded by a para-

pet, consisting of a continuation of the wall, a balustrading of stone or wood, or pierced stone or terra-cotta panels. Good examples of stone balustrades have been shown in the illustrations of Haddon, St. Catherine's Court, Brympton, Montacute, and Annesley; of pierced stone panels at the Hall Bradford-on-Avon and at Claverton Manor; of terra-cotta panels or balustrades at Hatfield.

It will be seen in all these examples that the character of the architecture placed on the terrace conforms with that of the overshadowing building. The arrangement of the steps plays an important part in the design.

To announce the approach to an entrance, to accent some especial form, or to break the monotony of a long stretch of wall, clipped trees and shrubs are often set out. The best evergreens for this purpose are the common Irish yew and its golden variety *taxus hibernica aurea*. Cypress and juniper can also be kept in good shape, and holly is easily preserved in pyramidal form. For elaborate topiary work the common yew and tree box are best. Yew is adapted to objects of large size, as is evident from the examples at Levens and Elvaston. Box is used for miniature designs. The curious Dutch specimens of topiary work at Ascott are clipped from dwarf box trees.

For cultivation in wooden cases, tubs, or large flower-pots, Portugal laurel, sweet bays, orange trees, and lemon verbena are frequently used.

Parterre, Castle Ashby.

Where the space for planting is limited, these are important accessories.

The beauty of the parterre must of course largely depend upon its wealth of flowers. For producing masses of colour perhaps the finest perennials are iris, peonies, roses, lilies, phlox, larkspur, Oriental poppies, helianthus, dahlias, carnations, and gladioli. Among the most effective annuals and biennials are columbine, campanula, poppies, asters, African marigolds, cornflowers, sweet-william, snapdragon, wallflowers, pinks, pyrethrum, pentstemon, and hollyhocks. For fragrance, lavender, mignonette, alyssum, nicotiana, and thyme are much cultivated. There are besides many tender or half-hardy plants which must be partly raised in a greenhouse and can be bedded out only in summer.

A few flowering shrubs may be admitted to the garden. Sweet almond, pirus japonica, azaleas, and rhododendrons are usually placed

Fountain, The Orchards.

Park, Newstead Abbey.

in the border, as they take up too much room in the flower-beds. Clematis, honey suckle, ivy, jasmine, and climbing roses are used to cover arbours and form festoons and garlands.

No novelties worthy of especial mention have been added to the architectural or sculptural ornamentation of the parterre. Classic statuary and classic or Renaissance designs for fountains are better models than any recently erected, while Elizabethan or Jacobean architectural features are superior to those evolved nowadays. It is strange how seldom a new and satisfactory note is struck in any of these directions.

The boundary, when not formed by a wall, usually consists of a hedge. The best and most durable of these barriers are constructed from evergreen holly, yew, tree box, or cotoneaster, and from deciduous trees and shrubs, like privet, sweetbrier, beech, hornbeam, thorn, and mirobella plum. To give the garden hedge a more ornamental appearance than if it enclosed a field or meadow, standard trees are sometimes introduced at regular intervals and allowed to rise above the rest with their tops clipped in balls or pyramids. In other cases the summit of the hedge is clipped in the shape of battlements as at Old Place and Holme Lacey, or surmounted by quaint figures as at Sudeley Castle near Cheltenham and at Brome Hall in Norfolk.

The prettiest openings through the hedge are made in the form of arches sometimes flanked by pilasters and overtopped by balls, obelisks, or a pointed pediment. A variety of the best examples are to be seen at Brockenhurst.

Tennis-courts, croquet-grounds, and bowling-greens are provided in connection with almost every modern garden, laid out within easy reach of the house. In planning these, seats are usually placed in positions convenient for watching the progress of the game. On a croquet-ground or bowling-green the best vantage point is above the goal, on a tennis-court beside the division line formed by the net.

The proper dimensions for a tennis-court are seventy-eight by thirty-six feet for the actual divisions marked out, and a margin of twenty feet on the ends and five on the sides. Dirt courts are easier to keep in order, but grassed ones are more attractive looking and pre-

Fountains at Brockenhurst and Ascott.

SUN-DIAL : OLD PLACE

ferred by many players. The ends of the margin are usually oval and protected by back-nets.

About the same area must be allowed for a croquet-ground, though its size is more variable; the surface, it need hardly be said, is always planted with grass.

Bowling-greens vary greatly in their proportions. Forty yards square is supposed to be the regulation size, but they are often much narrower. The green is usually enclosed by a wall or hedge, or sunken below the level of the lawn. Many new bowling-greens are being constructed, as bowling has lately begun to return into fashion.

As to style, modern taste is eclectic; it would be difficult to say whether the most inspiration has been recently derived from mediæval, Elizabethan, Italian, Dutch, or French authorities. Many modern instances contain selections from each, but unfortunately few of the former are really representative of the present century, or a fine expression of characteristic English taste.

In some of the best modern English gardens there is a combination of classic statuary, Renaissance fountains, French perspectives, Dutch topiary work, and flowers from all over the world. But in such a garden, when there is breadth given to the masses of colour and a proper regard to scale and proportion, the effect is not always incongruous.

Among the gardens where originality has been shown in the rear-

Kitchen Garden, Newstead Abbey.

rangement of quaint old features, that at Old Place, Lingfield, is an interesting example. It is not exactly a Tudor garden, though in perfect harmony with a well-restored Tudor manor-house. The most conspicuous ornament of the pleasaunce is the curious sun-dial shown in the illustration—a high column surmounted by a square block, on top of which a pelican is feeding its young. The various parts of the garden are well distributed in relation to the house, and skilfully accented by topiary work and appropriate architecture.

The Elizabethan style has been frequently reproduced, as in the gardens at Arley, at Camprey Ash, and Muntham. In many ways it is most in accordance with modern taste and worthy of imitation.

The gardens at Brockenhurst are beautiful examples showing French influence. Nothing better can be imagined than the treatment there of yew and holly hedges, serving to enclose the gardens and to form a background for the statuary and fountains. The green courts are independent of flowers for their beauty, which is retained throughout the year. One of these courts is intended to serve for a bowling-green; here a curious seat is placed at the base of a flowering tree. Several pictures are included [page 251] to furnish an idea of the good taste

GATE-WAY & TERRACE: BARROW CT

PAVILION BARROW COURT

evinced in the design of the archways and the position and proportions of the alleys, statuary, and fountains.

At Sedgwick Park, near Horsham, is a charming garden showing considerable originality. Its maker had travelled widely and found inspiration in many French and Italian gardens, but the features she borrowed from them were adapted in such a way as to give her garden a distinctive character. A pretty and unusual enclosure contains an oblong tank of water, so arranged that it can be used for a swimming-pool. Beside the water is an alcove in the wall retaining the terrace above, which forms a pleasant substitute for a grotto.

Some interesting gardens have been rearranged and supplemented by others, under the direction of Mr. F. Inigo Thomas, at Barrow Court. The alterations and additions were executed about the year 1892. Originally beside the old house there was a terrace, and beneath it a formal garden surrounded by yew hedges and enclosing a pond: these were slightly modified by Mr. Thomas.

The new work was accomplished in the park beyond the first garden. A wide strip of ground running east and west was levelled, leaving a high bank below the flower-garden with a drop of some six feet into the park, and was walled and balustraded with stone. This excavation formed a terrace at the northern edge of the flower-garden. At each end were erected "suntraps," walled enclosures differing in detail and decked out with a cloister and seats for garden tea. One of these smaller pavilions is shown in the illustration [above].

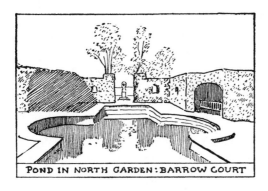

POND IN NORTH GARDEN : BARROW COURT

The arrangement of the tennis lawns is especially striking. They are divided from the park by a tall iron fence, supported at intervals by terminal figures, rising from a semicircular bastion. In the centre are wrought-iron gates, with piers and vases flanked on either hand by winged lions. The terminal figures are twelve in number and represent the months of the year, beginning with a child for January and moving round with the sun through advancing stages to an old woman for December.

Groves, cricket-grounds, etc., have been planned to occupy a space beyond the boundary walls, but have not as yet been carried out. The whole scheme would repay careful study.

One of the best of the more simply planned gardens is at the Orchards, near Godalming. The fountain, in the centre of the main garden, surrounded by festoons of roses, is good and original in design. Upright posts supporting chains for other garlands add to the composition by furnishing vertical lines, in contrast to the long horizontal contours of the low-lying hills, seen above the wall in the distance.

Miss Jekyll's garden, also near Godalming, contains the elements of both naturalistic and conventional gardens. The arrangement is very simple and largely depends for its beauty upon various delightful colour schemes. It is seldom that both wild and cultivated flowers have been grouped more successfully.

It is impossible to attempt to enumerate all the beautiful gardens in various styles, which have been laid out during the last few years. From

THE PARTERRE · LONGFORD CASTLE · WILTS
EARL OF RADNOR

SCALE

ROSE
TREES

HOUSE

WOODEN SEAT : SHRUBLANDS

the largest to the smallest, from the stiffest to the most unconventional, they go to prove that, just as there are beautiful shades of every colour, so any kind of garden may be made beautiful if its construction displays a knowledge of the principles underlying its particular fashion and if it is tended by loving hands. No wild garden can be made successful unless its designer has analyzed the characteristic aspects of nature, no romantic garden by one who lacks an appreciation of the picturesque, while to perfect the conventional enclosure a sense of scale and proportion, involving at least a rudimentary knowledge of architecture, is equally essential. Finally, a love of flowers is the natural foundation on which to build all gardens, whether formal or informal.

GARDEN-HOUSE : CASTLE ASHBY

Appendix

BEFORE the Norman Conquest the Anglo-Saxons showed a fondness for nature, although they had little opportunity to cultivate it. Appreciations of the beauty of the changing seasons and of the fragrance of the flowers were frequently expressed, as in the following verses:

Swecca swetast	Of odours sweetest
swylce on sumeres tid	such as in summer's tide
stincað on stowum	fragrance send forth in places
stappelum fæste	fast in their stations
wynnum œfter wongum	joyously o'er the plains
wyrta geblowene	blown plants
hunig-flowende.	honey-flowing.
	— *Exeter Book*, p. 178.

Fæger fugla reord	Sweet was the song of the bird
folde geblowen	the earth was covered with flowers
geacas gear budon.	cuckoos announced the year.
	— *Exeter Book*, p. 146.

But except what they learned from the monks their knowledge of horticulture must have been very slight, and apart from the monasteries, the enclosures where they grew plants must have been of the simplest description. That these plants were grown in enclosures is evident from the derivation of the words *wyrt-tun* and *wyrt-geard* applied to what might perhaps be dignified as a garden. Little more of these gardens is known, however, than the names of the plants to be gleaned from early herbaries. A few of these names are in pure Anglo-Saxon, but the majority are of Latin origin. The *Herbarium* of Apuleius, written in the fourth century, was translated into Anglo-Saxon and was probably considered as an authority about plant-lore.

Among vegetables the best known seems to have been the leek, as an enclosure for pot-herbs came to be ordinarily called the *leac-tun*, and a kitchen gardener as the *leac weard* or leek keeper. The other alliaceous plants, we are told, were considered as so many varieties of leek and were designated by such names as *eune-leak* or *yune-leac*, supposed to be the onion, and *gar-leac* for garlic. Bean and cress are also Anglo-Saxon words, but cabbage, peas, turnip, radish, parsley, mint, sage, rue, and other herbs, although in use, passed by Latin names.

Long lists of flowering plants might be appended from Anglo-Saxon writings. But as they are difficult to identify, and probably many of them grew only wild or were prized merely for medicinal qualities, they may have had no connection with a garden and do not help us to imagine its appearance. For the cultivated rose and lily, they adopted the Roman names *rose* and *lilie*; the latter appears to have been their favourite flower. Among other plants which apparently were grown in beds were *suthern-wude* (southernwood), the *turn-sole* (sun-flower) also called *sigel-hwerfe* (the gem-turned) or *solseace* (from the Latin *solse-quium*), the *clœfre* (violet), the periwinkle (from the Latin *pervinca*), *hu-nig-suckle* (honeysuckle), the peony (from the Latin *pionia*), the *dœges-eye* (daisy), and the laur-beam, more likely to have been the bay tree than the laurel.

The principal enclosure seems to have been dominated by fruit trees, hence the origin of the words *orc-geard*, *orc-geard*, and *orcyrd*. The apple was the chief fruit of the Anglo-Saxons, and known by the Anglo-Saxon name *œppel*. The apple tree was called an *apulder*, and was divided into two species—the *surmelst apulder* or souring apple tree, and the *swite apulder* or sweeting apple tree. An apple orchard was an *apul-der-tun*, and from the fruit was pressed *appel-win* or cider. Cherries (*cyrs-treow* or ciris-beam from the Latin *cerasus*) were also favourite trees, and the enclosure especially inended for them was called the *cherry-geard*. The pear (as its names *pera* and *piriga* from the Latin *pirus*, imply) was probably received from the Romans, as were the peach (*per-soc-treow* from *persicarius*), the mulberry (*mor-beam* from *moruvs*), the chestnut (*cysten, cyst* or *cystel-beam* from *castanea*), and perhaps the al-mond (*magdala-treow* from *amygdalus*), the fig (*fic-beam* from *ficus*), and the pine (*pin-treow* from *pinus*). The small kernels of the pine were used as relishes much as we eat olives. The plum has not changed its original Anglo-Saxon name, and the nut (*hnuter*) is nearly the same. Strawberries and raspberries (*strea-berige* and *hynd-beriges*) were also well known to the Anglo-Saxons, although perhaps only in their wild state. The vine was often cultivated and called the *win-treow* or wine tree, its fruit *win-berige* or wineberries, and a bunch of grapes, *ge-clystre* or a cluster.[1]

[1] Wright, *History of Domestic Manners*.

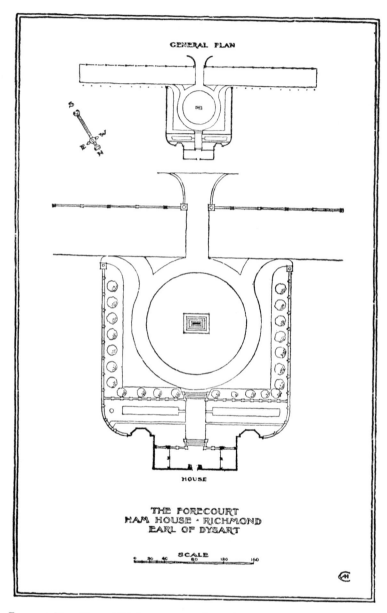

Forecourt, Ham House. This forecourt is good in scale and in proportion of its details. The driveway is paved with large stone flags, and there are leaden busts in the niches of the wall which are in pleasing contrast to the rich red brick. A number of plans for forecourts are shown in Blomfield's Formal Garden in England.

Bibliography

WORKS REFERRING TO GARDENS

CLASSIC

Arnold, B.
De Graecis florum et arborum amantissimis. Göttingen, 1885.

Barnabei, Felice.
La Villa Pompeiana di P. Fannio Sinistore Scoperto presso Boscoreale. Rome, 1901.

Böttiger, C.A.
Racemazionen zur Gartenkunst der Alten.

Browne, Sir Thomas.
The Garden of Cyrus. 1658.

Castell, R.
Villas of the Ancients. 1728.

Cato, M. Porcius.
De Re Rustica. c. 200 B.C.

Cicero, M. Tullius.
De Senectute. c. 1st century B.C.

Columella.
De Re Rustica: Scriptores Rei Rusticae. Leipsic, 1794.

Comes, Dr. Orazio.
Illustrazione delle piante rappresentate nei dipinti Pompeiani. Naples, 1879.

Dezobrey.
Rome au siècle d'Auguste. 1846.

Diodorus Siculus.
Bibliotheca. c. 50 B.C.

Falconer.
Historical View of the Gardens of Antiquity. 1785.

Gregorovius (trans. A. M. F. Robinson).
The Emperor Hadrian.

Homer.
The Odyssey, Done into English Prose by S. H. Butcher and A. Lang.

Joret, Charles.
Les Jardins de l'ancienne Égypte. 1894.

263

Les plantes dans l'antiquité et au moyen âge. 1897.
La rose dans l'antiquité et au moyen âge. Paris, 1892.

Koch.

Die Baüme u. Strauchen der Alten Griech. 1879.

Lafaye, Georges.

Article *Hortus* in the Dictionnaire des antiquités grecques et romaines.

Magoun, H. W.

Pliny's Laurentine Villa, Transactions of the American Philological Association. 1895.

Mangin.

Histoire des jardins anciens et modernes. Tours, 1888.

Mau-Kelsey.

Pompeii, Its Life and Art. By August Mau. Translated into English by F. W. Kelsey. New York, 1899.

Meyer, G.

Lehrbuch der Schönen Gartenkunst. Berlin, 1895.

Möller.

Die Botanik in den Fresken der Villa der Livia. Mittheil. d. k. arch. Inst., Rom. Abth. 1890.

Morgan, Thomas.

Romano-British Mosaic Pavements. London, 1886.

Niccolini.

Le case ed i monumenti di Pompéi disegnati et descritti. Naples, 1834.

Palladius, Rutilius.

De Re Rustica. 4th or 5th century A.D.

Plinius, Caius Secundus.

Natural History. 1st century A.D.

Pliny the Younger.

Letters. 1st century A.D.

Plutarch.

Lives. 1st century, A.D.

Seneca.

Epistolæ. 1st century A.D.

Simonis.

Ueber die Gartenkunst der Römer. Blankenburg, 1865.

Stengel.
Hortorum, Florum et Arborum Historia. 1650.

Tacitus.
Annals. 1st century A.D.

Temple, Sir William.
Miscellanea: Upon the Garden of Epicurus. 1685.

Theocritus.
Idylls. 3d century B.C.

Theophrastus.
History and Causes of Plants. 4th century B.C.

Varro, M. Terentius.
De Re Rustica. c. Ist century B.C.

Virgil.
Georgics.

Wantig, R.
Haine u. Gärten in Gr. Alt. pr. v. Chemnity. 1893.

Xenophon.
Œconomicus. c. 5th century B.C.

MEDIÆVAL

Albert the Great.
De Plantatione Viridariorumque. De Naturis Reris. Ed. Thomas Wright,
London, 1863.

Chaucer, Geoffrey.
Poems.

De Beauvais, Vincent.
Speculum.

De Garlande, Jean.
Le Ménagier de Paris, composé vers 1393 par un bourgeois parisien.

Delisle, Léopold.
Études sur la condition de la agricole et l'état de l'agriculture en Normandie
au moyen âge. Evreux, 1851.

De Loris, Guillaume.
Roman de la Rose. c. 1200.

De Ornatu Mundi.
Opéra ed. de Beaugendre. c. 1189.

Du Cerceau, Androuet.
Les plus excellents bastiments de France. 1576.
Dugdale .
Monasticon.
Gautier, Léon.
La Chevalerie. Paris, 1895.
Lacroix, Paul.
Mœurs, Usages, et Costume au
Moyen Âge et à l'Époque d' la Renaissance. Paris, 1872.
Mackenzie, Sir James D.
The Castles of England. New York, 1896.
Turner, T. H.
State of Horticulture in England. *Arch. Journal, Vol. 5.*
Walcott.
Church and Conventual Arrangement.
Walter.
Recueil de fleurs, fruits, etc., peints sur vélin par Jean Walter de Strasbourg,
de 1656 à 1665. (Bibliothèque Nationale Cabinet des Estampes.)

ITALIAN
Colonna, Fra Francesco.
Hypnerotomachia Poliphili. Venice, 1499.
Falda.
Giardini di Roma.
Montaigne, Michel de.
Journal du voyage de Michel de Montaigne en Italie par la Suisse et l'Alle-
magne en 1580 et 1581. Rome et Paris, 1774.
Percier et Fontaine.
Choix des plus célèbres Maisons de Plaisance de Rome et de ses environs.
75 plates. Paris, 1809.
Piranesi.
Vedute di Roma. 1765.
Platt, Charles A.
Italian Gardens. 1894.
Silvestro, Israell.
Alcune vedute di Giardini e Fontane di Roma e di Tivoli. Paris, 1646.

Taine, H.
Voyage en Italie. Paris, 1884.

Vitruvius, Pollio M.
Architectura Utini, 1825-1830.

DUTCH

Beudeker.
Germania Inferior.

Commelyn.
Hortus Amstelodamus. 1697.

De Hogue, Romeyn.
Villa Angiana.

Hoghenberg.
Hortorum ... formæ. Köln, 1665.

Rademaker, A.
Holland's Arcadia. 1730.

Van der Groen, J.
Le Jardinier des Pays Bas. 1672.

Van Oesten.
The Dutch Gardener. 1703.

Vredeman de Vries, J.
Hortorum Viridariorumque Elegantes et Multiplicis Formæ.
Antwerp, 1583.

FRENCH

Alphand.
Les promenades de Paris. Paris, 1868.

André, E.
L'Art des Jardins. Paris, 1879.

Blondel, J. F.
De la Distribution des Maisons de Plaisance. 160 plates. Paris, 1737–1738.

De Serres, Olivier.
Le Théâtre d'Agriculture et mesnage des Champs. Paris, 1603.

Dezallier d'Argenville, A. J.
La Théorie et la Pratique du Jardinage. Paris, 1713.

François, Jean.

L'Art des Fontaines. 1665.

Galimard, fils.

Architecture de Jardins. 68 plates, folio, 1765.

Gérardin, R. L.

De la composition des paysages et des moyens d'embellir la nature autour des habitations, etc., par R. L. Gérardin, vicomte d'Ermenonville. Genève, 1777.

Krafft, J. C.

Plans des plus beaux Jardins, 1810.

Laborde, Alexandre de.

Descriptions des nouveaux jardins de la France et des châteaux. Paris, 1808.

Laborde, A. L.

Descriptions des nouveaux jardins de la France. 1808-1821.

Langlois, N.

Parterres, 23 plans after Le Nôtre, Le Bouteux, etc.

Le Blond, A. J. B.

Engravings of Plans for Gardens. 1685.

Parterres de Broderie, 1688.

Leclerc.

Le Labyrinthe de Versailles. 1679.

Le Rouge, G. L.

Détails des nouveaux Jardins à la mode. 200 plates.

Recueil des plus beaux Jardins de l'Europe. 1776-1787.

Le Pautre.

Nouveaux desseins de jardins, parterres et fassades. Paris. N. Langlois.

Jets d'eau nouvellement gravis par Le Pautre. Se vende à Paris, etc.

Liger, Louis.

Le Jardinier Fleuriste. 1719.

Mariette, J.

Parterres de Broderie. c. 1730.

Mérigot.

Promenade ou Itinéraire des Jardins d'Ermenonville. 25 illustrations. Paris, 1788.

Mollet, André.

Le Jardin de Plaisir. Stockholm, 1651.

Morel, N.
Théorie des Jardins. 1776.

Nolhac, Pierre de.
Le Château de Versailles. Pavillon de Hanovre. 1900.
Articles about Versailles in the *Gazette des Beaux Arts.*

Perelle, Adam.
Collection of Engravings. 1685.

Sauval, Henri.
Histoires et recherches des antiquités de la ville de Paris. Paris, 1724.

Schabol, R.
Dictionnaire du Jardinage. 1767.
La Théorie du Jardinage. 1785.

Silvestre, Israel de.
Jardins et Fontaines. Paris, 1661.

Vallet, Pierre.
Le Jardin du Roy tres chrestien Henri IV. 1608.

Viollet-le-Duc.
Dictionnaire raisonné de l'architecture française du XIe au XVIe siècle.
Paris, 1868.

ENGLISH

Addison, Joseph.
An Essay on the Pleasures of the Garden. (*The Spectator*, No. 477.)

Amherst, Hon. Alicia.
A History of Gardening in England. London, 1896.

Bacon, Francis.
The Essayes or Counsels of Francis Lo. Verulam, Viscount
St. Albans. Newly enlarged. 1625.

Badeslade.
Views. London, 1720.

Barrington, Hon. Daines.
On the Progress of Gardening, in a letter to Mr. Norris. 1782.

Belcher, John.
Later Renaissance in England. London, 1897.

Blomfield, R.
The Formal Garden in England. London, 1892.

Borde, Andrew.

The boke for to Lerne a man to be wyse in buylding of his howse. (c. 1540.) Small 8vo.

Cavendish.

Life of Wolsey.

Chambers, Sir William.

A Dissertation on Oriental Gardening. London, 1772. 4to. Chinese Pavilions, Gardens, etc.

Cook, E. T.

Gardens Old and New.

De Caux, Isaac.

Wilton Garden. (c. 1645.) 4to.

De Lille, the Abbé.

On Gardening. 1783. 4to.

Dodoens-Lyte.

A Niewe Herball or Historie of Plantes. Antwerp, 1578. Folio.

Dugdale, Sir William.

Antiquities of Warwickshire. London, 1730. 2 vols.

Estienne and Liebault-Surflet.

Maison Rustique or the Countrie Farme, compiled in the French tongue by Charles Steuens and John Liebault, and translated by Ric. Surflet. 1600. Folio.

Evelyn, John.

The French Gardener. Translated into English by Philocepos. London, 1658.

Of Gardens. 4 books. First written in Latin verse by Renatus Rapinus; now made English by J. E. London, 1693.

The Compleat Gard'ner, etc., by J. de la Quintinye . . . made English by J. Evelyn. London, 1693.

Gatty, H. K. F.

The Book of Sun-dials.

Gerard, John.

The Herball, or Generall Historie of Plantes. London, 1597. Folio.

Gilpin, William.

Observations . . . relative chiefly to Picturesque Beauty. 1783–1809. 11 vols. 8vo.

Gotch, J. Alfred.
Architecture of the Renaissance in England. London, 1891.
The Architecture of the Early Renaissance in England. London, 1902.

Hentzner.
Itinerarium Germaniæ Galliæ, etc. Nuremberg, 1612.

Hill, Thomas.
The Proffitable Arte of Gardening. London, 1568. Small 8vo.

Holinshed, Ralph.
Chronicles of England, Scotland, Ireland. London, 1586–1587. 3 vols. Folio.

Kip and Knyff.
Britannia Illustrata. London, 1709. Folio.

Langley, Batty.
New Principles of Gardening, or the Laying-out and Planting Parterres. London, 1728. 4to.

Law, Ernest.
History of Hampton Court Palace. London, 1885–1891.

Lawson, William.
A New Orchard and Garden. 1618–1619. 4to.

Le Blond-James.
The Theory and Practice of Gardening. Translated from the French of A. le Blond by John James. London, 1703.

Lethaby, W. R.
Leadwork. London, 1893.

Logan, David.
Oxonia Illustrata. Oxford, 1675. Folio.
Cantabrigia Illustrata. Cambridge, 1683.

London and Wise.
The Retir'd Gardener. From the French of Louis Liger. London, 1706. 2 vols. 8vo.
The Compleat Gard'ner (of J. de la Quintinye), now compendiously abridged with very considerable improvements by George London and Henry Wise. London, 1699. 8vo.

Loudon, John Claudius.
Observations on the Formation of useful and ornamental plantations. Edinburgh, 1804.
Hints on the formation of Gardens and Pleasure Grounds. 1812.
The Encyclopædia of Gardening. London, 1822.

Macer-Linacre.

Macer's Herbal practysid by Doctor Linacro. 1530.

Markham, Gervase.

The Country Housewife's Garden . . . Together with the Husbandry of Bees . . . with divers new knots for Gardens. 1617. 4to.

Maison Rustique. 1616.

Mawson, Thomas H.

The Art and Craft of Garden-making. London, 1900.

Morris, Richard.

Essays on Landscape Gardening. London, 1825.

Mountain, Didymus; i.e., Thomas Hill.

The Gardener's Labyrinth. London, 1577. Small 4to.

Nichols, J.

The Progresses of Queen Elizabeth, etc. London, 1788–1821.

Parkinson, John.

Paradisi in Sole, Paradisus terrestris, or a Garden of all sorts of pleasant flowers . . . with a Kitchen Garden . . . and an Orchard. 1629. Folio.

Passe, Crispin de.

A garden of Flowers translated out of the Netherlandish. Utrecht, 1615. 2 parts oblong. 4to. 163 plates.

Platt, Sir Hugh.

Floræs Paradise. London, 1608.

Pope, Alexander.

Essay on Verdant Sculpture. (*The Guardian*, No. 173.)

Price, Sir Uvedale.

A Letter to H. Repton, Esq., on the application of the practice as well as the principles of Landscape Painting to Landscape Gardening. London, 1795.

An Essay on the Picturesque as compared with the sublime and beautiful, etc. London, 1794–1798.

Rea, John.

Flora, Ceres, et Pomona. London, 1676. Folio.

Repton, Humphry.

A Letter to Uvedale Price, Esq., on Landscape Gardening. London, 1894.

Observations on the Theory and Practice of Landscape Gardening. London, 1803.

An Enquiry into the changes in Landscape Gardening. London, 1806.

Robinson, William.
    The English Flower Garden. London, 1896.
    The Subtropical Garden. London, 1879.
    The Wild Garden. London, 1881.
Rye. W. B.
    England As Seen by Foreigners in the Days of Elizabeth and James I. London, 1865.
Scott, Sir Walter.
    On Ornamental Plantations and Landscape Gardening. Quarterly Review. 1828.
Sedding, John D.
    Garden Craft, Old and New. London, 1895.
Seiveking, A. Forbes.
    The Praise of Gardens. London. 1899.
Stephenson, David.
    The Beauties of Stowe. London, 1746.
Switzer, Stephen.
    The Nobleman, Gentleman, and Gardener's Recreation, etc. London, 1724. 8vo.
    Short Instructions very profitable and necessary for all those that delight in Gardening . . . translated out of French into English. London, 1592.
Tijou, John.
    A New Book of Drawings of Gates, Frontpieces, etc. London, 1693
Triggs, H. Inigo.
    Formal Gardens in England and Scotland. London, 1902.
Turner, William.
    Libellus de Re Herbaria novus . . . London, 1538.
Tusser, Thomas.
    Five hundred points of good husbandrie. Early English Dialect Society. London, 1878.
Walpole, Horace.
    Essay on Modern Gardening. Strawberry Hill, 1785. 4to.
Worlidge, John.
    Systema Horticulturæ, or the Art of Gardening. London, 1677.
Wotton, Sir Henry.
    The Elements of Architecture. London, 1624. 4to.

Wright, Thomas.

A History of Domestic Manners and Sentiments in England. London, 1862.

ANONYMOUS

A Plan of Mr. Pope's Garden and Grotto, etc. 1745.

The Grete Herbal. London, 1516.

The Maske of Flowers . . . upon Twelfth Night. 1613. 1614.

MISCELLANEOUS

Attiret-Beaumont.

An Account of the Emperor of China's Gardens at Pekin. By J. D. Attiret. Translated by Sir H. Beaumont, *i.e.*, J. Spence. London, 1752.

Burckhardt, J.

Der Cicerone. Leipsic, 1879.

Conder, J.

Landscape Gardening in Japan. Tokio, 1893.

Du Bled, Victor.

Les Fleurs. *Revue des Deux Mondes.* 1902.

Falke, J.

Der Garten, seine Kultur u. Kunstgeschichte. Stuttgart, 1885.

Girault de Prangey.

Souvenirs de Grenade et de l'Alhambra. Paris, 1836.

Jäger, H.

Gartenkunst und Gärten sonst und jetzt. Berlin, 1888.

Pueckler-Muskau, H. L. H.

Andeutungen über Landschaftsgärtnerei. Struttgart, 1834.

Riat, Georges

L'Art des Jardins. Paris, 1900.

Tijou, John.

New Booke of Drawings Invented and Designed by John Tijou: 1693. Reproduced by B. T. Batsford, 1896.

Index

A Note on the Type

ENGLISH PLEASURE GARDENS has been set in Robert Slimbach's Adobe Jenson, a digital version of a much-admired roman type first cut in 1470 by Nicolas Jenson. Called "the most Venetian of the Venetian faces," Jenson's types were among the most admired early type designs, exerting an influence that would last well into the twentieth century. More recently, the types have inspired numerous attempts at revival and reinterpretation, the earliest being William Morris' Golden type, the most beautiful (perhaps) being T. J. Cobden-Sanderson's Doves type, and the most famous being Bruce Rogers' Centaur. It is interesting to note that unlike the majority of typographical revivals of the period, which hewed closely to acknowledged standard sources, the many Jenson-based romans issued in the late nineteenth and early twentieth centuries varied dramatically in appearance. This was due in part to the disparity among their designers' root sources but was ultimately due more to a desire not to produce (as Morris put it) a "servile" copy of the original. ❡ As Rogers did in creating Centaur, Slimbach turned to Jenson's edition of Eusebius' *De Evangelica Præparatione* as his model, enlarging the printed letters photographically and retouching them prior to final redrawing. This process reduced the roughness of the inked impression while preserving the irregularities of a hand-cut type—that is, the features that gave the originals much of their charm and warmth. ❡ Because Jenson never produced an italic face, designers of revivals found themselves forced to fill this need by adapting other sources. The most successful have been the types modeled after the types of Ludovico degli Arrighi, the sixteenth-century printer and writing-master. Frederic Warde was the first to adopt this model, and his elegant Arrighi was adapted to accompany Centaur. For his "Jenson italic," Slimbach based his lower-case characters on Arrighi's *cancellersca formata* letters, substituting the forms of *cancellersca corsiva* for the upper-case and swash letters. ❡ With its impeccable history and inimitable elegance, Jenson's type – in all its incarnations – continues to test the mastery of its interpreters. Its elusive beauty stands as a challenge to type designers still seeking to create "the perfect roman."

Book design and typography by Dean Bornstein